D1523456

The Complete Book of Puppet Theatre

The
Complete Book
of
Puppet Theatre

David Currell

BARNES & NOBLE BOOKS
TOTOWA, NEW JERSEY

First published in the USA 1987 by
BARNES & NOBLE BOOKS
81 Adams Drive
Totowa, New Jersey, 07512

ISBN 0-389-20865-7

Originally published 1974 as *The Complete Book of Puppetry* by Pitman
Publishing Ltd.; reprinted 1976. Completely revised, updated and
published 1985 by A & C Black (Publishers) Ltd., 35 Bedford Row,
London WC1R 4JH

Library of Congress Cataloging-in-Publication Data
Currell, David.
  The complete book of puppet theatre.
Rev., updated ed. of: The complete book of
puppetry. 1974.
  Bibliography: p.
  Includes index.
  Summary: Introduces the history of puppetry and
gives instructions for making various types of puppets,
creating stage sets, and producing plays.
  1. Puppets and puppet-plays. [1. Puppets.
2. Puppet plays] I. Currell, David. Complete book of
puppetry. II. Title.
PN1972.C87   1986   791.5'3   86-22246
ISBN 0-389-20685-7

Printed in Great Britain at The Bath Press, Avon

Contents

To my mother and 'Auntie Florrie'

Preface

It is inevitable as materials and techniques develop over the years that any 'complete' book gradually becomes the 'incomplete' book, so I welcome this opportunity to revise *The Complete Book of Puppetry* as *The Complete Book of Puppet Theatre*. The original seems to have stood the test of time fairly well, but the substantial revisions reflect a number of influences.

First, the need to up-date information, revise the bibliography and other appendices. Secondly, the past ten years have seen a much more rigorous and professional approach to the use of puppets in education, which has progressed accordingly. Thirdly, soon after the publication of the first edition, the Puppet Centre was established in London; this has brought ten years of contact with puppeteers nationally and internationally on a scale not previously possible.

Ten years of teaching puppet theatre courses at all levels, together with developing materials and techniques, have brought considerable additions and refinements to the constructional sections. Finally the greater awareness, by puppeteers and public alike, of puppets as *theatre* warrants a much more thorough consideration of the performance – which is reflected in the amended title. The performance has always been the most neglected area of the art; books on puppetry focus almost exclusively on construction techniques and hardly ever attempt seriously to answer the question: *I've made a puppet but what do I do now?*

This new edition endeavours to discuss the nature of the puppet and set it in the context of the worldwide puppetry scene; to describe a wide range of construction and presentation techniques and to draw out principles which will enable these techniques to be applied to the reader's particular needs; to outline significant related puppetry arts; and to draw all these threads together in a practical consideration of the many aspects of the performance, illustrated by reference to the philosophies and approaches of two highly regarded puppet masters; finally, to provide new revised appendices to support the enthusiast's puppetry activities. If the verdict is that we have succeeded in this task, perhaps the reader may feel that we are justified in calling this *The Complete Book of Puppet Theatre*.

My thanks are extended to all those who helped to make the first edition a reality – not least among them Gordon Straight who introduced me to puppet theatre, guiding and encouraging me for many years – and to those acknowledged elsewhere in the text who have contributed to the present edition. In particular the contributions of Ray DaSilva and Barry Smith excited and inspired me in preparing the text and to them my very sincere thanks are due. Also to Sally and Ann Snook for their help in preparing the manuscript and typescript. Finally to Judith Holden and Anne Watts of A&C Black for their support throughout this major undertaking.

1 Introducing puppet theatre

Throughout the world the puppet show is a popular entertainment. Sometimes it is an ancient heritage, a last reminder of an age long past; sometimes a medium for the contemporary artist's experiments with shape, colour and movement. For centuries it has been used to relate myth and legend and enact simple traditional farces. Now, as well as undergoing a tremendous revival as entertainment for both adults and children, it is becoming more and more widely used in education and as therapy.

What exactly is a puppet? Perhaps it might best be described as 'an inanimate object moved in a dramatic manner by human agency', a definition which includes a wide range of figures, but not dolls and automata.

The puppeteer is an artist, a unique combination of sculptor, modeller, painter, needleworker, electrician, carpenter, actor, writer, producer, designer and inventor who in the course of preparing a show calls upon a host of diverse skills. He may take on all of these tasks himself and, with luck, achieve a high degree of artistic unity. Alternatively, he may be just one of a group or company, pooling their many and varied talents.

Puppetry itself is essentially a folk art which from time to time has become a fashionable craze. Because of its ephemeral nature its history must be largely a matter of conjecture. Its origins, which like those of most of the arts are confused, are generally thought to lie mainly in the East. Certainly puppetry in Asia was highly sophisticated at a very early date and Asia is the source of many of the ideas and techniques of the puppetry of the West. Cult figures with moving parts survive from the very earliest times, but whether or not these were used in a 'dramatic manner' can never be definitely known.

In all the early Mediterranean civilisations and under Roman rule the puppet drama undoubtedly flourished and vestiges of this dramatic tradition may possibly have survived the Dark Ages. (The characters of the *Commedia dell' arte* may well owe something to it.) In the Middle Ages wandering showmen travelled all over Europe with the puppet show and puppets were widely used to enact the scriptures – until they were banned by the Council of Trent.

Since the Renaissance puppetry in Europe has continued as an unbroken tradition, though experiencing many rises and declines in popularity. In seventeenth-century England it reached the height of popular appeal as the only entertainment allowed by Parliament; and again in eighteenth-century France when *Ombres Chinoises* not only flourished as a fairground entertainment but were also a fashionable craze amongst artists and nobles. Puppetry has always been popular in Italy, and the magnificent Sicilian Orlando marionettes are one of the most famous puppet traditions of the West.

Figure 1 Rapunzel and the Prince from John Wright's production of Rapunzel *at the Little Angel Theatre, London*

In the nineteenth century the puppet show was taken to America by emigrants from many European countries and their various national traditions were the foundations for the great variety of styles to be found there today.

In contrast to the changes and developments which are taking place in Europe and America the Far Eastern countries cling to their ancient, unchanging traditions. In Burma, a dancer's skill is still measured by his ability to imitate the movements of the marionette and in Japan the Bunraku puppets, which once overshadowed the Kabuki in popularity, survive unaffected by the general, if ambivalent, turning towards the West.

Throughout its long and world-wide history the puppet show has remained essentially characteristic of the country that produces it, reflecting something of the national temperament and psychology of different peoples. Compare for example the elaborate refinement of shadow puppets, most popular in the East, with the earthy knock-about glove puppets of the West. Similarly, within Europe itself, the main protagonists of the traditional farces – Karagöz of Turkey, Caspar of Germany, Guignol of France – embody many aspects of the national character.

Most types of puppet in use today fall into one of four main categories: glove puppets (and hand puppets), rod puppets, marionettes and shadow puppets. There is also a wide range of other techniques from masks to finger puppets, from the toy theatre to animated puppet film.

The glove puppet is, as the name implies, used like a glove on the operator's hand; the term 'hand puppet' is sometimes used synonymously but now tends to be used more specifically for Muppet-type figures where the whole hand is inserted into the puppet's head. The rod puppet is held and moved by rods, usually from below but sometimes from above; the Japanese Bunraku puppets have recently given rise to the development of a similar style of rod puppet, usually requiring two or three operators and held in front of them. Sometimes a combination of hand and rod control is used for a puppet. Glove puppets are usually quite simple in structure but a rod puppet may vary in complexity from a simple shape supported on a single stick to a fully articulated figure with moving eyes and mouth.

The marionette is a puppet on strings, suspended from a control held by the puppeteer. Its construction can vary from the extremely complex to the very simple; from a figure with any number of moving parts controlled by a multitude of strings to a simple figure with only a few strings.

Shadow puppets are flat cut-out figures held by a rod or a wire against a translucent illuminated screen. The term is also used loosely for a form of full-colour, translucent, cut-out figure operated in the same manner.

Glove and rod puppets are usually presented from within a booth. The traditional covered booth is still used for 'Punch and Judy' but the open booth has become more and more popular, affording as it does far greater scope for performance and a wider viewing angle for the audience.

Marionettes are also commonly presented on an open stage with the puppeteer in view of the audience. The traditional marionette stage with a proscenium front to hide the operators is still used, but size, portability and setting-up time are factors which influence the trend towards open-stage performances. Greater awareness of the performance in recent years has led to increasing exploration of the use of space instead of the confinements of the conventional booth or stage.

Marionettes are versatile puppets which may be constructed in a wide variety of ways. Performances with marionettes can be uniquely graceful and charming but fast and forceful action is generally ruled out by the danger of tangles. In inexperienced hands marionettes can be highly unpredictable as their movement is largely governed by their centre of gravity and the natural swing of their parts. The experienced puppeteer draws upon this natural movement to great advantage.

Rod puppets, like marionettes, offer a great potential for creativity in design and presentation. The range of possible swift and subtle movements makes the rod puppet ideal for sketches that depend on precision timing. Unlike the marionette, a well-made rod puppet goes where you put it and stays there. Rods can be used to illustrate beautifully and they can also handle large dramatic pieces. The glove puppet, although limited in gesture to the movement of the figures, is ideal for quick, robust action and the live hand inside it gives figures a unique flexibility of physique. It can be most expressive and can handle surprisingly challenging pieces, as demonstrated by Theatre of Puppets' *Faustus* (see Chapter 15).

Shadow puppets are often used to illustrate a narrated story, for which they are ideally suited; however, the traditional Greek and Turkish shadow shows demonstrate how suitable the shadow puppet can be for direct dialogue and vigorous knock-about action.

Figure 2 Sortir, en quelque sorte *by La Citrouille (Alain and Annie Lecuq), France*

It is perfectly possible, of course, to combine or alternate the use of different types of puppet in one performance. The combination of marionettes with rod puppets is particularly satisfactory as the stylised movement of the rod puppet is closely related in effect to that of the marionette. Shadow play, which can be used very successfully to show scenes and actions taking place in the distance while three-dimensional figures carry on the main action in the foreground, can also be used to illustrate linking narrative in a three-dimensional show and for such things as dream and memory sequences.

The combination now occurring more frequently of masked actors and puppets has attracted a great deal of interest. Clearly masks and puppets are closely related: when you put on a mask you surrender your personality and, in a sense, become a puppet. In both, the set expression portrays a dramatic essence with peculiar power and invites us to see beyond this. In puppet theatre we have drama intensified.

The puppet is a unique concept; it is not an actor, and puppet theatre is not human theatre in miniature. It is important to try to understand the puppet 'as puppet'; it is this uniqueness which helps to justify its existence: if the puppet is used to try to replicate the human actor, then it destroys the reason for its own existence. To try to understand the puppet in terms of the human actor fails to get at the essence of the puppet. In fact, in many ways, puppet theatre has more in common with dance and mime than with acting.

When an actor makes his entrance, he *represents*; when a puppet makes its entrance, it *is*. The puppet brings to the performance just what you want and no more; it has no identity outside its performance, and it does not bring other associations onto the stage.

The puppet is free from human limitations: it can throw itself to the ground in a way which no human actor or dancer could do. It can speak the unspeakable and deal with taboos, deal with all our dark sides; it can portray an ideal or emotion which cannot be expressed in any other way.

Artists such as Molière, Cocteau, Klee, Shaw, Mozart, Gordon Craig, Goethe and Lorca have all taken a serious interest in this form of art. Yet,

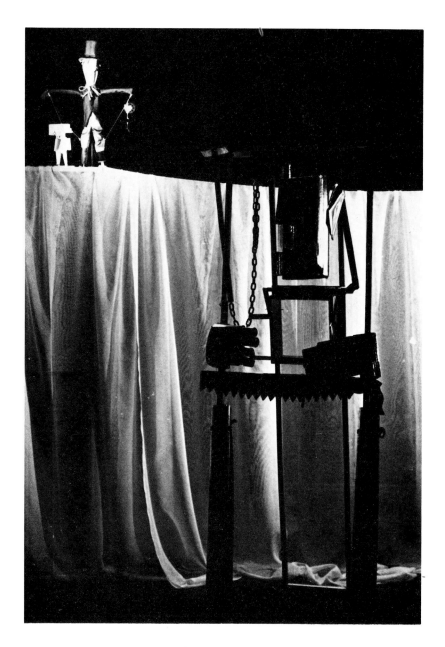

Figure 3 Dorothy and the Scarecrow meet the Iron Man in Le Jardin des Magiciens *by Théâtre Sur Le Fil, France*

despite all this, in the West puppet theatre is highly popular but remains lowly regarded. The reasons for this include the tendency this century to focus almost exclusively upon the craft aspect and to fail to give due consideration and time to the performance. The fact that it has become entertainment for children often carries the erroneous assumption that it is therefore not something for adults. And the puppet theatre has a great need of good writers and directors; it needs some of the preciousness, pretentiousness and pomposity knocked out of it.

The puppeteer must remember that the actor does not walk onto the stage and stand there implying: 'Look at me, aren't I clever?' He has a *reason* for being there. So it is with puppets; we do not want to see a puppet just jiggling around the stage as a sort of animated gimmick. It must serve a dramatic purpose. Puppet theatre cannot successfully deal with psychological concepts as can the human theatre: the puppet cannot generally be used for complex soul-searchings and it is devoid of many aspects of non-verbal communication available to the actor. But the puppet, still or moving, can be equally powerful. The audience strikes a compact with the performer, that it will suspend its disbelief – and when that audience is dramatically involved, it 'reads in', investing the puppet with emotion and movement; it can see the puppet breathe.

Many people do not understand how much work goes into puppet theatre; a production is a big undertaking, as will become apparent in the following chapters. There are so many disciplines involved, so many areas of expertise demanded, that probably the best advice that can be given to anybody starting in puppetry is to see as much theatre, dance and mime as possible, as well as puppet theatre; to take classes in those areas of performance that are most relevant to puppet theatre (movement, mime, voice, etc.); and to experiment with materials and techniques. Study people: people at rest and people in motion, people when happy, when sad, when bold, when shy, when weary. What characterises them, their moods, their ages? Do not attempt to reproduce these human movements but draw out the essence. Simplification and selection are important aspects of the puppeteer's art.

Most of all, remember that there is no *one* way of doing it, no rules or formulae. Puppetry is a theatre art which offers considerable scope for experiment and adventure. It may be considered as one of the most liberating forces that can be used in theatre.

2   Puppetry past and present

Puppetry is a visual and dramatic art which has continued for thousands of years. Exactly when or where it originated is not known, and even its comparatively recent history in many countries is obscure.

In one country puppetry may be a living folk art; in another it may be used as a means of teaching simple or illiterate people; in a third it may be considered a high art form. In one manner or another it is practised throughout most of the world by young and old.

This chapter gives in outline something of what is known of the development of puppetry throughout the world, and also brief descriptions of the work and activities of contemporary puppeteers.

Puppets in ancient times

The origin of puppetry remains the subject of dispute. Some authorities claim that puppetry was practised in India as long as four thousand years ago. It is widely held that puppets were in use before human actors as religious taboo forbade impersonation. Supporting evidence for this is found in the fact that the leading player in Sanskrit plays is titled *sutradhara* which means 'the holder of strings'.

In China puppetry is thought to have begun some two thousand years ago and marionettes were in use by the eighth century AD. There seem to have been several types of 'puppet' in ancient times, among them 'living puppets' – which may have been children acting as puppets – and 'water puppets' – possibly akin to the Vietnamese figures which perform on wooden rafts floated on a lake and are controlled from a distance by a complexity of strings. Some authorities, however, suggest that shadow puppets were the earliest form of puppet used in China; they certainly date back well over a thousand years.

The Greeks used puppets possibly as early as 800 BC. Undoubtedly puppetry was a common form of entertainment by the fourth century BC. Marionettes were the type of puppet used, as can be deduced from the fact that the Greek word for puppet is *neurospastos*, *neuron* meaning cord. Glove puppets may also have been in use, the Greek word *koree* meaning both a long sleeve that covers the hand and a small statue.

The first puppeteer known by name is Potheinos, a Greek who performed in the theatre of Dionysys in Athens. He is referred to by Athenaeus, a Greek writer of the second century, in a miscellaneous work called *The Deipnosophists*, but nothing is said of the content of his performance.

Puppetry was certainly established in Rome by 400 BC when there start to appear references to puppets in the writings of the time. The nature of

Figure 1 Odysseus: A Tale of the Sea *by Marionetteatern, Sweden, directed by Michael Meschke*

these references point to the use of marionettes and glove puppets but the allusions are not specific so we know nothing of the nature of the performances. When the Roman Empire came to an end in the fifth century the circuses fell into disuse and the entertainers were driven out. Among them were the puppeteers who then wandered over Europe with their shows.

Puppets in Western Europe

Puppets were used all over the Mediterranean in ancient times and it seems reasonable to assume that the tradition was kept alive through the Dark Ages by wandering entertainers. By the thirteenth century puppetry was well established in many parts of Europe. It has since experienced many changes in popularity which at times has rivalled that of the live theatre.

Free exchange between the countries of Europe has produced in them similar trends and styles in puppetry. The Belgian puppets, for example, are very similar to the large Sicilian marionettes and most countries have a counterpart of Mr Punch. In Holland he is Jan Klaasen (originally Pickle Herring), in Belgium Tchantches, in Spain Don Christobal Polichinello, and so on.

All European countries currently have puppet theatre but those discussed below have more significant historical traditions and a generally higher level of puppetry activities. Nonetheless most of those countries which do not have a specific mention in the text have puppet masters and companies of note. Among these are Triangel (Henk and Ans Boerwinkel) from Holland and Michael Meschke in Sweden, who established the Marionnetteatern and, more recently, the Dockteaterinstitutet (Swedish Institute of Puppet Theatre). Both Michael Meschke and the Boerwinkels have broken new ground with revolutionary ideas in puppet theatre and achieved international recognition.

Italy

In Italy at the end of the fifteenth century there appeared a form of drama known as the *Commedia dell' arte*. Amongst the stock characters of these plays were buffoons, or *zanni*, who went under such names as Pulcinello, Arlecchino, Scaramuccia and Burattino. The travelling entertainers often had puppet representations of the characters but it is not possible to determine whether they appeared first as puppets or live actors, though the term *burattini*, meaning glove puppet, was in use before the dramas of the *Commedia dell' arte* emerged.

One of these buffoons, Pulcinello, travelled as a puppet character throughout Europe and became a popular figure in many countries though taking on other names and adapting to the nature or styles of the region. It is from this character that Punch derives.

By the end of the fifteenth century puppets seem to have become well established as a popular form of entertainment in Italy. The types of puppet used were marionettes, probably supported by a rod fixed to the head with the limbs manipulated by strings or fine wire; *marionnettes à la planchette* which were jigged to music; a type of rod puppet which moved in grooves made in a plank; and glove puppets.

In the late eighteenth century Italian *fantoccini* (puppet) plays, which incorporated a great many spectacular effects and ingenious tricks and transformations, were tremendously popular and travelled widely throughout Europe and to England.

In recent times the popularity of puppets was greatly influenced by the famous Teatro dei Piccoli of Vittorio Podrecca which, founded in Rome in 1930, flourished for over twenty years and travelled extensively.

In the past few years puppet theatre in Italy has enjoyed a considerable revival with major companies comprising up to eight members and receiving subsidies from their municipalities and arts associations. Signora Maria Signorelli, who until recently held the chair in puppet theatre at Bologna University, directs the Nuova Opera dei Burattini based in Rome; also in Rome is a permanent marionette theatre, the Acciattella. In Turin the Compania Lupi continues with its seventh generation of puppeteers, whilst Teatro Gioco Vita (Piacenza) with its dramatic shadow spectacles is among a substantial number of young companies throughout Italy who are quickly establishing an international reputation.

Sicily

Sicilian marionettes are renowned for their magnificent productions which dramatise the conflict between Christianity and Islam. The most famous of these plays is *Orlando Furioso*, Orlando originating from an eighth-century knight called Roland.

The legend of Roland, which evolved over several hundred years, was finally embodied by the Italian poet Ludovico Ariosto in his poem, *Orlando Furioso*, in 1532. Orlando, the perfect knight, is the leader of the Paladins (the twelve peers who accompanied King Charlemagne) but is distracted from his duty by his love for Angelica. After many adventures,

Figure 2 A 19th century Sicilian Orlando Furioso

Angelica marries another and Orlando goes mad, hence the title. Eventually Orlando returns to Charlemagne's camp, is cured of his madness and in battle kills Agramante, King of Africa and leader of the Saracens.

This story, made up of hundreds of smaller episodes, was improvised by puppeteers until it became the story it is today – a tale of knights, witches, giants and dragons. The Orlando marionettes became more popular in Sicily than anywhere else and Sicily has become the permanent home of this traditional puppet drama.

The Sicilian puppets are made of wood and have beaten armour, shields and swords, their height being determined by their rank. Those in the Palermo tradition stand some 3 feet high, whilst the Catania figures are around 4½ feet. A heavy rod passed through the puppet's head from

Figure 3   Karaghiosis

above supports the whole body and another rod works the sword arm. The shield arm is moved by a string. By lifting and turning the one centre rod, the puppet walks and can even be beheaded.

The first reference to the story of Orlando being played by puppets dates from the sixteenth century, but this type of puppet had been in use since Roman times. Today the two leading companies are the Cuticchio family of Palermo, where also Antonio Pasqualino runs the Museum of Puppets, and the Fratelli Napoli of Catania, recipients of the respected Dutch Erasmus Award.

Greece

Today in Greece shadow puppet shows are the most popular, featuring a Punch-like character, Karaghiosis, introduced to Greece by the Turks. The figures, approximately two feet high and traditionally made of leather, are now often made from plastic or acetate. The shadow screen may be up to twenty feet long and five feet high. The lighting is arranged from below the screen and the figures operated from behind.

One of the best known contemporary Karaghiosis puppeteers is Spatharis, a talented performer whose father and grandfather were both Karaghiosis performers. His latest venture is the establishment of a museum in the Amaroussion area of Athens.

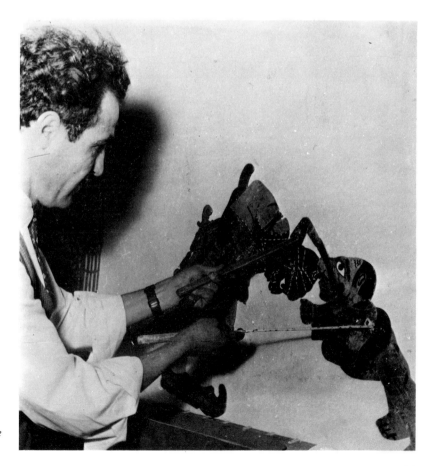

Figure 4   Spatharis manipulating Karaghiosis (right) and Veligekas, the brave man of the Turkish Pasha

Figure 5 Rod puppets of Richard Teschner, showing the early influence of the Javanese wayang golek *puppets*

Figure 6 A later rod puppet by Richard Teschner

Austria

The most important contribution of Austria to the development of puppetry was made comparatively recently by Professor Richard Teschner who considerably influenced the development of rod puppetry in Europe. Inspired by the Javanese *wayang golek* figures, he developed his own very intricate type of rod puppet, often with a complicated system of control strings inside the supporting rod. From 1925 until his death in 1948 Teschner presented shows in his *Figurenspiegel* theatre, the proscenium of which was a gold-framed concave lens surrounded by the signs of the Zodiac.

The Salzburg Marionette Theatre presents some of the most beautiful puppetry spectacles the world has ever seen, with productions ranging from *Don Giovanni* and *Die Fledermaus* to *The Tempest* and *Rumpelstiltskin*. Performances, which have been given since 1913, include operas, operettas, ballet, plays, musical plays and pantomime. The company employs hundreds of craftsmen, designers, musicians, etc., to meet the demands of these elaborate productions.

Other puppet companies in Austria today struggle to develop, hindered by the lack of official recognition of puppetry as a theatre art.

Figure 7 Madonna and Child by Richard Teschner

Figure 8 Mozart's Il Seraglio *by the Salzburg Marionette Theatre*

Figures 9, 10   Scenes from Mozart's
The Magic Flute *by the Salzburg*
Marionette Theatre

Germany

Since the beginning of the nineteenth century Germany has shown a special affinity with the puppet theatre. In 1802, Christoph Winter founded in Cologne the Haenneschen Puppet Theatre which, over a century and a half later, still performs in the original style with a distinctive type of rod puppet. The puppet is supported by an iron rod, the end of which is held in a thick wooden rod which stands on the floor. Nowadays both legs hang free but in older figures the rod passed through one leg. One arm is controlled by a wire, the other hangs loose.

13

Figure 12   *Professor Doctor Freidreich Wilhelm Ambrosius of Albrecht Roser*

In 1858 Joseph 'Papa' Schmid acquired a small Munich theatre, the Heideck Theatre, in which he performed with such success that in 1900 a new theatre was built for him by the Municipal authorities.

In 1905 the Munich Artists' Theatre was founded by Paul Brann and in 1911 Ivo Puhonny's theatre at Baden-Baden. Max Jacob, who, until his death in 1967, was the President of UNIMA, had one of the finest German puppet companies, the Hartstein Puppets, later to become the Hohnsteiner Troupe. Today one of the most active German puppeteers is Albrecht Roser of Stuttgart, a skilful performer who has travelled the world with his puppets and achieved universal recognition as a marionettist.

Germany's traditional puppet play is *The History of Doctor Faustus*. Puppets have performed the play ever since it was first published in 1587. Originally these performances included a comic character called Hanswurst (Jack Sausage) but after the publication of Goethe's *Faust* in 1832 he was replaced by a rather less vulgar character called Kasper, or Kasperle. The popularity of Goethe's *Faust* had a reviving effect on the puppet show and Kasper survives to this day as a counterpart of Punch.

Germany has the finest collection of puppets and puppet theatre exhibits in the world, housed in the Munich City Theatre Collection, and the German puppetry institutes and organisations are among the strongest in the world.

Figure 11   *An old German marionette: the dwarf flower seller transformed into the wizard*

Figure 13 Clown Gustaf with his horse Alize Zizipée: marionettes by Albrecht Roser

Figure 14 Albrecht Roser's Clown Pünktchen

Figure 15 Sendrine, a French marionette (c 1910) supported by a rod to the head

France

The fourteenth-century *Li romans du bon roi Alexandre* (in the Bodleian Library) contains an illustration of hand puppets used in a portable booth with castle turrets on either side, the arrangement termed a *castellet* or *castello*.

Marionnettes à la planchette were used in France before the sixteenth century and puppet theatres existed in Paris by the beginning of the seventeenth century.

In the eighteenth century marionette operas were so popular that bitter rivalry arose with the live theatre and in 1720 an attempt was made to have the puppet productions restricted by law. This failed, and puppet performances continued with added vigour and even greater popularity.

Shadow puppets, called *Ombres Chinoises*, were also popular in the eighteenth century, not only as fairground entertainment but also among artists, and a theatre founded in 1776 by Dominique Seraphin was much patronised by the fashionable world. Again, at the end of the nineteenth century, a shadow theatre flourished in the Chat Noir club of Rodolphe Salis.

Figure 16   Guignol (right) and Gnafron (c 1906)

In about 1630 Italian travelling showmen brought Pulcinello to France where he became Polichinelle and gradually acquired the exaggerated physical characteristics of Punch. Polichinelle's popularity, however, was surpassed by that of Guignol, a glove puppet dressed in the style of a Lyonnais silk weaver and of typically Lyonnais character, who appeared at the beginning of the nineteenth century. Guignol in fact became so popular in France that the name is now the common French term for 'glove puppet'.

Today France has a host of talented performers, some well established in traditional performance styles and others taking initiatives with more experimental work. The most exciting development in recent years is the establishment of the Institut International de la Marionnette in Charleville -Mézières, a major international centre for all aspects of puppet theatre including training and research.

Figure 17   Théâtre Sur Le Fil *of Claude and Colette Monestier, France*

Figure 18   *Abstract figures by Philippe Genty, France*

Puppets in Eastern Europe

Most countries of Eastern Europe had an early tradition of travelling showmen who included puppets in their entertainment. In these countries too there was a Punch-type character: in Russia he was Petrouchka (or Petrushka), in Hungary Vitez Laszlo, in Czechoslovakia Kasperek, in Rumania Vasilache and in Yugoslavia Pavliha.

With a few exceptions, puppetry in East European countries did not develop very much until the twentieth century but when the development began it progressed at an impressive rate. Now there are thousands of amateur puppeteers and many State puppet theatres employing large numbers of professionals.

The Rumanian Tandarica Theatre in Bucharest has won international acclaim for its puppet presentations while, in Yugoslavia, the State Puppet Theatre Lubliana is outstanding. The German Democratic Republic, of course, shares many traditions with West Germany but the most prominent figure on the recent scene is Peter Waschinsky who has a solo show and also directs the Neubrandenburg state-supported puppet theatre.

Figure 19   A modern Kasper by Frieder Simon of East Germany

Figure 20   Three robbers by Frieder Simon

Figure 21 A scene from The Chief: A Balkan Western *by the Central State Puppet Theatre, Sophia, Bulgaria*

Czechoslovakia

Czechoslovakia had a long tradition of marionette presentations but since the Second World War has been more concerned with rod puppetry. Considerable work has also been done in the sphere of 'black theatre' presentations and some of the black theatres of Prague have received world-wide recognition.

One of the most famous Czech puppeteers this century was the late Joscph Skupa whose father-and-son creations, Spejbl and Hurvinek, are known throughout the world. The Hurvinek and Spejbl Theatre in Prague was forced to close during the Second World War and Skupa was imprisoned in Dresden when it was discovered that he had continued to perform secretly. He escaped during a fire in 1945 and after the war re-opened his theatre which still presents puppet productions today.

One of Joseph Skupa's pupils, the late Jiří Trnka, won international accalim for his puppet films. Although his early ventures in professional

*Figure 22 Kasparek of Czechoslo-
vakia*

*Figure 23 A puppet from the Black Theatre of Prague of Hana and Joseph
Lamka*

*Figure 24 Spejbl (right) and Hur-
vinek*

puppetry were a failure, his later outstanding work on cartoons, puppet
films and book illustrations earned him the title of National Artist.

The greatest influence on the development of modern puppetry in
Czechoslovakia is attributed to the late Professor Jan Malik, who was for
forty years the Secretary-General of UNIMA, the international puppetry
organisation. A Holder of the State Prize Laureate, his career covered the
roles of author, editor, producer and director.

The puppet companies are subsidised by the State and since 1948 the
puppet theatre has enjoyed equal status with the live theatre. Puppeteers sit
on the State Theatre Council. A Chair of Puppetry has been established

and a four-year course is offered for training in all aspects of puppet theatre.

The present Director of the Puppet Theatre Department of the University is Jan Dvorak who is also Director of Drak, a leading avant-garde company formed in 1958 in Hradec Kralove, East Bohemia.

Hungary

There are indications of a very modest tradition of puppet theatre in Hungary. Towards the end of the eighteenth century, Haydn directed a puppet opera company, playing in German, as part of his duties as musician at the court of Prince Eszterhàzy. This was the only 'artistic' puppet theatre before this century, but there exist nineteenth-century documents giving permission for puppeteers to perform and pictures depicting scenes from the 'live picture shows'. The only real tradition of puppet theatre apparent into the twentieth century is that of Vitez Laszlo (Lancelot the Brave) but there are some folk customs involving puppet-type figures and masks.

Early this century attempts to establish puppet theatres failed because of lack of finance and public interest but, between the wars, puppetry developed in education as a powerful means of 'instruction'. Then in 1947 Mesebarlang (The Cave of Tales) was formed, two years later to become the Hungarian State Puppet Theatre, Allami Bábszinház. Its early years

Figure 25 The Lovers from Petrouchka *by the Hungarian State Puppet Theatre*

Figure 26 The Hungarian State Puppet Theatre's production of Háry János (John the Hero)

saw the development from a naturalistic, scaled down version of the human theatre to a more stylised puppet theatre, but for a while it became a rather contrived imitation of Obraztsov's State Central Puppet Theatre in Moscow. By the late fifties, notable Hungarian poets and writers took an active interest and a growing band of writers for puppet theatre emerged. Now the Budapest-based company extended its scope to provincial performances and by 1964 it covered the whole country.

In the same year a highly successful version of *A Midsummer Night's Dream* paved the way for the staging of dramatic and musical classics which continue to feature prominently in the company's repertoire. Now the company, under the artistic direction of Dr Dezső Szilágyi, has two fully equipped theatres and a company of over two hundred and fifty, which includes sixty performers who work in eight groups, each with its own repertoire. Between them they give eight to ten performances at five or six different places each day. It is a unique national cultural institution.

Poland

Polish puppet theatres date back at least to the fifteenth century. The traditional *szopka* theatres were first used in the churches and then, in the seventeenth century, played in the streets. These small, portable stages were used for Nativity plays rather like medieval miracle plays. Each tiny puppet is held by one small rod or wire which moves in grooves in the stage floor, the stage usually being constructed to represent a church. This form of puppetry is still practised. Today it is not unusual to see live actors and puppets in the same play and 'black theatre' technique is commonly practised.

In the last thirty years more than thirty State puppet theatres have been formed. Their presentations, which are of a high technical standard, are mainly for children, drawing upon Polish poetic fairy tales and some foreign material.

Figure 27 A rod puppet from the State Theatre Lalka, Warsaw

Figure 28 A Polish szopka

Figure 29 Winter and Roses from What the Four Seasons are Talking About *by the Polish State Puppet Theatre Pinokio, Łodź*

23

Among the notable Polish figures is Dr Henryk Jurkowski, professor of puppet theatre at the Universities of Bialystok and Wroclaw, training puppet theatre directors. The President of UNIMA, he is an eminent writer, director, academic and an influential ambassador for world puppet theatre.

Russia

Russia's only puppeteers before the Revolution were the travelling Petrouchka men, the last of whom, Ivan Zaitsev, died in 1930. Zaitsev was the first puppeteer to receive the Soviet title Merited Artist.

Early experiments in puppetry had an emphasis on performances for children but today there are presentations for audiences of all ages. Especially through the influence of Richard Teschner of Austria, the Russian interest in rod puppetry grew and Russia is considered to be one of the leading countries for this type of presentation.

The finest puppeteer Russia has ever had is generally thought to be Sergei Obraztsov, an expert in all forms of puppetry. Originally a teacher and actor, then solo puppet performer, in 1931 he became the Director of the first State Puppet Theatre, now the State Central Theatre in Moscow which is one of the largest puppet companies in the world with some 350 members.

The State Central Theatre, still directed by Obraztsov, is now housed in a magnificently equipped puppet theatre with two auditoria – one for children and one for adults. There are two performances a day for children and evening performances for adults. This theatre also has a museum and is now a training centre for actors and directors.

Among the other notable companies is the Leningrad Bolshoi Puppet Theatre which has similarly achieved wide recognition. Throughout the Soviet Union there are over a hundred permanent State puppet theatres as well as thousands of puppeteers with travelling companies.

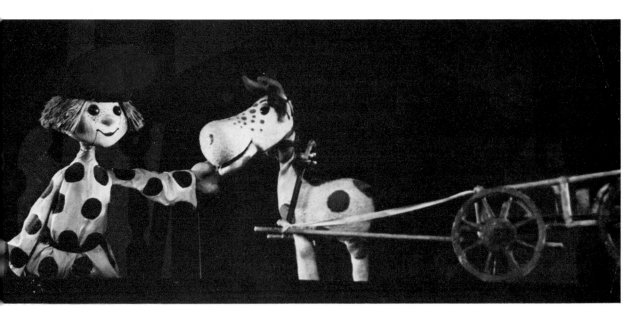

Figure 31   The Fairy Story of Emilio
*by the Leningrad Bolshoi Puppet
Theatre*

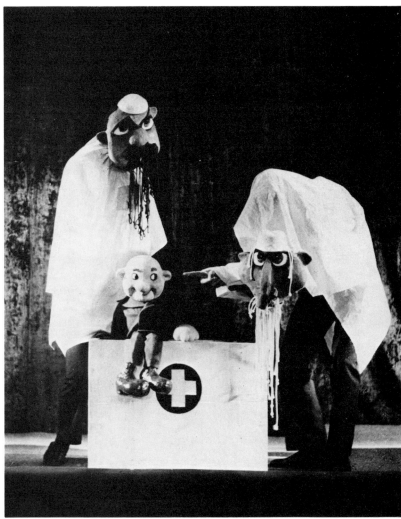

*Figure 32   The Leningrad Bolshoi
Puppet Theatre production of* The
Adventures of the Good Soldier
Schwejk

25

Figure 33   A scene from The Adventures of Burattino *by the State Central Puppet Theatre, Moscow*

Figure 34   Two characters from A Straw Hat *by the State Central Puppet Theatre*

Figure 35   The new State Central Puppet Theatre, Moscow

Puppets in the Middle East

In most parts of the Middle East, little of the early traditions appear to have survived and it is only recently that steps have been taken to re-establish puppet theatre, particularly for use in education and teaching about religious heroes.

Egypt

Herodotus refers to puppets in Egypt as early as the fifth century BC and there are clear indications that there was widespread use of puppets for religious purposes such as fertility rites. Today the Cairo Puppet Theatre, founded in the 1950s, flourishes in an excellent modern building and Aragoz, a cousin of the Turkish Karagöz, is still to be seen performing.

Iran

Few documents about Iranian puppet theatre survive but reference to the art is found in the eleventh-century poems of Omar Khayyam, who compares man to a puppet and existence to its manipulator.

Today one finds Gharégose, a shadow puppet akin to the Turkish Karagöz, and other figures similar to those of the fifteenth century. These are used for evening performances in tents, the main character being a negro who has many different names – such as Mobarak or Almasse – and represents the defender of the oppressed. Modern trends include the

Figure 36   Mr. B, a television puppet by Iraj Emami, Iran

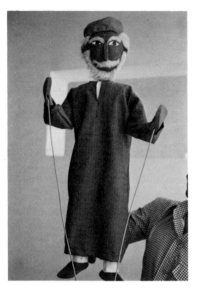

Figure 37 A character from The Woodcutter's Donkey *by the Department of Drama, Ministry of Education, State of Qatar*

introduction of puppets into television. Puppets now perform only for children and adolescents and there is insufficient activity, awareness and exposure to puppet theatre for there to be much work of a high artistic calibre.

Israel

There is a good deal of interest in puppet theatre in Israel at present and 1983 saw its first major puppetry festival. The most notable of the Israeli companies is the Train Theatre which, as the name suggests, has been created in a railway carriage.

Jordan

Puppet theatre in Jordan is progressing very quickly, due in large part to the dedication and talents of Miss Wafa Qusous who developed it at the Haya Arts Centre in Amman and is now spreading her work further afield.

Figure 38 The Turkish Karagöz (left) and Hacivad

Qatar

Qatar has just created its first puppet theatre under the direction of Hassan Ibrahim, Head of the Department of Drama in the Ministry of Education, aided by Mohammed Kishk from the Cairo Theatre and with advisory support from UNESCO. The project to develop puppet theatre includes an initiation into the art for young people. Already they are showing a great deal of commitment, enthusiasm and talent.

Turkey

The traditional Turkish puppet show is a shadow puppet knock-about comedy. The plays centre around a Punch-like character called Karagöz ('Dark-Eye').

The Turkish shadow figures are only six to twelve inches high, and the screen is about five feet wide. The figures are traditionally made of tough camelskin, specially treated to make it translucent and brightly coloured with dyes, but modern materials for construction are now to be found as well.

The origins of these puppets is unknown but it is possible that they came from India or Arabia. The script, like that of Punch, is traditional and was never written down. The plays are presented most frequently during Ramadan; for twenty-eight days there is a different Karagöz play each night.

Puppets in Asia

In general, puppetry in the Eastern countries is very unlike that of Europe. The Asian puppet theatre often has close connections with human dance and drama and frequently draws upon classical literature or religious sources for its themes.

There is a great variety of puppetry styles in Asia. Every type of puppet is to be found and there are many unique types of presentation.

India

All forms of puppetry are practised in India, the type varying with the area. An interesting style of marionette is to be found in Southern India: the figures are made of wood and are approximately four feet high with an unusual stringing arrangement. The main control, to which head and waist strings are attached, consists of a cloth-covered ring which fits onto the puppeteer's head. Rods held by the puppeteer are used to control the puppet's hands.

In contrast, the *Kathputli* marionettes of Rajasthan have a very simple control. The puppets have carved heads and bodies with stuffed cloth arms; instead of legs, they have long skirts which twirl and sway expressively. The control is a single loop of string, one end of which is attached to the puppet's head, the other to the back of the waist. Occasionally an extra string is added to control the arms. The Rajasthani marionettes have high-pitched voices produced by the performers speaking through bamboo and leather reeds.

Figure 39 An old Rajasthani Pan
figure

Figure 40 An Indian shadow figure from Andhra

The *tolu bommalata* (there are a variety of spellings) shadow puppets are found in the Andhra region and may be the origin of the Javanese *wayang kulit* puppets. The name *tolu bommalata* means 'the play of high-fashioned toys', the figures being made of intricately pierced deer or goatskin, treated to make it translucent, coloured with dyes and held by split cane. The arms are controlled by thin canes whilst the legs hang free. The figures are all over five feet high, relative size being governed by the character's importance. The shadow screen is usually made of two saris, fastened together and attached to poles.

The plays, frequently performed throughout the night every night for a few months, are often taken from the Hindu epics, *The Mahabharata* and *The Ramayana*, both written some two thousand years ago. These great works lend themselves to puppet productions, containing as they do supernatural beings, gods, magical monkeys and other similar ingredients for successful puppet entertainment.

In recent years the traditional styles of puppetry have been practised increasingly by part-time puppeteers. As elsewhere, puppetry's educational possibilities have been recognised and puppets are used in the villages to teach the people about health and hygiene as well as to entertain.

Figure 41 A Rajasthani marionette operated by only one loop of string

Burma

Puppetry in Burma is given full recognition as a serious form of art. The traditional puppets are marionettes which may have as many as fifty or sixty strings, although the majority have far fewer. The characters of the traditional show are always the same; they include votaresses, a horse, two elephants (one black, one white), a tiger, a monkey, parrots, a necromancer, a yogi, a king, a prince, a princess, two prince regents (one white faced, one red faced), four ministers, an astrologer, a hermit, clowns and ogres.

The stage is a bamboo platform with curtains to hide the puppeteers. The acting area is divided into a court and a forest, one on either side of the stage. The characters are referred to as either 'left' or 'right' puppets, depending on which side of the stage they take; the 'left' are ugly and evil whilst the 'right' are good and honourable.

The plays number hundreds, drawing mainly upon the *jatakas*, the stories of the Buddha's previous incarnations, either as animal or human. They are concerned chiefly with virtuous life and constantly stress moral retribution.

31

These marionette productions were created and developed by U Thaw, a Minister of Royal Entertainment in the eighteenth century. They have had a considerable influence on the human dance drama, to the extent that the dancer's skill is measured by his ability to recreate convincingly the movements of the puppet.

Thailand

Thailand's form of shadow play, the *Nang*, is said to have come originally from India. There are no individually operated puppets, the characters and scene being cut in the same large piece of hide which is fastened to two poles. These scenes are held against a large white screen and the shadows cast by firelight are used to accompany the narration of the story. Although the characters remain static, the performers holding the 'scenes' dance.

The plays are based upon Thai dance dramas and musical accompaniment is provided by percussion and stringed instruments.

A similar form of presentation is also found in Kampuchea, though now mainly on special occasions only.

Vietnam

Vietnam has for centuries used all the familiar types of puppet and also one that is unique – the 'water puppet'. Each puppet is between thirty and thirty-six inches high and is manipulated by a long bamboo pole with a complexity of strings. A raft forms the stage, which floats on a lake. The puppeteers operate the puppets from approximately twenty to thirty feet away and often have to stand in the water, behind a screen, for many hours whilst performing. The audience watches these presentations from the waterside.

For the plays, the puppeteers have drawn upon traditional materials – often religious or didactic – but now more modern themes are blended with the traditional ones as propaganda and morale boosters.

China

Chinese puppets are usually small but very elaborate. The marionettes are made of wood, ivory, or bone and sometimes have as many as forty strings,

Figure 43   The Fishgirl and the Official: 17th century Chinese shadow puppets

though this is not common. The use of rod puppets has increased as a result of Russian influence.

An old style of glove puppet presentation, *Ku Li Tzu* ('the Coolie Show'), is still in existence. The tiny puppets perform in a small booth styled like a house; it is fastened on the end of a pole that is used to carry it about. For the show, this fit-up is propped against a wall and drapes attached to the booth are released so that they hang down and hide the puppeteer. Sometimes the drapes are tied around the puppeteer's ankles.

There appear to be two main traditional types of shadow puppet: the Peking shadows, intricately made of leather from the belly of a donkey and just over twelve inches high; and the Cantonese shadows which are larger and of thicker leather.

The leather is treated to make it translucent and then dyed to produce delicate colouring. The faces, which are stylised, are always in profile. Those of heroes, rulers and women are mostly cut away, leaving only a thin outline, whilst those of other characters have only a few features cut away. With the large number of characters in each play, the puppet maker must be able to produce a great variety of heads that are immediately distinguishable.

Each figure is controlled by three wires (held in bamboo rods); the wire that supports the figure is fastened by thread to the front of the neck and is held by the operator in one hand while, with his other hand, he holds the rods that control the puppet's hands. Heads are often interchangeable. Limbs hang freely, usually in two sections with joints fastened by knotted thread.

Figure 44   A 'Good Honest
Dragon'(Chinese)

The shadow screen is made of white translucent cloth or strong paper approximately five feet wide and three feet high. It is supported by a framework of bamboo poles with bright drapes hung around the screen. Scenery is extremely simple, and symbolic rather than realistic. Light, traditionally from lanterns, is increasingly provided by electricity.

A shadow puppet company usually consists of up to eight performers, some also acting as musicians. Their plays are akin to the classical theatre's productions, not raucous comedy like Punch and Judy. Traditional themes from Chinese history and legends still survive, but contemporary plays contain much propaganda with workers and peasants among the heroes.

Japan

Japan's puppets are centuries old, having originated, probably, in Korea. Originally they were used mainly for religious presentations but by the middle of the sixteenth century puppet shows had assumed sufficient dramatic form to draw audiences with performances of *noh* plays and *kyogen* comic interludes at religious festivals.

By the middle of the eighteenth century *Bunraku* puppetry completely overshadowed the *kabuki* as popular entertainment and the human theatre regained its position only by emulating the puppet drama. Towards the end of the century, however, the puppet theatres went out of fashion and most closed. Today small shows of all types (drawing upon Japanese and European material) are to be found in the provinces, and the Bunraku puppets still survive, aided by various subsidies.

Bunraku puppets are usually between three and four feet high and are manipulated by three men. The leading operator, the *omo-zukai*, with his left hand holds the puppet in front of his body and works the head, mouth, eyes and eyebrows; with his right hand he operates the right arm and hand of the puppet. He has two assistants: the *hidari-zukai* who works the left

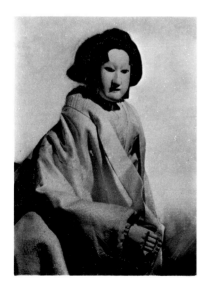

Figure 45   A puppet from the Bunraku Puppet Theatre of Japan

35

Figure 46   A Bunraku performance

hand and arm, and the *ashi-zukai* the junior assistant who manipulates the legs.

All three work with perfect co-ordination and precise timing. Usually they all wear black gowns (*kurogo*) and black hoods, the black costume traditionally representing invisibility or 'nothingness'. In some presentations the main manipulator may wear a brightly coloured robe but, except in gay dance dramas, this is usually regarded as unorthodox.

Less important characters are usually simpler to operate and may have only one or two puppeteers. The Bunraku puppeteers only manipulate the puppets and do not speak. In addition to certain realistic movements there are exaggerated and stylised actions that are unique to Bunraku and detailed rules and forms to be adhered to in conveying all emotions.

The plays presented are often by Chikamatsu Monzaemon (1653 – 1725). He is said to have been the finest dramatist Japan has ever had, specialising in *joruri* plays for the puppet theatre. As the puppets act, the *joruri* (a story in the form of a dramatic epic poem) is told by the *tayu* (the narrator). He explains all the dramatic elements: the story, the action and the personality and psychology of the characters of the play. Musical accompaniment and atmosphere are provided by a *samisen* player.

The roles of *tayu* and *samisen* do not exist just to support the puppets' acting: each stands in its own right and Bunraku depends upon the perfect harmony of these arts with that of the puppet.

Among the notable modern Japanese puppet companies is the PUK Theatre, formed in 1929 by Taiji Kawajiri and which now numbers some hundred members, with a strong influence in television as well as live stage performances. The Takeda Marionette Troupe also has a worldwide reputation and performs with beautifully created string puppets. The company was formed by the late Kinnosuke Takeda, who died in 1979 and was regarded by many as one of the finest exponents of puppet theatre this century.

Figure 47 Wayang golek *wooden rod puppets of Java*

Java

Javanese puppetry is famous for its beautiful *wayang* figures. The term *wayang* is a general term referring to the theatrical performance and is qualified by a further word which defines the particular type of puppet. A great variety of presentations is encompassed by this term; the main ones are as follows.

Wayang golek, wooden rod puppets. This style of puppet probably came to Java from Bengal with the spread of Hinduism.

Wayang klitik, flat, wooden rod puppets with leather arms. The figures are carved in low relief and exquisitely painted. This type of presentation is not often seen today.

Wayang kulit, shadow puppets, the most common of all the *wayang* figures. They are about two feet high and are made from delicately patterned buffalo hide, the design being chiselled out of the leather and then the whole figure painted and gilded. Every aspect of the puppet's design is set down by tradition and is related to the character portrayed.

37

Figure 48 Arjuna, a Javanese wayang kulit *shadow puppet*

Thus the audience gathers all the necessary information about the puppet's character simply from its appearance. Even the angle of the head is significant.

The Javanese puppeteer, the *dalang*, presents his shadow show from dusk to sunrise. The role of the *dalang* has been likened to that of the priest as in Java puppets are thought to be the incarnation of ancestral spirits, and thus the *dalang* is a medium between these spirits and his audience. He manipulates the puppets, speaks all the dialogue, and conducts the *gamelan*, the percussion orchestra which sits behind him.

The *dalang's* cotton screen, or *kelir*, is supported by bamboo sticks and is about five feet high and up to fifteen feet long. Two long stems of banana plant, placed along the bottom of the screen, are used to hold the puppets' rods when they are off stage, the good characters on the right, the evil on the left.

Until recently it was traditional for the men of the audience to sit behind the *dalang* and watch the actual puppets whilst the women sat in front of the screen and watched the shadows cast by the light of an oil lamp on the beautiful figures.

Puppetry in the English-speaking countries

Great Britain

Puppets were known in England by the fourteenth century, possibly introduced by French entertainers in the thirteenth century. By the time of Elizabeth, marionettes and shadow puppets were in use, although glove puppets were the most popular as they were easy to pack and carry around. During this period vagrancy was a serious problem and acts were passed which made these wanderers criminal. Actors and puppeteers were included unless they could find a patron amongst the nobility or were granted a royal licence.

In 1642, with the outbreak of the Civil War, the theatres in England were closed. Puppet performances, however, were not restricted. Thus the eighteen years of the Parliament were a period of unsurpassed popularity for the puppet theatre.

When Charles II returned to England in 1660 entertainers from the Continent, including puppeteers, came with him. These puppeteers brought with them a character called Polichinelle, originally based on the Italian Pulcinello. In England Polichinelle became Punchinello, a name soon shortened to Punch. At that time Punch was a marionette, not a glove puppet.

By the early eighteenth century puppetry was a fashionable entertainment for the wealthy, the puppet show being one of the places at which to be 'seen'. Punch, by then an established and popular character, was included in all manner of plays and had now acquired a wife, Joan, later to become Judy. Later in the century, when interest in puppetry was flagging, the Italian *fantoccini* marionettes made a timely arrival. With their tricks and 'transformations', the *fantoccini* plays gave fresh impetus to the art of puppetry. This was accompanied by new interest in shadow play through the influence of the French *Ombres Chinoises*.

By the end of the eighteenth century the novelty of tricks and transformations began to wear off and Mr Punch came back into the limelight, now as a glove puppet performing for parties and in the streets. By 1825 Punch was at the height of his popularity and the story he played had taken on a standard basic form. Until now puppetry had been an adult entertainment but by 1820 the puppeteers were catering for children.

Marionette performances were still to be seen but as the permanent theatres closed they, like the glove puppets, took to the streets. Their success here was only short-lived and they soon performed in the pleasure gardens, following the example of Punch and Judy for whom this had proved to be a profitable venture. Also to be seen after dark were the street *galanty* shows, a form of shadow show, presented in a Punch and Judy booth, but with a white sheet across the proscenium, illuminated by candlelight.

The travelling marionette companies now took up the melodramas of the live theatre as well as presenting the old traditional tricks in pantomime-style shows. Toward the end of the nineteenth century the puppets' popularity had risen once again and reached a point when England's marionette troupes were considered to be the best in the world.

Figure 49   Punchinello as he was when he first came to England in 1662. This character was recreated by Waldo S. Lanchester, using the head of the late Max Jacob's Casper (of the Hohnstein Puppet Playhouse)

Figure 51 The Cures: collapsible clowns from a 19th century English troupe (probably the Tiller Clowns)

Figure 50 (Left) John Styles, a leading Punch Professor, with a collection of old Punch figures

Great companies toured the globe with wagons carrying large theatres for elaborate productions. This popularity was to decline again, however, with the arrival of the cinema.

The twentieth century has seen yet another revival, and with the advancement of scientific knowledge there has been a parallel development in the techniques and materials used in puppetry, both in construction and in presentation. Interest in the toy and model theatres in the early part of the century led to the formation of the British Model Theatre Guild in 1925 by H. W. Whanslaw and Gerald Morice. This organisation, which subsequently became the British Puppet and Model Theatre Guild, is still active.

In 1943 the Educational Puppetry Association was formed. Much of the credit for the success of the EPA is due to the work of the late A. R. Philpott (the puppeteer 'Pantopuck') who steered the organisation through to its involvement with the Puppet Centre which was formed in 1974. The Puppet Centre (and its Education and Therapy Unit, as the EPA later became) is a charitable trust which is a national and international

Figure 52   Columbine, a marionette of the famous 19th century Barnard Troupe

reference point for all aspects of puppet theatre (see Appendices). The establishment of the Puppet Centre and its subsequent work has been one of the major reasons for the heightened awareness of puppet theatre in Britain today.

There is also a British Centre of UNIMA, the international puppetry organisation. The past President of UNIMA is Jan Bussell, a first-class puppeteer who, with his wife Ann Hogarth, one of the finest marionette operators, has been presenting the Hogarth Puppets for over fifty years. Though known best to the public for their work with 'Muffin the Mule' their work has many facets and they have been very influential ambassadors of puppet theatre worldwide.

There are now a number of permanent puppet theatres of note in

Figure 53 *Wispa the Wizard by the DaSilva Puppets, Norwich Puppet Theatre*

Figure 54 *The Hogarth Puppets'* Macbeth

Figure 55 *(top right) Characters from* The Arabian Nights *by Polka Children's Theatre, London*

Britain, among them, the Harlequin Theatre at Colwyn Bay, directed by Eric Bramall and Christopher Somerville, experts in puppet technique and manipulation, and John Wright's Little Angel Theatre at Islington in London. The Little Angel has been the training ground for a number of well-known puppeteers and here the beautiful presentations cater successfully for both children and adults. Puppet theatres have also been established within recreation halls and arts centres, the most active of these being that directed by John Blundall in the Midlands Arts Centre, Birmingham. John Blundall is also Chairman of British UNIMA.

Recently two new theatres have been founded: the Norwich Puppet Theatre, the home of the DaSilva Puppet Company, and the Polka Children's Theatre in Wimbledon, London. Both are ambitious enterprises which have met with great success under the direction of two well established directors, Ray DaSilva and Richard Gill respectively.

It is impossible to mention all the puppet performers who deserve acknowledgement of their skills and talents. They range from 'suitcase puppeteers', who can pack all of their equipment into one or two cases, to

Figure 56 Zeus and Hera from Of Gods and Greeks *by the Caricature Theatre, Wales*

Figure 57 A scene from Two Magic Cows *by Cannon Hill Puppet Theatre, Birmingham*

those who are fortunate enough to have their own permanent theatre. Their presentations vary from the old traditional acts, such as Punch and Judy and the fantoccini-type shows to pantomimes, plays, ballet, opera and experiments in modern art forms.

Others are actively engaged in making puppet films, especially for television, where puppets have cut themselves a fairly large slice of viewing

Figure 60 Chinese Kites, *an item from* Playspace *by Theatre of Puppets*

time. Apart from educational television, they are to be seen frequently in the programmes for young children, in the 'space-age' series, often referred to as *supermarionation*, in variety shows, satirical programmes and a large number of advertisements.

The tremendous possibilities of puppetry, not only as an art form but also as an educational and therapeutic agent, have been realised in recent years, and are being thoroughly explored by teachers, social and medical workers and many professional bodies.

Figure 61 Camberwick Green, *a 'stop-action' television series by the Gordon Murray Puppets*

Figure 64   Giant Bird by Majorie Batchelder McPharlin for Weapons of Lightning, *a Navajo Indian play by Virginia Lee Comer*

The United States of America

The first American puppeteers were the Indians, the puppets they used probably a development of the mask. The Northwest Coast Indians are known to have used beautifully carved cedar wood masks in religious ceremonies of a dramatic nature. The Hopi Indians of the American Southwest also used both human and animal figures in forms of puppet drama. In these and many other societies a development from the mask to the marionette may be clearly discerned.

There is no one tradition that typifies American puppetry for it has drawn upon the puppetry styles of many nations. When in 1524 Cortes went to Honduras in search of gold there was a puppeteer in his entourage. The first English-style marionette show that can be traced in America was presented by a puppeteer named Holt in New York in 1738 and was *The Adventures of Harlequin and Scaramouche*.

When Maximilian became Emperor of Mexico in 1864, Guignol was introduced to the American continent. In the nineteenth century the Greeks came to North America with Karaghiosis, and immigrants from all parts of Europe brought with them their own styles and traditions. Such were the influences upon American puppetry, but the presentations were very much 'patriotic' affairs, with the Greek showmen playing in Greek and for Greeks, and so on. Only with the third and fourth generations did the puppeteers begin to play to audiences of a more international flavour.

Towards the end of the nineteenth century a few American puppeteers began to gain international recognition. Probably the most outstanding of these was Walter Deaves. One of his world tours lasted seven years and it was he who developed the idea of having an elaborate puppet theatre, with boxes for the puppet audience and a puppet orchestra, in which to present puppet shows on the vaudeville stage. In fact, the whole fit-up could fill a live theatre stage.

By the twentieth century it was recognised that puppetry was capable of being a much more intellectual form of artistic expression than it has previously been and European fashions influenced the puppeteers to produce plays rather than variety. One of the foremost performers of the age was Tony Sarg (1880 – 1942), the son of a German consul. Sarg set out as an illustrator in London, took up puppetry and moved to New York in 1915. Although he designed and operated his puppets, they were in fact made by other puppeteers. His productions were so successful that the majority of American puppeteers followed his lead.

Remo Bufano (1894 – 1948), born in New York of Italian parents, was one of the experimental puppeteers who developed their own individual styles during this period. Probably his most successful creations were the giant marionettes which he designed and made for Robert Edmond Jones' production of *Oedipus Rex*.

Bufano was a travelling performer with no permanent theatre, like most puppeteers of the period. By the late twenties there were about a dozen large travelling companies in North America but most were destined to close with the Depression.

One of the leading puppeteers this century was Paul McPharlin, a key figure in the formation of the Puppeteers of America organisation in 1937. He wrote *The History of the Puppet Theatre in America* which was

Figure 65 The Kuklapolitans *by Burr Tillstrom*

Figure 66 The Frost Giant and the Spirit of Spring from Holiday on Strings *by Bil Baird*

Figure 67 One of the Pod People from Henson Associates' film of The Dark Crystal

Figure 68   Two items by Bruce Schwartz, U.S.A.

completed by his wife, Majorie Batchelder McPharlin, also an accomplished puppeteer.

After the Second World War, American puppeteers began to delve into the possibilities of 'modern puppetry'. Many of the large puppet companies had disappeared but a new army of solo performers emerged, often performing in full view of the audience in the now familiar cabaret-style or open-stage presentations.

Developments were made in educational and therapeutic puppetry and many puppeteers, among them Bil Baird and Burr Tillstrom, kept pace with modern trends in television, advertising and films.

Burr Tillstrom with his creations Kukla and Ollie began making television shows – *The Kuklapolitans* – in 1939. He was among the first of the television performers and went from strength to strength. Today the Kuklapolitans still hold their position in American puppetry.

Bil Baird at one time toured with Tony Sarg, then formed his own show which he has directed for over fifty years, performing for night-clubs, films and television. He has established himself as an international puppeteer of high repute and his book, *The Art of the Puppet*, is a magnificent work.

One of the biggest impacts on puppetry in recent years has been made by Jim Henson, creator of the Muppets and President Emeritus of UNIMA-USA. His work is discussed in more detail in Chapter 11. Peter Schumann's Bread and Puppet Theatre is another revolutionary puppet company, often working with giant figures in the style of street theatre, which sharply contrasts to the art of Bruce Schwartz whose exquisite masterpieces capture at one moment the quiet power of the oriental tradition and at another the finest raucous glove puppetry.

These performers represent the wide scope of the American puppetry scene which reflects the international influences upon it over the years.

Canada

Many Canadian companies are quickly establishing a reputation for high quality puppet theatre. Notable amongst them is Felix Mirbt who works with actors and large puppets, drawing upon such sources as Ibsen's *Dream*. Another company using larger-than-life-size puppets is Théâtre Sans Fils whose performances for adults are based on Canadian folk legends. These legends are also the source of inspiration for the Manitoba Puppet Theatre which uses a combination of puppets and masks. In a suburb of Toronto a puppet centre has been established in a converted school building and the Canadian Government is extremely supportive of puppet theatre which is progressing accordingly.

Australia

Australian puppet theatre in recent years owes much to the work of Edith Murray whose Clovelly Puppet Theatre has been the training ground for a number of established puppeteers. Now internationally acclaimed for his shadow puppetry, Richard Bradshaw is the most prominent personality in Australian puppetry today. He has also been the Director of the Marionette Theatre of Australia which has acquired a new theatre in the Sailors Home Building in Sydney.

Handspan Theatre, based in Melbourne, has a very distinctive contemporary philosophy and style and is committed to extending the boundaries of visual theatre. The company creates a very powerful and appealing blend of images, music and dialogue which gives the audience a unique experience in puppet theatre.

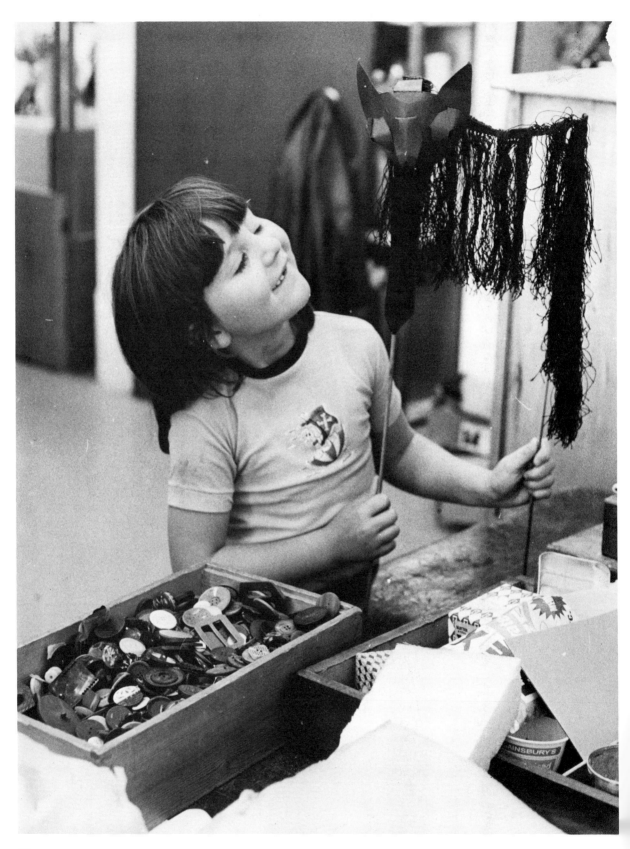

3 Puppetry in education

Puppetry and learning experiences

Children demonstrate tremendous enthusiasm for using puppets and puppetry can contribute greatly to many aspects of the child's learning and development. It provides opportunities to meet, explore and understand a wide range of concepts, knowledge, skills and situations, but one must distinguish between *learning* with puppets and *teaching* with puppets. It is in the hands of the children themselves that the real value of puppetry in education is to be found. There are those who set out to 'teach the concept of ...' using puppets but this is a very dubious activity which does not match what we know about how children attain concepts and the role of *experience* in learning.

Puppetry provides a stimulus for, and reinforcement of, the child's learning as he engages in a wealth of concrete experiences which are linked to a purposeful activity. As such it is the sort of activity that should consistently be available in the classroom rather than something just for special occasions.

Puppetry incorporates all manner of art and craft activities, but also opens up the whole realm of performance possibilities – which may be anything from a child sitting with two puppets in a quiet corner to a full production. It is when puppets are made but not used that puppetry becomes a dead-end and children's enthusiasm is lost.

It brings together children of widely differing abilities and interests to contribute to the common purpose. It also integrates different areas of the curriculum, though teachers should take care not to engineer artificial links where there is no real logic to such integration. The underlying principles apply throughout the whole educational range; the actual concepts involved and the techniques used may vary in complexity or depth but the ways in which puppet theatre permeates the curriculum are basically the same, whatever the level.

The mathematical aspects include such activities as measurement, sorting, classifying and matching; dealing with shape, proportion, weight, designs and scale drawings, plans and elevations; spatial relationships such as things being 'beside', 'behind' and 'around'; sight lines and viewing angles, etc. Similarly the child may be exploring levers, pivots, counterbalance, pulleys, sound and light, electricity (with batteries) and properties of colour or perhaps looking at scientific concepts of ourselves.

Environmental studies provide the background knowledge to the performance – the period, the people, their ways of life, and so on. Not only is knowledge gained in this way but children learn how to seek and handle knowledge, and it is linked to a very definite purpose which they

Figure 1 (Opposite) A class workshop session at the Puppet Centre, London

Figure 2 Exploring possible materials: a co-operative activity at the Puppet Centre

understand. This also provides opportunities to explore other people's situations and points of view, and the performance encourages children to decentre and to explore notions of intentions and consequences, which is a strong element in moral development. But, again, the 'using puppets to teach morals' approach, which depends on the power of the puppet to convince, is quite inappropriate, for it encourages the child to look to the puppet as a powerful authority determining what he thinks and does, rather than to look for *reasons* for moral decisions.

The performance requires the child to explore and develop not only the puppet's movement but also his own, for one's own bodily awareness is a significant part of performing with puppets. He can be invited to achieve variety and quality of movement, to explore the puppet's bodily movement, its movement in space and in relation to other characters. Choosing music by listening, reflecting and discussing may be appropriate for some; also improvisations and the use of published music with self-made and school instruments. Music may be used too as a stimulus for the action or as a background, providing mood and atmosphere.

Through the drama the children may explore and represent imaginative fantasies, everyday situations, and the realities of the wider world. It helps to heighten understanding, awareness and insight. The children bring spoken language to bear upon their experiences, from the negotiation of the materials needed, their properties, colour, shape, texture, through to the story, characterisation, etc. Written work will follow with the writing of the story or scenario, planning the performance, details of characters, the props list, lighting and effects details, invitations, posters, programmes and a record of the project and its progress. Second language teaching benefits from all of these activities but also from the motivation to talk in a foreign tongue, and it is widely recognised that working with puppets helps to overcome inhibitions.

Fundamental to all of this work is a need for puppetry to be a challenge, whether physical, technical, intellectual or social. The problem with much educational puppetry is that the children are not extended; they continue year after year to make the same sorts of puppet and perform the same sorts of performance, so it becomes a trivial activity. It can be undertaken at any level so it is suitable for any child and *can* and *should* always be a challenge.

Children with special needs

Children who have behaviour problems and learning difficulties suffer particularly from a poor self-image. Many do not like themselves and are convinced that they have nothing to offer, yet with puppets they can be successful with an activity which they, their teachers, parents and other children value. *They* can have something to offer too.

It is very important for them to be allowed to make a contribution to the community. Very often we deny them this opportunity by providing everything for them. If they can produce a show and can go and give it to other people, they can regain their self-respect. They benefit from the same puppetry experiences as any other children as outlined above, but for these children such concrete experiences are even more important and fundamental to their learning.

Puppetry can be additionally helpful to maladjusted children in that they can be violent with puppets and enjoy this without guilt – it is those grotesque puppets doing it to one another, not actual human beings. They can express feelings against society and authority and can escape from the front that they need to maintain before their peers. Puppetry gives them the opportunity to make a different statement: to say things they would not otherwise say. Maladjusted children often have something to say and perhaps nobody has ever listened to them. They take their puppets and make their statements, and there is no need for the teacher to go back over it and try to discuss it with them, to pursue it as a sort of 'therapy'. They have made their statement and that is it; the therapy has taken place in making the statement.

This raises the whole question of therapy, which must be left to the properly qualified person. The value of puppetry here is considerable, but not well defined; puppetry as therapy can release some very powerful forces, the implications of which are not widely understood. There is too much loose talk about puppets in therapy and too many people who dabble in it in an undesirable way.

Disabled children also benefit from the experience of puppetry, for the same reasons as any other child. Puppets can be operated from hospital beds, from wheelchairs, with the feet and by deaf and blind children. They can be held with all manner of necessary attachments and the child can play any character, whatever capabilities the role demands. It is used very effectively to encourage children to exercise fingers, hands, limbs and muscles to an extent which they would otherwise reject.

There are also a few companies specialising in performances for 'normal' children with themes aimed at increasing awareness, acceptance and integration of children with handicaps. Kids on the Block is one such American company whose puppet characters have all manner of disabilities. Out of context, the idea of 'disabled puppets' may seem questionable but this company handles the themes with care, sensitivity and taste.

Some controversy exists in this area for there is one school of thought which maintains that effective integration and acceptance occurs when those with special needs perform and, thus, have something to offer which is valued by others. They maintain that these other approaches to increase awareness, however well-intentioned, highlight differences and disabilities rather than promote integration. At the time of writing, a British research project to appraise such approaches is planned in co-operation with the Education and Therapy Unit of the Puppet Centre.

Introducing puppetry

Children will be aware of puppets on the television and may be used to having them available in the classroom from the time they enter school. The initiative for puppet activities may then come from them and the idea very quickly spreads. Perhaps the teacher has used puppets for story-telling (the one occasion when it is appropriate for the teacher to do so) and will suggest that some children might like to make their own. Otherwise the impetus might come from a performance or a demonstration which is to be followed by a workshop and the children's own performance.

It may be desirable to start a few children on the activity, as they may need a good deal of attention, and then to open up the work to an increasing number of the class. Providing it is very well organised, there is no reason why suitable puppets should not be made as a whole class activity. It is recommended that the children are not shown *the way* to make puppets, but possibilities are explored together. For example, take a yogurt pot: 'What could this become? ... the head? ... which way would you use it? ... what else do we need? ... eyes? ... can you see anything suitable in the box? ... where shall we put them? ... can you see anything else we could use for eyes? ...', and so on. Identify the possibilities, then set the children to work using whatever materials are to hand.

It is essential to have a collection of materials suitably sorted and labelled (see Chapter 5), good tools (there is more danger of accidents with

Figure 3   An impromptu glove puppet performance by nine-year-olds

Figure 4   Mask puppets made by children in an Indian village near Madras

blunt tools than with sharp ones) and good adhesives suitable for the range of materials to be used. Newspaper to cover the tables can be rolled up and thrown away so things can be quickly cleared up, and the organisation of particular tables, for gluing, sewing, painting, etc., helps to prevent accidents like paint getting spilt on somebody's material. The momentum of the construction should be kept up so as to leave sufficient time for the performance.

What type of puppet?

Clearly, much will depend on the ages and abilities of the children and the requirements of the purpose for which puppets are to be used. It is

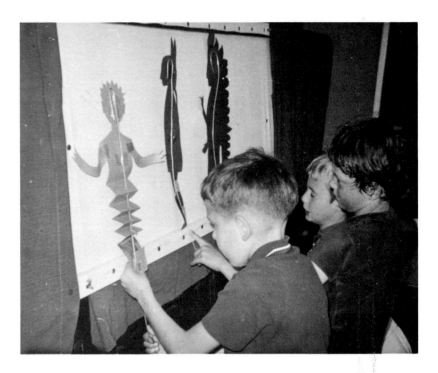

Figure 5   A class shadow puppet show

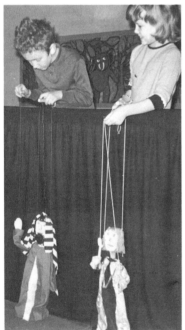

Figure 6   Mark and Diana manipulate junk-box marionettes with only four strings

Figure 7   Junior school children operating shadow puppets with illumination from a window behind the screen

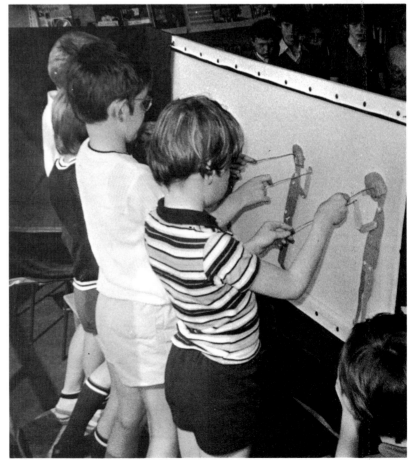

popularly thought that glove puppets are the most suitable for young children, but this is not necessarily the case. Remember that each type can be as simple or as complicated as desired.

Glove and rod puppets have an intimacy with the operator that *is* particularly suitable for young children, but the glove body is quite difficult to make and its gestures are limited to the movement of the tiny fingers inside it. These manipulation skills may be appropriate but some little hands are better holding a simple rod puppet, which also offers considerable scope for creative use of materials.

Marionettes and more complicated rod puppets are generally suitable for older children but simple ones are possible. Shadow puppets are quick to make, easy to operate and powerful in their effect. They are appropriate from the time the child is able to understand the concept and to work seeing the puppet but not seeing the shadow he is creating, for only the audience will see this. Shadow puppets deserve much more attention than they receive at present.

When working with older children one has to overcome the trivial image of puppetry. One way is to introduce larger puppets: those which require two operators to co-ordinate their movements or whole body figures which the young person works from inside and moves or dances with. These help to get away from the 'dolly' image. Some people use huge puppets; though these do have fabulous presence, there is not a lot one can do with them.

Whatever the type of puppet, the construction techniques and performance possibilities are detailed in the following chapters. 'Instant' puppets are suitable for many purposes, and these can be quite complex despite the rather misleading term. There is no need today to take two or three weeks to make a head, waiting for each stage to dry while the enthusiasm dwindles. However, while maintaining technical progression, older children should be challenged appropriately with the construction and the performance.

The performance

The 'performance' may be a child representing an everyday situation, it may be based on a child's story, a nursery rhyme, a song, a folk tale, a published story, etc. It is advisable to start with a theme or story, rather than with puppets in search of a story. If the children commit themselves by holding up the puppets for an improvisation, and then dry up, not knowing where to go, a crisis point arises and the usual outcome is to make the puppets fight. This applies particularly to children without experience of using puppets; once they have discovered the possibilities and limitations, they are better equipped to improvise, though they will still require support.

Usually it pays to work from a scenario as some structure is needed, but a script to be learned word-for-word is generally to be discouraged. It prevents spontaneity and the vitality and freshness achieved when some freedom within a framework is possible; moreover, forgotten lines and technical hitches can result in terrible confusion if the performers are not used to improvisation. Tape-recordings have many of the same disadvantages and do not have the power of the live voice to hold attention. To get

Figure 8 The Laundryman and his Wife from The Secret of Fire, *a play by ten-year-olds*

the best performances from children, and for them to get the most out of the activity, it is important for the child who operates also to speak for his puppet, to achieve the identification and concentration that is so typical of good puppet theatre. Further considerations for the performance are detailed in Chapters 14 and 15.

Booking a professional show

Headteachers:
    'It was not at all what we expected.'
    'The show was not suitable for infants.'
    'The puppets were beautifully made but the manipulation and acting were disappointing.'

Puppeteers:

> 'We arrived in good time to set up but the hall was full of children eating lunch.'
>
> 'The headmistress was a lovely lady but, by the time she had finished telling them to behave and be quiet, we had difficulty in getting them to participate.'
>
> 'They wanted us to perform on the school stage but it was not big enough for our fit-up.'

These are just a sample of the comments heard frequently from schools and puppet companies but there are ways to avoid most misunderstandings and to find a suitable show. The places to start are your local newspaper advertisements, your professional publications, or your local or national puppetry organisations (see Appendices or consult the telephone directory). When you have obtained publicity brochures from a number of companies, study them carefully – and read between the lines. You can learn quite a lot from the quality of their leaflets and the statements that they make.

It will help if you are clear about what *you* expect and why you want a puppet show. Is it for a Christmas party, a school fête, to launch, boost or round off a topic, a way of introducing 'story' in another form, a means to extend language work, or perhaps the lead-in to your own puppetry activities? Just the experience of theatre is so valuable to very many of our children and serves as a springboard for a wide range of activities. If you are clear about what you are trying to achieve and where you think the value lies for your children, you have more chance of selecting a suitable show.

Have you any preference (or prejudices) about the type of puppet? Try to keep an open mind as the puppeteers will have chosen the medium to suit that particular performance. Glove puppets are splendid for fast-moving action and, well handled, can be quite charming. The fit-up is usually moderate in size but so too are the puppets, so take care over the size of audience and seating arrangements (especially, do not push very young children up close to the booth as the viewing angle and sight-lines will be impossible for them). Rod puppets have a particular grace and can be any size; it is worth exploring them if the children are familiar only with glove puppets. The staging is usually more elaborate and will take a little longer to set up. Marionettes are not often seen in schools, partly because of the complexity of travelling a large fit-up with a bridge for operators, and visibility can be difficult unless they are sufficiently raised above the floor (check the headroom for the puppeteers). However, some companies have less conventional methods of presentation which overcome these problems. Finally, shadow puppets have a great deal of scope and with recent innovations can be very colourful presentations, especially good for story-telling. Shadow shows followed by workshop sessions are increasingly popular, both because of the speed of construction and the effectiveness of the puppets.

You also need to consider whether you want the performance for a class, various classes or the whole school, for some are clearly more suitable for intimate groups whilst others can play in large theatres. Sometimes it is a good idea to have the show twice – for different age groups – rather than

Figure 9 Pluto, King of the Under-world, from a story-telling project with nine-year-olds by Froebel College students, London

Figure 10 Barbara Aiello with some of the Kids on the Block

having one large audience: some companies present slightly different versions with language, action and length tailored to the age group.

Do you want just a performance? A performance and brief demonstration? A performance and a workshop session? This decision may make a big difference to your choice of company. But beware! Not all those offering performances and workshops have the experience or ability to handle the latter successfully though they may present a good show.

What else do you need to ascertain before approaching a company? Where is the show to be given and what space, including headroom, is available? Do you have *total* blackout? (This is important if you want a show using ultra-violet lighting and fluorescent colours). How long do you want the performance to be? One of the most common faults with puppet shows is that they are too long, so if you were thinking of an hour and the performer suggests forty minutes, he probably does know best! Be cautious if it is the other way round. Finally, how much do you want to pay? By and large you get what you pay for and you may reckon on anything from £35 for a reputable small one-man show to much larger sums for a well-known company (travel expenses will depend on location). Whatever the size of the show, if you want the best, you will have to pay for it.

Having decided upon your priorities, it is inevitable that you will have to be flexible and make some compromises, as you identify those who appear most appropriate. But how do you know they are as good as they would have you believe and, however competent they may be, that they are suitable for your needs?

You may write for further information and raise any queries, but a brief telephone call to the Director or Administrator may help you more to determine what you want to know. Most established companies depend on their reputation and on word-of-mouth recommendations so it is not in their interests deliberately to sell you an inappropriate show. However good a company, the quality of different items in their repertoire will vary, so ask them to send with their literature copies of any reviews of the current show and details of other schools or venues where they have performed. Another quick telephone call to one or two previous bookings will be well worth the effort. Also ask them to provide details about their technical requirements and about the show (a précis of the story, suitability of age-range, size of audience, duration, type of puppet). Also check whether the fee is inclusive of travel, accommodation (where necessary) and tax.

In conclusion, please look after the puppeteers and make sure you have everything ready for them to set up when they arrive. They might also welcome a cup of tea or coffee. You would be amazed at some of the situations they encounter and the demands made upon them (though some of them do need to be more professional too). Do not rush them in and hustle them away – you will be missing a lot if you do. Many of them have much to share and *you* will find it valuable to entertain *them*.

*Figure 1   A design by Brian Froud
for one of the Mystics in* The Dark
Crystal

*Figure 2   A Character from the
Cannon Hill Puppet Theatre production of* The Tales of Hoffmann

4 Puppet design

Principles of design

The newcomer to puppet theatre often begins by making a puppet, with no particular idea of what the puppet is to be or what it is to do. He sees what the head starts to look like as it progresses and develops whatever seems to emerge. There is, understandably, a need to explore the materials but the product of such an approach may be less satisfactory than it could have been and its potential is often limited to practising manipulation. This also tends to reinforce the all too common practice of making puppets as a craft activity and not following up with the performance.

It is a good idea to start with a project in mind, however simple, and to know what the puppet is to be and do. Then you can design a specific puppet for a specific purpose. At times it will be necessary to explore different techniques as the puppet progresses; some decisions cannot be made at the design stage. Having tried one possibility, some adjustment or alternative method may prove necessary, but here the construction methods are subservient to the overall design rather than the emerging puppet's character being dictated by the techniques employed.

The two main aims when creating a puppet are to construct a figure that embodies the character you wish to convey and to operate it so that its movements convey character and emotions to the audience.

The puppet is an essence and an emphasis of the character it is intended to reflect. The puppet artist has to create and interpret character, not imitate it: he selects those characteristics that he considers most suitable to express the personality he has imagined. He has considerable freedom for not only does he design the costumes of his actors, he also creates their heads, faces, body shapes, etc.

Whatever the puppet represents, it must be distinctly and boldly modelled, for delicate features, however beautiful, will be lost on the puppet stage. The puppet that lacks bold modelling and exaggerated design will appear nondescript to an audience only a matter of feet away.

The artist studies natural form but he does not simply copy what he sees; he interprets it by searching for the underlying structures and then working on these. So must the puppet maker. To take the example of the face, he must look to the basic structure, to see what is happening 'behind' the face and how it gets its form.

Study different people in all kinds of moods, not with the idea of copying a particular head or body shape but to see how it 'works'. Take the person in a thoughtful mood: what is it in his face and bearing that characterises his mood? Now he looks happy, but what changes have occurred to his face? What is it that produces the happy expression? What makes that same face look sad? And so on. This kind of study leads to greater understanding not only for the artist and sculptor but also for the puppeteer.

It is an excellent plan to keep a scrapbook of drawings, pictures, and ideas. Pictures of people of all ages and types, people in uniform or costume, features, cartoons, greetings cards, advertisements and magazine articles (e.g. on eye make-up or hair styles) are just a few examples of useful reference and inspiration sources. Hansjürgen Fettig (*Glove and Rod Puppets*, Harrap, 1973) suggests some excellent exercises which may be adapted to use with such a reference collection.

1 Pick out a selection of pictures of heads and pair strikingly different ones.
2 Taking each pair in turn, try to identify the characteristics of each partner and list the ways in which they differ, in terms of overall impression or character and more specific detail of shape, features, etc. What sort of profession, temperament, intelligence, leisure pursuits would you attribute to each? What else could you say about them?
3 Having completed the exercise for about eight pairs, reflect on the list; not only will you see how much we 'read into' a face but you should try to identify what information you make most use of in arriving at such decisions. That is, the most significant aspects to bear in mind.

Similar exercises can be carried out in relation to body types and the changing shape with increasing age. Often the beginner makes his puppet, drawing upon what he thinks he 'knows' about people: he makes children smaller, adults bigger, and tries to convey all the character in the face. The result is a puppet that is not convincing. He needs to conceive the puppet design as a whole and for this he needs to *observe* and analyse what he sees.

It must be emphasised that the purpose of these exercises is to enhance awareness and not to create a puppet that tries to replicate human proportions and movement. The puppet will look unnatural if given human proportion; it is the variations on such proportions that are important in creating a caricature which will be dramatically effective in the puppet theatre.

Attention must be drawn particularly to the importance of the puppet's eyes. Brian Froud, the artist and illustrator who produced the designs for the Jim Henson film *The Dark Crystal*, explains that his designs always start with the eyes: 'Once I have got them right, the rest follows naturally.' They are so important to human and puppet communication, and it is the eyes which, perhaps more than any other single feature, bring the face to life.

Proportion and design

Although strict adherence to the 'rules' of proportion does not make for an interesting and effective puppet, there are useful guidelines which form a basis upon which to work, and certain principles which apply to humans and puppets.

Whilst the head is approximately a seventh of the total height of an adult human, for a puppet it is about a fifth (figure 3) but might be as much as a

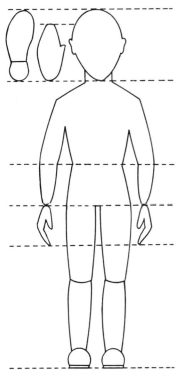

Figure 3 Proportion

66

Figure 4 Two sentries from The Soldier's Tale *by the Little Angel Theatre*

quarter or as little as a sixth. With humans and puppets, the hand is approximately the length from the chin to the middle of the forehead and covers most of the face. The hand is also the same length as the forearm and the upper arm, the feet a little longer. Elbows are level with the waist, the wrist with the bottom of the body and the finger tips halfway down the thigh. The body is generally a little shorter than the legs.

Attention must be given to body shape as well as proportion. Common mistakes are to make the puppet too tall and thin and lacking any real body shape, particularly the profile. It is useful to hold the puppet between a strong light and a blank wall and to examine the shadows it casts as it moves; strongly designed puppets will create strong and interesting shadows too. Figure 4 illustrates deliberate variations on the norm for dramatic effect.

The importance of the unity of the design becomes clear when one sees mistakes such as a fat head and body coupled with neck, arms and legs that

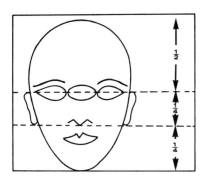

Figure 5 A guide to suitable proportions for the head. Top of ears align with eyes. Bottom of ears align with nose. The eyes are approximately one eye's width apart

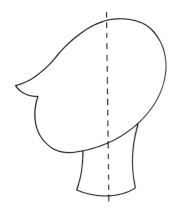

Figure 6 Setting the head on the neck

are too long or too skinny. Though they may be covered with clothes it is very noticeable if there is insufficient bulk.

The angle at which the head sits on the body and the way in which it moves are essential to characterisation, so there are important considerations for the positioning of joints between the head, neck and body.

The head can be divided into four approximately equal parts: the chin to the nose; the nose to the eyes; the eyes to the hairline; the hairline to the top of the skull which is slightly less than the other sections. Thus the eyes are approximately halfway between the chin and the top of the skull (slightly nearer to the top). The top and bottom of the ears are normally in line with the top and bottom of the nose.

It is a common mistake to make the eyes too high in the head or too close together, foreheads too low and ears too high or too small for the head. Ears should be studied from the side and from behind: they contribute to characterisation more than is generally realised. Viewed in profile, the neck is not in the centre of the head but set further back depending on character (figure 6).

Again it is the variations from the norm which are usually most significant. For example, the eyes are shown as approximately one eye's width apart, but the spacing in fact depends upon the width of the nose and the characterisation required. The age of a character affects the proportions of the head, and the addition of hair can completely change its apparent shape.

When considering head proportions, pay special attention to the bulking of hair on the head. Keep this in mind from the initial stages of head making, as the shape of the skull may need to be related to the bulk of the 'hair'. This contributes to the eventual size and shape of the head and, obviously, thick fur and dyed string will have different influences upon size, shape and, therefore, character.

It is not always appreciated that small variations on a shape can create a wide range of characters. Too often the face has too much detail, which clutters up the design and interferes with the effective conveying of character. In principle, keep it bold and simple with clean lines to achieve greater dramatic effect.

Costume

Research costumes carefully and try to identify the essential characteristics of a period. It is the simple costume design which captures the essence of the line that is usually the most effective, so do not let the design become too fussy or cluttered. One can often reflect the shape of the puppet – or perhaps the head – in the costume, so that there is some unity to all aspects of design.

Suits of clothes made for a puppet as one would for a doll are not likely to be successful and will probably restrict movement. It is usually much more satisfactory to create the costume directly onto the puppet, gluing or stitching as appropriate. Gluing tends to be quicker and leaves no seam edges inside the clothes to hinder movement; any seams which are subject to strain will need a few stitches however. The glue used depends on the material. UHU, Bostik No 1 or Sobo glues are suitable for most materials.

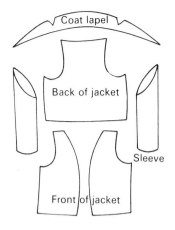

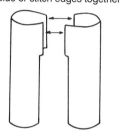

Glue or stitch edges together

Figure 7   Costume construction

To make a hem, smear glue sparingly but evenly along the edge, turn it up and press firmly. To make a seam, glue one edge and press it on top of the other. The use of glue prevents the outer edge fraying. The glue method is not suitable for costumes such as flowing robes with gathers as glue will stiffen the hem and prevent it falling in the desired folds.

The basic shape for trousers are two tubes of cloth fastened together at the top (figure 7). For a jacket, begin with the front and back panels, then add the sleeves, collar and lapels. A shirt under a jacket needs only a wide strip of material glued down the front of the body and a narrower strip around the neck for the collar. Period styles follow a similar process, with the shapes modified to achieve the intended line.

Dresses usually require front and back panels for the bodice, and sleeves added; the skirt may be cut in one piece or in a number of panels. Some costumes are created by simply draping, stitching and gluing a single piece of fabric onto the puppet.

The fabrics used should stand up to wear but they should also be soft and fairly lightweight. If they are too heavy they will hinder movement; if too thin, light will shine through. They should also drape and move well: jersey fabric cut on the cross is particularly suitable for full, flowing robes (see Chapter 15, figure 3).

When choosing a fabric, see how it hangs on the straight, on the cross and try the right and wrong sides. Note differences in texture, considering especially its appearance from a distance, and use combinations of textures to achieve variety and set off one another. Puppets dressed only in jersey fabrics or in polyester cottons will not look so interesting.

Felt is useful for trimmings but puppeteers hoard all manner of fringing, braids, ribbons, lace, fur, beads, costume jewellery, etc. for their costumes.

The colours for a costume will depend on how suitable they are for the effect you want to achieve. Certain colours do tend to suggest particular characters or moods such as gaiety or evil, but one is not limited to stereotyped conventions of colour symbolism: there are successful exceptions to most rules. It may be useful to consider the colour wheel (figure 8) showing the primary and secondary colours. To create harmony in a costume, having chosen one colour, one would then look to the *analogous* colours (the neighbouring colours and the tertiary shades in between them). But one needs also to accentuate colours by the use of a little of a *complementary* colour (that opposite your predominant colour on the colour wheel). It is not usually appropriate to combine complementaries in equal parts or they will clash.

It is worth exploring the use of nets and sheer fabrics over another material – for example, a pale voile over a deeper colour or a dark lace over a vibrant colour. Try using different shades of the same colour, contrasting colours and the effects of a white overlay on darker colours.

While black works well for stage drapes, it is seldom successful for costumes as it tends to look flat; good substitutes are dark blue, dark green or dark brown.

Avoid large prints as these often look ludicrous on small puppets. Sometimes it will be necessary to stencil or paint a required pattern on a plain fabric, using textile paint or very thin acrylic paint. Despite the vast range of available fabrics, it is still difficult to find the right colour in the particular fabric, so it might be necessary to dye the fabric. Always test a

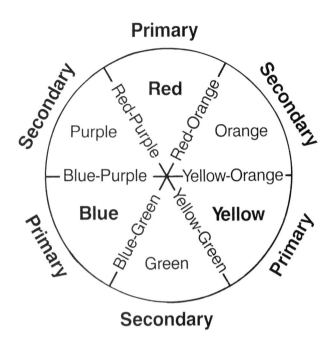

Figure 8 Colour wheel. See previous page

small piece of the fabric first: see how it looks when it is dry as it is impossible to judge while it is still wet. Dye the fabric before making it up into the costume and treat sufficient material to allow for errors in cutting and making up the costume, as it is difficult to match the colour with another batch of dye.

Finally, but by no means least, remember that coloured lighting has a tremendous influence on the colour of costumes so, when selecting the fabrics, have regard for the settings in which the character will appear. You might be able to adjust the lighting a little, but it is no use, for example, to have a red costume in what is conceived as an eerie scene utilising a good deal of green light. One soon develops a knowledge of these things, but it is wise to try swatches of possible materials under stage lights before purchasing the fabric.

A note on methods

Enthusiasts have been known to get bothered when confronted with conflicting advice on the same topic in different books. In a sense this is like trying to cook whilst following two different recipes. There is seldom any *one* way of doing anything in puppet construction; some techniques work for one person but never quite suit another. This knowledge is gained only by experience and each puppeteer develops his own style and methodology.

There are occasions in the text when a particular approach is recommended, but many others when alternatives are offered to allow for individual preference and differences in availability of materials.

However, there are basic principles which are inherent in all the

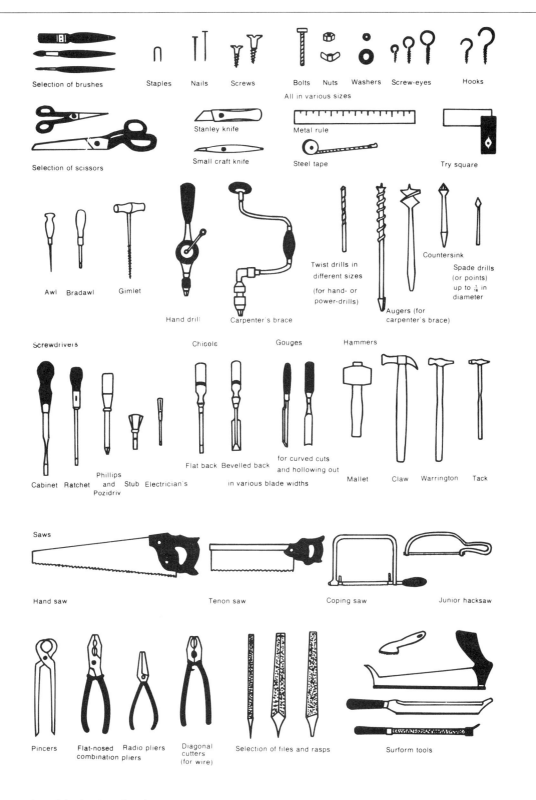

Figure 9 A useful selection of tools

Selection of brushes   Staples   Nails   Screws   Bolts   Nuts   Washers   Screw-eyes   Hooks

All in various sizes

Selection of scissors   Stanley knife   Metal rule   Try square

Small craft knife   Steel tape

Awl   Bradawl   Gimlet   Hand drill   Carpenter's brace   Twist drills in different sizes (for hand- or power-drills)   Augers (for carpenter's brace)   Countersink   Spade drills (or points) up to $\frac{1}{16}$ in diameter

Screwdrivers   Chisels   Gouges   Hammers

Cabinet   Ratchet   Phillips and Pozidriv   Stub   Electrician's   Flat back   Bevelled back   for curved cuts and hollowing out   in various blade widths   Mallet   Claw   Warrington   Tack

Saws

Hand saw   Tenon saw   Coping saw   Junior hacksaw

Pincers   Flat-nosed combination pliers   Radio pliers   Diagonal cutters (for wire)   Selection of files and rasps   Surform tools

71

techniques. Once you understand these you will find that you too acquire your own nuances of construction as you follow the techniques outlined and develop or adapt them to your particular purposes.

These days it is only Mr Punch who says: 'That's *the* way to do it!'

A note on tools

One of the splendid things about puppet theatre is that it is suitable for all ages and abilities. You can take up puppet theatre at whatever level is appropriate to you and it can always provide a challenge. Similarly a workshop can function with just a pair of scissors, glue, thread and tape, but for those who wish to explore beyond instant puppets a small collection of tools is essential. Figure 9 illustrates a good selection to work towards. Puppeteers are notorious for improvising – for example, using a headless nail, sharpened with a file, instead of a small drill bit – but care should be taken for reasons of safety and respect for your tools. A chisel that is used to open tins of paint will have a very short life as a decent wood working tool and brushes are expensive to replace when they have not been properly cleaned. Scissors need to be sharp and will stay so only if used for appropriate materials, keeping the fabric scissors separate from those used for card, etc. Clogged up files and pliers with chewed-up jaws will make for frustration and hard work.

For those embarking upon woodcarving, ordinary woodworking tools will do, but woodcarving tools are recommended; they *can* be very expensive but sets of basic tools are reasonably priced and better suited to the beginner. These must be treated with the greatest respect at all times.

A note on measurements

The standard widths and thicknesses of wood, quoted throughout this book and in shops, are by convention the sizes of the wood unplaned. The actual dimensions of the wood as sold (i.e. planed) will usually be at least ⅛th in (3 mm) under the quoted dimensions. Examples of the equivalent imperial and metric measures referred to in the book are:

Imperial	Metric
1 × 1 in	25 × 25 mm
1½ × 1½ in	38 × 38 mm
2 × 2 in	50 × 50 mm
⅜ in diameter	9 mm diameter
½ in diameter	12 mm diameter

If you need to convert lengths into metric measures, calculating 25 mm to the inch gives sufficiently accurate results.

5 Instant Puppets

The term 'instant puppets' is in some respects a euphemism for 'junk puppets', the latter term carrying with it unfortunate connotations and not encouraging a lively and creative attitude in approaching the materials and their potential.

Today goods of all descriptions come in a wide variety of containers, in all manner of shapes, sizes, colours and textures. Many of these have been designed not only for their functional requirements but also their appeal to the shopper, so the articles already have a good deal of potential which the puppeteer can draw upon.

There is a need to be bold and adventurous in trying out ideas; one of the problems with instant puppets is that many people do not progress but continue to make the same puppets in the same way. Whatever method is used, do take care to make the puppets look crisp, clean and bright. Junk materials that are tatty and dirty or pieces of crumpled fabric just will not do; they will look like 'junk puppets' and will deserve to be regarded as such.

Figure 1   A simple glove puppet: an old ball with features made from felt, buttons and a toothpaste tube cap

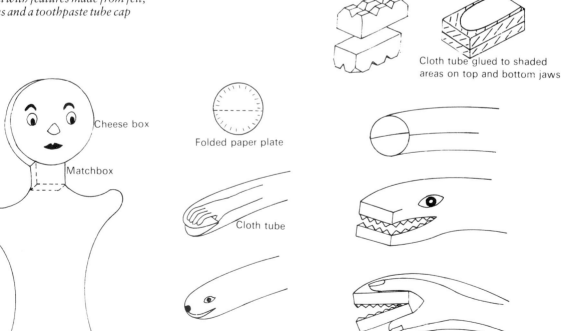

Figure 2   A cheese box puppet head   *Figure 3   A simple sleeve puppet*   *Figure 4   A sleeve puppet with snapping jaws*

Figure 5　An African teacher displays puppets made from local materials

Figure 6　A puppet head made entirely of banana fibre by an African student

Figure 7 (Opposite) An owl created from off-cuts of wood by Frieder Simon, DDR

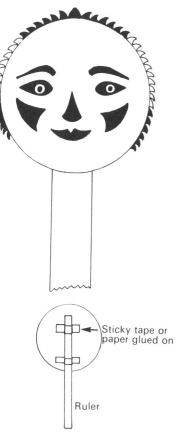

Sticky tape or paper glued on

Ruler

Figure 8 A paper plate puppet with coloured paper or felt features

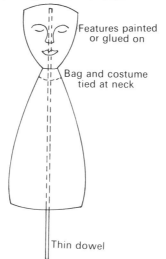

Paper bag stuffed with paper

Features painted or glued on

Bag and costume tied at neck

Thin dowel

Figure 9 A paper bag rod puppet

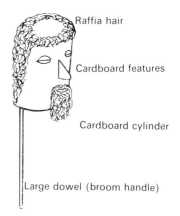

Raffia hair

Cardboard features

Cardboard cylinder

Large dowel (broom handle)

Figure 10 A cardboard head for a rod puppet

Figure 11 John, four years, with simple rod puppets made from dish-mops, plastic balls and clothes-pegs

Figure 12 An animal rod puppet

75

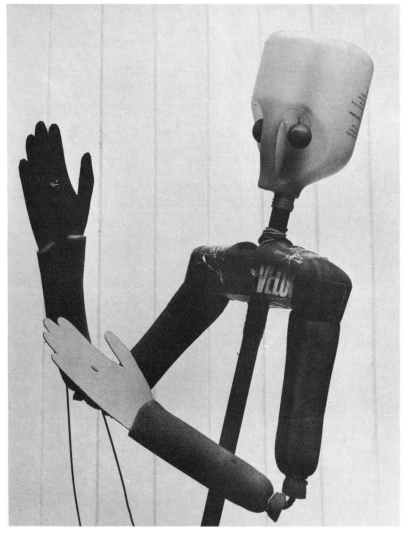

Figure 13 Horace, a junk-box rod puppet

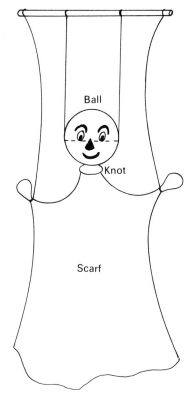

Figure 14 A scarf marionette

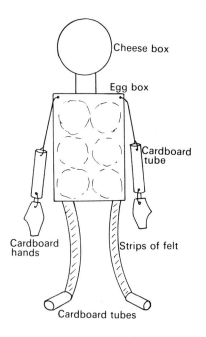

Figure 15 A cardboard marionette

Figure 16   A watering can marionette. Legs and arms: rope. Feet and hands: foam rubber

Figure 17   A junk-box marionette nears completion at the Puppet Centre, London

The illustrations included in this section are generally self-explanatory, demonstrating the possibilites and principles of this type of puppet construction. Most of the construction relies upon a good quality contact glue suitable for the materials used, strong cord or thread, sticky tape (masking tape is preferable) and the occasional stitch with needle and thread. It is good practice to reinforce 'hinges' (such as snappy jaws made from an egg box or other cartons) with a strip of strong fabric glued along the join.

A well organised collection of 'junk' makes exploration and construction much easier: sort your collection into boxes or other containers which are clearly labelled – large clear coffee jars are excellent for smaller items so you can see the contents at a glance. The illustrations give a good indication of the sorts of items to collect.

Fabric needs to be fairly soft as stiff or thick fabric will restrict movement, though it is useful for trimming. Young children's clothes acquired cheaply from jumble sales often provide suitable puppet costumes, especially for rod puppets. Having made an 'instant' puppet one does not wish to spend hours on the clothes and anyway this is often counter-productive. The most effective costumes are often lengths of fabric draped and stitched in place just here and there, allowing the natural movement of the fabric to enhance the puppet's movements. Just draping a piece of fabric over your hand or attaching it to a rod with an elastic band enables it to be used for different purposes on different occasions.

Instant glove puppets are best made with draped material rather than the standard 'glove' for the body as it is more difficult to make this well, and a comfortable fit, than is generally appreciated. It is possible to have a selection of glove puppet bodies with elasticated necks for use with different heads; a few trimmings may be added temporarily to help establish the character.

If clothes are to be made – and instant puppets sometimes have none at all – the techniques are described in Chapter 4. This helps to underline the point that the basic principles apply whether it be an instant puppet or any other type, so it is equally necessary to pay attention to these principles, to explore the medium and to understand the nature of the puppet and puppet theatre.

Remember that shadow puppets, described in Chapter 10, can be very quick and simple to make, so these too might be regarded as instant puppets.

6 The Puppet Head

The techniques described in this chapter may be used to make heads for marionettes, rod puppets and glove puppets. The choice of material and method will depend upon the type of puppet, what it is to do, the effect you wish to achieve, and what material suits you.

Exploring materials

The first encounter with some materials may prove a little frustrating until you have come to terms with the medium but perseverance is recommended. For example, some people take to plastic wood very quickly; others find it infuriating because they expect it to behave like plasticine or they have more stuck to their hands than to the puppet! However, once they have explored its properties and mastered the techniques, they find it an excellent medium for puppet making.

You need to explore a number of materials and give each a reasonable try, so that future choices can be made through knowledge and experience rather than from long-established attitudes. So many exciting materials have developed in recent years, there is no longer any need to spend countless hours with papier mâché (though even that technique is described below so that you can choose for yourself).

As new materials come onto the market, do explore their potentials for puppet making. They will need to be flexible in their applications, easily modelled, moulded or sculpted, lightweight but strong and durable, not prone to chipping or cracking, nor tending to shrink excessively or distort when drying, easily cut with appropriate tools when dry and amenable to use with a variety of paints and adhesives. Though the techniques for handling different media will vary slightly, the principles will be the same as those outlined in this chapter.

Which technique to use?

The construction techniques for heads may be grouped under four broad categories: fabric or sewn puppets, sculpted puppets, modelled puppets, moulded puppets. Generalisations about the relative merits of the techniques are difficult because much depends on the skill and ingenuity of the craftsman. If one were to state, for example, that fabric puppets are more limited in their scope for characterisation, within a week or two one would be sure to see an excellent example which would contradict such a comment. Even the texture achieved depends considerably on the puppeteer. However, the following guidelines are offered:

Figure 1   The Man and the Devil
from The Soldier's Tale by the Little
Angel Theatre

Figure 2   Wolf and Rabbit, cloth
glove puppets by Ian Allen, Playboard
Puppets

Fabric puppets generally require a basic sewing ability but this is not difficult to acquire. They tend to lack the strong modelling that creates character and carries effectively to a large audience; for a beginner, getting the pattern right is difficult unless one is simply following published designs.

Sculpting depends very much on which material is used – for example, there is a need to be very bold when hacking away at foam rubber (a more fiery temperament seems to help!) compared with wood where the mastery of the tools and techniques plays a more important part. Sculpting essentially requires the ability to start with a block, visualise what you want to achieve and know what to cut away and what to leave. At first this may be a rather difficult skill to master, though with some materials it is easy to glue pieces back on if you cut away too much.

Modelling is the technique that appeals to most people as you can get the basic structure right in the model upon which you make the head and then continue to build up the features in the chosen material until the desired effect is achieved. Some materials also permit you to cut away during the modelling or when the head is dry. Most modelling materials, used in an appropriate thickness, are both strong and lightweight.

Moulding (or casting) involves taking a plaster cast of the model and then using the cast to make copies in the chosen material. It offers the possibility of making a number of identical heads easily; this is helpful for the same character in different dress or if required, as a rod, glove and marionette, or with minor subsequent changes to the heads for family members such as brothers. But more particularly, some puppeteers would

80

Figure 3　A head modelled in plastic wood by the author: it also has moving eyes

Figure 4/1　Neck for a glove puppet

Figure 4/2　Neck for a rod puppet or marionette

Figure 4/3　Neck for a rod puppet or marionette

Figure 4/4　Recommended neck for a marionette

use this method for all their needs because it is then possible to renew heads – and puppets do take a lot of wear with a busy company – and because it is the only construction method which permits one to get the finished product exactly right in the initial plasticine model. Because the head is hollow it also tends to be lightweight. This is probably the messiest of the techniques and when used with materials which dry rigid it is not possible to have any undercutting in the initial modelling. Shrinkage of the medium can also pose some difficulties.

Note 1: Heads for glove puppets should have slightly bell-shaped necks or at least a ridge around the bottom of the neck so that the body can be fastened more securely. The hole in the neck is usually oval to accommodate two fingers (figure 4/1).

Rod puppet heads can be modelled either with necks (figure 4/2) or without, in which case the neck is built onto the body and joined inside the head (figure 4/3). Marionette heads tend to move most effectively if the necks are made separately from head and body, with a joint inside each (figure 4/4), though the methods illustrated for rod puppets may be adopted.

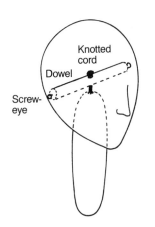

Figure 5/1 A dowel insert for securing the neck and the head strings

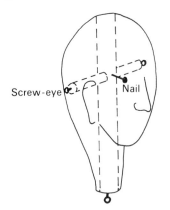

Figure 5/2 A dowelling 'cross' built into the head

Note 2: If a head is to be used for a marionette, the ears should be strong enough for attaching head strings to them. If they are not, or if it is a cloth or rubber marionette, secure a strong dowel across the head for attaching screw-eyes, and fixing the neck (figure 5/1). If the head and neck is built in one piece, build a dowelling 'cross' into the head. This consists of a large vertical dowel with a hole drilled across it to accommodate a horizontal dowel which is glued and nailed in place (figure 5/2). Screw-eyes are again used for the head strings and another in the bottom of the neck facilitates the joint between neck and body.

Fabric heads

A sock or stocking head

Take a sock or stocking and stuff if with *either* an old tennis ball, *or* a piece of fabric or foam rubber. (Foam rubber may cause a lumpy surface if the pieces are too large.)

If the head is intended for a marionette, knot the sock and then cut it off at the heel (figure 6/1); if for a glove or rod puppet, cut off the sock at the heel then glue and tie it round a conical cardboard neck tube or a rod (figures 6/2 and 6/3).

Stitch or glue on features.

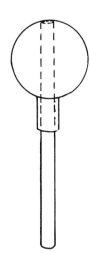

Figure 6/1 A head for a marionette
Figure 6/2 A head for a glove puppet
Figure 6/3 A head for a rod puppet

A felt head

Cut out two side pieces (figure 7/1) and a central gusset (figure 7/2). Place the two side pieces together and oversew them together between the chin and the top of the nose (Y to Z).

Make crossed cuts in the gusset as marked (figure 7/2). This is for the neck.

Oversew the gusset to the two side pieces (Y to Z) leaving a gap in the seam to allow the head to be stuffed.

Stuff the head with foam rubber (or any other suitable material) and stitch up the seam.

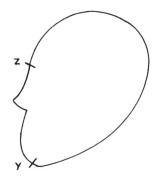

Figure 7/1   The felt side shape

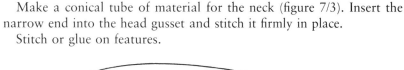

Figure 7/2   The head gusset

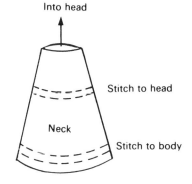

Figure 7/3   The conical neck tube

Make a conical tube of material for the neck (figure 7/3). Insert the narrow end into the head gusset and stitch it firmly in place.

Stitch or glue on features.

Sculpted heads

Sculpted heads are usually made from foam rubber, from polystyrene or from wood.

Foam rubber heads

Foam rubber heads can be made very quickly, but it is a tougher material to cut than it appears. Suitable tools are a bread knife (preferably electric), a hacksaw blade, a craft knife or very sharp scissors – Wilkinson Sword dressmaking scissors or similar brands with the large plastic handles are excellent. The use of unsuitable scissors can result in a crushed finger nerve and a loss of sensation for a substantial time. For a smooth finish, use a

Figure 8   Rosie Dear from To See the Queen: *a rod puppet with head and hands cut from foam rubber by Violet Philpott*

83

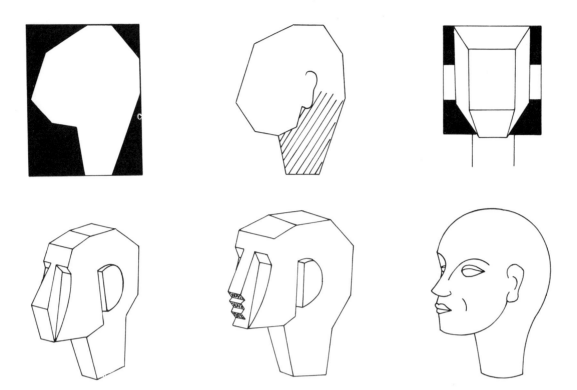

Figure 9   The main stages in sculpting a foam rubber or polystyrene head

small Surform rasp. Use quite a good quality foam or it may crumble with age.

It is a good idea to sketch the outline and essential features full-face and in profile on the block; these will disappear with cutting but provide a useful starting point for the basic shaping. (If you use a felt pen, take care that it does not rub off onto your clothes.) A common mistake is to make the profile too flat, particularly the back of the head; remember that you usually need a greater distance from back to front of the head than from side to side.

Figure 9 illustrates useful stages in developing a head by this method. It is not uncommon with some people's finished puppets to be able to see the shape of the block from which the head was cut. This indicates either a lack of boldness in the cutting or that the block was too small for the intended head.

For best results, establish the shape with an electric bread knife and then do more detailed shaping with the scissors and a sharp knife, finishing with a rasp. For a rugged finish just pull pieces of foam from the block. If you cut away too much or wish to add features to a basic shape, simply glue on pieces of foam.

Be sure to use a suitable adhesive. Electric glue guns are available but should be used with great care as the emerging glue is extremely hot and can give severe burns.

For eyes, it is usually best to carve out the sockets and glue into them large wooden balls, appropriately painted and varnished. It is, of course, possible to install a mechanism for moving eyes as described elsewhere.

To open deep holes for rods or other internal fixtures, use a thin, long, coarse and raspy round file.

Sometimes the foam is left in its natural colour but most foam tends to fade with age so, unless it is to be covered with fabric, fur fabric, etc., painting is usually preferred. Spray paints are useful for large areas. Paint applied with a brush tends to soak into the foam which then remains wet and squelchy for a long time; instead, having mixed the paint, spread it on to the surface of the foam with your finger tips.

A polystyrene head

Polystyrene (Styrofoam) is an excellent medium for the puppeteer as it is very light. Blocks of it can be shaped into heads, and even large hands, by melting or cutting it. Be sure to use fire-resistant polystyrene.

Make the basic shape with a heat gun, a rasp, a hand saw, a hacksaw blade or any hot implement. Rasps and blades are preferable, for the fumes caused by heat require good ventilation. Follow the same stages as illustrated for the foam rubber head (figure 9).

Carve finer details with a sharp craft knife. Deep modelling is necessary or detail will be lost when the head is covered.

Cover the surface of the polystyrene with small pieces of brown paper or newspaper, using PVA or a carpenter's pearl glue. Three layers should be sufficient; allow each layer to dry before applying the next. Change the colour of alternate layers to ensure full coverage of the head. If the neck is to be hollow line it, too, with glue and paper. Cover the last layer of paper with a coat of glue, then sand it. Exercise care over choice of glues to be used with polystyrene. Many glues will dissolve it.

Carving a head in wood

Woodcarving is an art in itself and for advanced techniques the reader is recommended to consult books specifically concerned with the subject. However, many puppeteers with no special knowledge of carving make beautiful wooden heads, having developed their own individual techniques through practice. They manage with a few sharp knives (or a craft knife with interchangeable blades), a selection of files and glasspaper.

The surform range of rasps is excellent for much of the shaping that needs to be done; they are efficient tools, easy to use and very safe. With some woods a considerable amount of modelling may be done with glasspaper.

A small selection of woodworking chisels are helpful; John Wright (*Your Puppetry*, Sylvan Press, 1951) recommends as a starter set a 1 in flat chisel and a ¾ in gouge for 'clearing' (creating the main shape), a ½ in flat chisel and a ½ in shallow gouge for finishing, and a ¼ in gouge for grooving plus a woodcarving mallet and a pair of callipers for comparing measurements. A set of woodcarving tools, properly used, is a great asset of course.

For effective carving you also need a sharpening stone and oil, and a strong rigid workbench or table with a wooden vice (metal jaws may be padded with wood). Today, powered band-saws are much more commonly accessible and very useful for cutting basic shapes.

Use a well-seasoned, close-grained, hard wood. Fruit woods are generally recommended but limewood is the most widely used; it is easily

Figure 10 Bastien by John Blundall, Cannon Hill Puppet Theatre: notice the design of the eyes

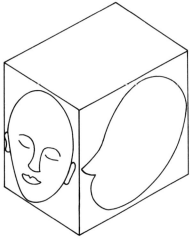

Figure 11 Allow for the depth of the head when carving from a block

worked, does not splinter readily and is quite light in weight. American white wood has similar qualities but lime is preferable. Jelutong, a Malaysian wood, has become very popular recently, especially for heads. Loose-grained light woods such as balsa are not at all suitable. Needless to say, all suitable woods are comparatively expensive, so select your wood carefully; look for a straight grain, and avoid knots if you can.

If carving a puppet for the first time it is a good idea to carve the head last; use the body and limbs to get the feel of the tools and the material before tackling the most difficult parts.

When designing the head and transferring this to the block to work on, remember the head is much deeper than it is wide so allow plenty of wood for the front to back dimension (figure 11). As the block is carved, your outlines will disappear; keep redrawing these as necessary. Occasional sanding of the surface can also help in studying your progress on the face.

Use the wood so that the grain runs vertically down through the whole puppet (except the feet) and make your chisel cuts in the same direction as the grain or the wood will split and vital parts of the figure will be lost.

Figure 12 John Wright (Little
Angel Theatre) carving

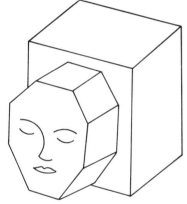

Figure 13/1 Remove the major part
of the waste with a saw and chisel

Figure 13/2 Use a chisel to establish
the actual shape

Strike the chisel with a series of firm, sharp taps of the mallet rather than
with heavy blows. For fine paring, hold the chisel with both hands (figure
12) with the end of the shaft in the palm, against the heel of one hand and
the other hand over the shaft and blade, helping to guide it. Always keep
both hands behind the direction of the cutting edge.

It is advisable first to carve the face and front half of the head, back
almost as far as the ears, using the bulk of the other half of the block to
hold the head firmly in the vice. Begin by using a saw and chisel to remove
the major part of the waste (figure 13/1) and then a chisel to establish the
actual shape (figure 13/2).

Next carve the face in the stages illustrated for a foam rubber or
polystyrene head (figure 9). Rub it down to a smooth finish, starting with a
coarse grade of glasspaper on the roughest parts and working down to a
very fine one.

When the face is complete work towards the back of the head, leaving
blocks for the ears so that the head can continue to be held in the vice.
Finally, carefully shape the ears and hollow out the socket for the neck and
as much of the head as possible through this hole in order to reduce its
weight.

If you encounter problems in holding the partially shaped head in the
vice, it is possible to screw a block of wood securely to the bottom of the
head and to hold this block in the vice, removing it when it is no longer
needed.

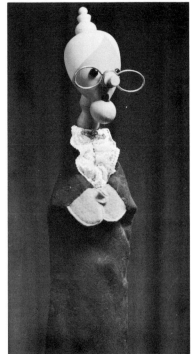

Figure 14 Amahl's Mother carved by John Wright for the Little Angel Theatre production of Amahl and the Night Visitors

Figure 15 Grossmutter

Figure 16 Mephisto.
Carved puppets by Frieder Simon, the Larifari Theatre, DDR

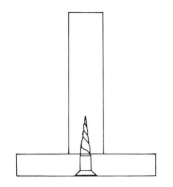

Figure 17 A modelling stand

Modelled heads

A head is modelled in plasticine (plastilene) and then covered in some material (e.g. plastic wood) that will form a shell. This is then split, the plasticine removed and the shells joined together again.

To model the head, make a modelling stand of suitable proportions by screwing together a dowel and a block of wood (figure 17) and model the basic form of the head around the dowel. It is unwise to model very fine detail as this will tend to be lost in the following process. Modelling can be heightened at the finishing stage.

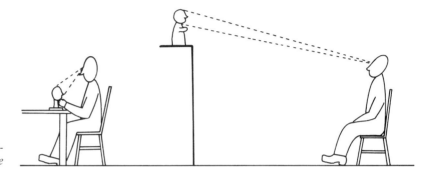

Figure 18 The relationship of puppet to maker and puppet to audience

Whilst modelling the head, take account of the different spatial relationships between puppet and maker and between puppet and audience (figure 18), particularly for rod and glove puppets. Take care not to angle the puppet head upwards (a common tendency) or its focus will be above the audience. It is a good idea to tilt it slightly forwards, but not noticeably. When using a modelling stand, lift it up occasionally and view the puppet from the angle of the audience.

Most of the materials described for modelling may also be used for moulding heads, as detailed later.

Modelling upon a cardboard base

This type of head is extremely strong and particularly suitable for animal characters.

Draw the profile shape on strong cardboard and cut it out. Glue on cardboard 'ribs' to give the head its shape (figure 19/1). Strengthen the ribs with strips of cardboard glued on as braces (figure 19/2).

Cover the whole shape with layers of thin card (figure 19/3), then cover the cardboard with a thin layer of the desired modelling material and build

Figure 19/1 The cardboard shape with 'ribs' glued on

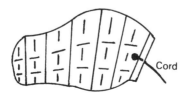

Figure 19/2 Braces glued between ribs

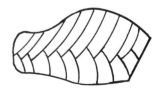

Figure 19/3 Shape covered with strips of thin card

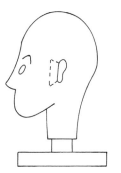

Figure 20/1 Plasticine model with cardboard ears

Figure 20/2 Model covered with plastic wood

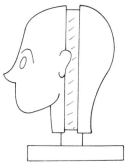

Figure 20/3 When dry, the head is cut open and the plasticine removed

up detail as required. With plastic wood, first smear the card with glue. If moving eyes or mouth are desired (see pages 98 and 99 for how to make these), cut away the cardboard as necessary to accommodate these.

Note: It is possible to use this method and cover the cardboard framework with cloth or fur fabric.

A plastic wood head

Plastic wood is a pliable material which, when left exposed to the air, sets hard and can be cut, drilled and sanded just like wood. When used with acetone as a solvent, it becomes easier to model and a smoother finish is achieved.

Cut out cardboard ears and fasten them in the plasticine model (figure 20/1). It is easier to build the ears on card and these solid ears are very strong. Smear the plasticine (but not the cardboard ears) with petroleum jelly to prevent the plastic wood sticking to it.

Cover the head with a layer of plastic wood about ⅛ in thick; apply it in small pieces (figure 20/2), having dipped them in acetone so that they blend together easily. When working on the ears, smear the cardboard with glue, then add the plastic wood. Model finer details with modelling tools or any other suitable implement (such as a small knife blade or even the end of a paintbrush).

When the plastic wood is dry (at least twenty-four hours), cut open the head, making the cut behind the ears and over the top of the skull (figure 20/3). Cut through the plasticine with strong thread or fine wire. Scoop the plasticine from the plastic wood shell, taking care not to apply any leverage against the shell.

Hold the shells up to the light to see if there are any weak points which need strengthening (under the nose and around the eyes are common weaknesses). Scrape away any grease before applying plastic wood to the inside of the shell.

At this stage any moving parts, described in detail later, should be completed. Finally, glue the two hollow shells together again. Any gaps that may be caused by the two shells shrinking at different rates can be filled in with plastic wood. Smooth the head with glasspaper. For a very smooth finish, mix the plastic wood down to a thin paste with acetone and spread thinly over the head. Dip your finger in the acetone and rub it over the surface. Very fine sanding is all that is necessary to achieve an excellent finish.

A slightly different method is first to create a basic head shape, rather like a hollow egg or sphere, in plastic wood by the method described. Then model all the features solidly in plastic wood once the hollowed shell is really dry, again liberally using acetone as a solvent.

Note: Not all glues can be used with plastic wood. Clear multi-purpose contact adhesives such as UHU and Bostik No 1 or Sobo, a white resin glue, are recommended.

A papier mâché head

Make the head in exactly the same way as a plastic wood head.

To prepare the papier mâché, tear newspaper into very small pieces and soak them in a bucket of water. Rubbing the paper and heating the bucket will help the paper to disintegrate. When all the paper has turned to pulp, drain off the excess water. Mix powder-paste with the pulp and add water to produce a consistency like porridge.

After modelling the head, it may be warmed to dry it, but carefully and slowly. When dry, the head may be sanded lightly and cracks filled in with more pulp.

The main disadvantages with this method are the time involved in the preparation and later drying of the pulp and its limited modelling properties compared with a material like plastic wood.

A plaster and bandage (or paste and paper) head

Make the head in the same way as a plastic wood head. The modelling (such as eye sockets) must be deep for this method or they will tend to flatten out and disappear as the material is applied.

Cover the modelled head with *either* ordinary surgical bandage or muslin (mull) dipped in plaster filler, *or* thin paper stuck with PVA glue or cellular paste. Muslin is preferable to paper as it stretches over modelled detail more successfully.

First cover the plasticine head with overlapping 1 in squares of damp tissue paper. This will prevent sticking. Then apply 1 in squares of muslin or paper, the squares overlapping slightly. If muslin is used, three layers are recommended; if paper, a minimum of four. Press each layer firmly into the previous one. With paper, allow each layer to dry before applying the next.

A little paint in the plaster for alternate layers of muslin or different colours for alternate layers of paper helps to ensure that each layer is completely covered by the next.

When thoroughly dry, cut open the shell, remove the plasticine, rejoin and cover the head with another layer of muslin or paper. With muslin, detail can be built up with finely teased cotton wool saturated in plaster filler and further shaped when dry with a knife or glasspaper.

Figure 21 Stages in the construction of three Alabastine and muslin heads

A Celastic head

Celastic is the trade name of an impregnated woven cloth which can be bought by the yard in varying thicknesses. The name has become a general term used by puppeteers to describe all brands of this material. It is strong, unbreakable, waterproof, very light and fast drying.

It is softened with acetone or the Celastic medium, modelled onto a basic shape as with a plastic wood head, and allowed to dry hard. The use of rubber gloves is recommended, as is good ventilation; if using acetone for long periods, wear a suitable face mask to avoid inhaling the fumes.

Cover the plasticine head with a layer of damp tissue paper to prevent the Celastic sticking to it. As an alternative to plasticine the basic shape may be made from polystyrene: this must be covered with strips of sticky brown paper if used with acetone rather than the Celastic medium (acetone dissolves polystyrene).

First apply the Celastic to large areas – the back and top of the head – and then continue with the face. Dip strips of Celastic in acetone or the Celastic medium and press them firmly onto the shape, modelling the Celastic into the hollows with your fingers or a modelling tool moistened with acetone. If thicker Celastic is used, butt the strips together rather than overlap them. Press joins together and they will tend to disappear.

Should the Celastic start to dry out while you are still working on it, damp it down with a little acetone and then proceed. Whilst the first layer is still damp (but not sticky), add another layer. Continue until the required thickness is reached. To develop features, paint acetone onto the area to be worked and add Celastic in the usual way.

When dry, cut open the head and carefully remove the plasticine. If polystyrene is used, it need not be removed; a few drops of acetone will dissolve it if necessary, but take care not to soften the head. Rejoin the shells with a clear contact glue and cover with more Celastic and acetone.

The hard shell may be cut away with a sharp craft knife and smoothed with glasspaper. If this leaves a 'fuzz' on the head apply a coat of lacquer and sand again when dry. In order to paint the Celastic apply a coat of emulsion first and then proceed as usual.

A fibreglass head

Fibreglass matting is supplied in various grades and is used with polyester liquid resin in much the same way as Celastic and acetone. The use of rubber gloves is recommended.

Cover the model with damp tissue paper before applying the fibreglass. Saturate pieces of the matting in the liquid resin, press out all bubbles and then press the matting onto the model with the pieces overlapping. Use 'finishing matt' for the first layer so that the inside of the head is smooth.

Build up the head and features in coarse matt, then apply a final layer of fine-quality matt.

To remove the plasticine, cut open the head with a sharp knife before it is completely hard. If it is allowed to harden, a saw will be needed to cut it.

Join the two hollow shells with saturated matting, sand the head, (it may be filed if necessary) and paint it.

Moulded heads

It is possible to use a range of materials for creating heads by this technique. The latex rubber method is described but, with the exception of plaster filler and alabastine, all of the materials detailed for modelled heads have been used successfully with plaster casts.

When making the original model, remember that many materials have a tendency to shrink as they dry, so the original should be large enough to allow for this.

Undercutting (figures 22/1 and 22/2) can cause the rigid materials to lock in the moulds and it will be impossible to remove the shell without breaking either the head or the mould. A means of overcoming this is suggested if needed. However the flexibility of latex rubber (provided it is not allowed to become too thick) permits undercutting.

With the rigid materials, it is necessary to use a 'separator' to prevent them sticking to the mould. For plastic wood and papier maché use petroleum jelly (this will need to be cleaned off the head before finishing and painting; for paste and paper and Celastic, use damp tissue paper; for fibreglass a separator is manufactured. Each half of the head is cast separately by pressing the material firmly into the half moulds, in accordance with the directions for use given previously. When dry, the two shells are joined in the same way as a modelled head.

Making a plaster mould

The mould may be made from plaster of Paris, but quick-setting 'stonehard' dental plaster is far superior, though considerably more expensive. One has to work quickly once it starts to set, but it dries out ready for use in a very short time and is remarkably strong. When mixing the plaster, add the powder to the water, fairly thinly at first. A chemical action takes place and it will thicken very quickly, feeling warm to the touch as it does so. Always ensure that you have mixed sufficient; it is better to waste a little rather than risk not having enough. Three techniques are available:

The hand-held model for the application of plaster is suitable for moderate size heads, divided from ear to ear, for use with latex rubber. Rigid materials can be used for casting provided there is no undercutting.

The box method also divided for ear to ear, has the same limitation with rigid materials. It is suitable for larger heads which are not easily held in the hand to work on. For smaller puppets the former method is more economical on plaster.

The split-head method overcomes the undercutting problem with rigid materials by dividing the model down the centre of the face. However, the need to join the resultant shells in the middle of the face can pose problems in retaining the original modelling, and makes this a not very popular method. It is unsuitable for rubber heads.

Note: With the first two of these methods, it *is* possible to divide the face down the line of the nose to permit undercutting but, without considerable experience, it is very difficult to obtain a clean finish to the resulting head.

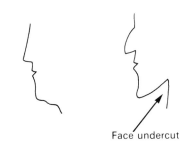

Face undercut

Figure 22/1 A face not undercut

Figure 22/2 A face undercut

The hand-held model

Insert thin metal (e.g. tin) strips into the plasticine model, over the head and down the sides across the line of the ears. The strips should overlap each other by about ⅛ in to form a fence (figure 23/1). Smear the plasticine and the metal strips with petroleum jelly.

Mix up the plaster. Then, hold the back of the head in your hand and work on the other half. As soon as the plaster starts to thicken, scoop it up with a spoon and fill in all the hollows (figure 23/2). As the plaster turns creamy, pour it all over this half of the head. The plaster should be about 1½ – 2 in thick.

Allow this half to harden for about thirty minutes, then remove the metal strips with tweezers.

Make a few shallow holes in the clean edge left by removing the metal strips (figure 23/3).

Cover the edge of the cast with petroleum jelly and take a cast of the other half of the head.

When the mould is hard, take the two halves apart and remove the plasticine. The second half of the cast will have knobs around the edge to fit into the holes in the other half; this allows the two shells to be aligned accurately for casting the rubber head. Clean the inside of the mould carefully with a rag soaked in methylated spirit (wood alcohol). Clean the ears, nose and other awkward cracks with loops of fine wire.

Leave the moulds to dry out until they no longer feel cold and heavy.

The box method

Make the plasticine model on a modelling stand. Remove the dowel in the head from the wooden base and screw it to a larger board so that the head is held securely.

Roll out a long strip of plasticine, approximately 2 in wide and ½ in thick; ensure it has a neat edge and use this to divide the head in two (figure 24/1). Press it into place firmly but taking care not to spoil the modelling.

Build out the corners and trim the divider into a rectangular shape (figure 24/2). Smear the back of the head and the divider with petroleum jelly.

Use a folded piece of strong card to create a box around the back of the head; seal the edges of the card with fairly large strips of plasticine to ensure that the plaster cannot leak out and the box does not collapse (figure 24/3).

Mix up the plaster. As soon as it starts to thicken, pour it steadily into the box, gently shaking the board with your free hand in order to release any air bubbles that might be trapped.

When the plaster has set, carefully remove the card and the divider and attend to any marks made on the head. Scoop shallow holes in the inside edge of the plaster block (figure 24/4) and smear the front of the head and this edge of the block with petroleum jelly.

Turn over the block so that the head is face upwards and fix another piece of folded card around it to box in the front of the head (figure 24/5). Secure the card with plasticine and pour in the plaster whilst shaking the model, as before.

When the second half of the mould is set, remove the card, scrape away

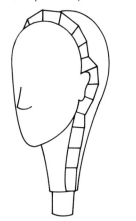

Metal strips overlap each other

Figure 23/1   The plasticine model with metal strips inserted

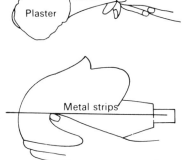

Plaster

Metal strips

Figure 23/2   Making the first half of the plaster mould

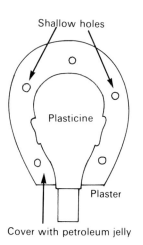

Shallow holes

Plasticine

Plaster

Cover with petroleum jelly

Figure 23/3   Making the second half of the mould

Figure 24/1 Dividing the head with plasticine

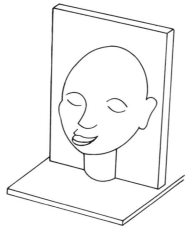

Figure 24/2 The divider trimmed into a rectangle

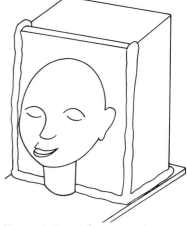

Figure 24/3 A box created to contain the plaster

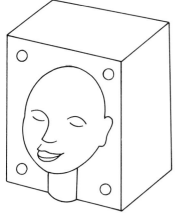

Figure 24/4 The first half of the cast with holes scooped out

any surplus plaster covering the join, and carefully prise the two blocks apart. Finally, remove the plasticine, clean the mould and allow to dry.

The split-head method

Model the head in plasticine then carefully cut it in half through the centre of the face along the nose line with a very fine wire.

Lay the two pieces onto a wooden board; cutting off the corners saves a lot of plaster. Build a retaining wall around the board with card and plasticine (figure 25), as for the previous head. It should be deep enough to contain the required depth of plaster.

Smear the models and the board with petroleum jelly, mix the plaster and pour it into the box as described previously. When it is set, remove the cardboard, scoop out the plasticine models, clean the mould and leave it to dry.

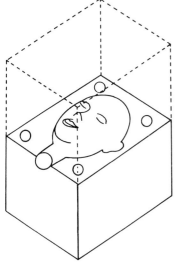

Figure 24/5 Making the box to cast the front of the head

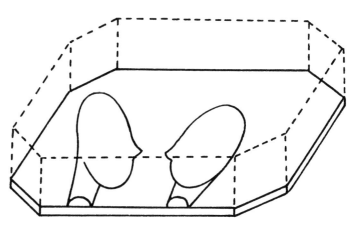

Figure 25 The split-head casting method

Figure 26 A latex-rubber character from Faustus *by Theatre of Puppets*

The latex rubber head

The latex rubber is obtained in a liquid state; different qualities and types of mix are available. Most puppeteers use a fairly strong, soft toy mix which is sometimes identified by the numbers A360W or A443W – A330 is also used, but this may be too flexible for some purposes.

Secure the two halves of the mould together with strong rubber bands and cover the join with plasticine. Pour the rubber into the mould through the neck until it is approximately a quarter full. Roll the mould to fill in all the cracks and continue to roll it as it is being filled to remove air bubbles.

Top up the level of the rubber as it drops slightly. It forms a skin on the inside surface of the mould. The longer the rubber is left in the mould, the thicker the head will be. About 45 minutes to an hour will usually be sufficient but it depends on the thickness of the rubber mix and the thickness required of the head. The larger the head, the thicker it will need to be to retain its shape (see Note 3 below). Some experimenting with the rubber may be necessary at first.

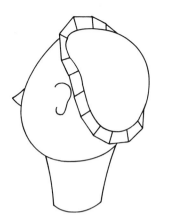

Figure 27 Dividing the head within the hairline

Figure 28/1 Wooden bead glued in eye socket

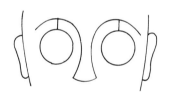

Figure 28/2 Wooden balls suspended from the eyebrows

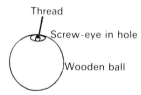

Thread

Screw-eye in hole

Wooden ball

Figure 28/3 Attaching the thread to the wooden ball

Figure 28/4 Sticky black paper pupil on a pearl button

At the end of the required time, pour the excess rubber in the centre of the mould back into the container to be used again.

Leave the rubber in the mould to dry. Twenty-four hours is usually enough but it depends on the thickness of the rubber, so be careful not to open the mould before the rubber is dry.

Put a little powder in the head, through the neck, and blow it around inside. This prevents the inner surfaces of the rubber sticking together.

Pull the plaster mould apart and remove the head. If there is a 'flash', or ridge, around the head from the join in the mould, trim it off with sharp scissors. Allow the head to dry for at least a further twenty-four hours before painting it.

Note 1: Some puppeteers add a hardener to the rubber to make it rigid, but this removes the possibility of undercutting and can make the head rather fragile.

Note 2: Because a rubber head can be manoeuvred out of a mould, it is possible to use the first of the techniques described above, with the metal strips taken around the back of the head under the hairline (figure 27). This avoids an unsightly flash down the ears and neck.

Note 3: Very large, flexible rubber heads may need some form of internal support to maintain their basic shapes. Glue to the inside of the head *either* a layer of foam rubber of appropriate thickness *or* a skull shape created in fibreglass, leaving exposed any areas which are required to be flexible.

Eyes

Eyes can be modelled and painted with the other features, or they can be suggested in one of the following ways.

Hollow eye sockets (figure 14) can be painted in a dark colour – and varnished if required – or covered with a reflective material such as metallic spangles.

Deep slits can be made in the eye sockets to produce heavy shadow, or the shape of the eyeballs can be cut out and a small wooden head (often black), glued top and bottom, placed in the centre of the hole (figure 28/1).

Painted wooden balls can be suspended from the eyebrows on fine, strong thread (figures 28/2 and 28/3).

Sticky black paper (for the pupil) can be glued on to a large pearl button. This is especially effective for animals (figure 28/4).

Glass medical or dolls' eyes *can* be used, but are too naturalistic to be in keeping with most puppets.

Illuminated eyes

Fit torch (flashlight) bulbs into the eye sockets. Screw the bulbs into bulb holders fixed to a block of wood; fasten the block into the head before the two pieces are joined together (figure 29/1).

Connect the bulbs in parallel (figure 29/2) for maximum brightness. The battery and a small switch may be contained within a hollow body (but there must be access to change the battery). The wires run into the body through the neck.

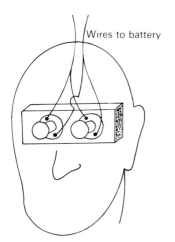

Figure 29/1 *Fixing the eyes in the head*

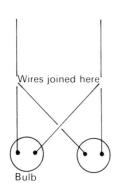

Figure 29/2 *Connecting the bulbs*

Figure 30/1 *Wooden eyes built into a plasticine base before the head is modelled*

If the lights are to be switched on and off during the performance, the switch must be attached to the control.

Moving eyes

Moving eyes are most often made for marionettes, occasionally for rod puppets, but seldom for glove puppets. Eye movement can be most expressive but is only effective for intimate performances as it will not show from a distance.

Make the eyes from two wooden balls (the size depends on the size of the head) with a hole drilled through the centre of each ball. Pivot the balls on a piece of strong galvanised wire (12 or 14 gauge), using ½ in diameter dowelling to give the necessary spacing between the eyes.

Build the balls and wire into the plasticine model (figure 30/1) and model the head over this shape, leaving the eyeball uncovered and the ends of the wire projecting through each side of the head. When the head is cut open and the plasticine removed, remove the balls and fix a screw weighted with lead into the back of each ball (figure 30/2). This acts as a counterbalance to open the eyes after they have been closed. They are closed by means of a string attached to the end of each screw.

Replace the balls in the head, cut the wire to the required length and secure it in the head by covering the ends with the same material as that used to model the head.

To stop the eyes opening too far, fix a thin dowel rod across the head for the screws to rest on. If the eyes jam in the head this can usually be put right by running a sharp knife around the inside of the eyelids.

Paint the eyes on the wooden balls when the face is painted.

Control For a marionette, the eye strings pass through two holes in the head. To prevent the thread fraying, it is a good idea to glue a piece of plastic drinking straw into the hole.

For a rod puppet, the strings pass over another dowel, fastened across the head, and then run down to the control (figure 30/3).

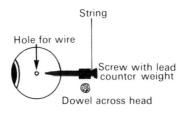

Figure 30/2 *The mechanism for opening and closing the eyes*

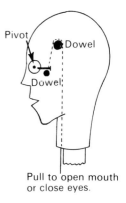

Figure 30/3 *Moving eyes for a rod puppet*

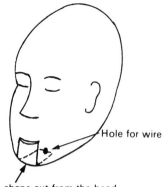

Figure 31/1 *The shape cut from the head*

L shape cut from the head.

Hole for wire

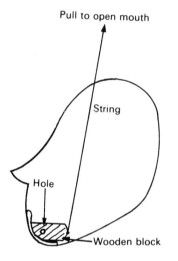

Pull to open mouth

String

Hole

Wooden block

Weight of block closes mouth

Figure 31/2 *The mechanism with a wooden block as a counterweight*

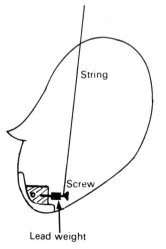

String

Screw

Lead weight

Figure 31/3 *The mechanism with a lead counterweight*

Mouths

Hand puppets in the style of the Muppets feature a moving mouth as a major part of the construction. However, a moving mouth is not very often required for the type of heads described in this section and, indeed, can be a liability. It must not move indiscriminately with no regard to speech, yet it would be impossible (and undesirable) to move it with every syllable. Its most effective use can be to give a gasp or similar reaction.

Moving mouths, like moving eyes, are most appropriate to marionettes but can be made in rod puppets. The method described is usually the most practical way of making moving mouths. Other methods, used in the construction of specific types of puppet, are described on pages 108 and 110.

Model a head over a plasticine base. When the head is cut open and the plasticine removed, carefully cut the mouth (i.e. the lower lip and chin) from the head in an L shape (figure 31/1).

Glue a wooden block inside this L-shaped piece (figure 31/2) and strengthen the bond with the material used to make the head.

Drill a hole through the block and pivot it on a piece of galvanised wire (12 or 14 gauge). Drill holes in the sides of the head to accommodate the ends of the wire.

Attach a string to the back of the block for opening the mouth (figure 31/2). The weight of the block acts as a counterbalance to close the mouth. A screw weighted with lead may be attached to the back of the block to increase the weight (figure 31/3).

Control As with moving eyes, the string passes through the top of the head for a marionette, and over a dowel secured in the head then down to the control for a rod puppet.

Painting and finishing the head

In order to match the basic skin tones, it is a good idea to paint the head, hands and, if bare, the feet at the same time. Painting should not be undertaken until the necessary joints have been completed.

Materials

The various types of paint available today offer a good choice for different purposes but you should avoid a glossy finish. Shiny faces do not look convincing and they glare under lighting. For most needs, acrylic paints such as Reeves Polymer Colours or Rowney Acrylacolour are recommended. Mixed with water, they produce a matt finish; mixed with acrylic medium, they have a slightly shiny appearance. For mixing larger quantities of colours which require a lot of white paint, white emulsion is a cheap substitute for the acrylic paint.

It is necessary to use polyurethane paints on fibreglass. With rubber heads, the medium must be used and the paint should not be too thick or it may tend to crack as the rubber flexes. To avoid the shiny finish, mix the paint with water and add *just a little* medium.

A useful technique to obtain a matt finish with shiny paint is, just before it dries, to dust it lightly with talcum powder. Shake, and then blow, the

Figure 32   Madam Butterfly by Ken Barnard

surplus from the head and finally dust off the remainder with a *very* soft ¼ to ½ in paintbrush. Continue to add powder and dust off as necessary, but take care not to smudge the paint.

Acrylic varnish may be used to enhance any parts which need emphasis such as eyeballs and some lips. When wet, the varnish has a milky appearance but it dries clear.

Principles of painting the head

Natural colour tends to detract from the face's modelling and its dramatic effect. It is better to consider the face in terms of stage make-up and to take account of the effects of stage lighting, especially coloured lighting. It is a

100

Figure 33 One of the Kings from Amahl and the Night Visitors *by the Little Angel Theatre*

good idea to paint the head under artificial light rather than daylight. Fettig provides a particularly good discussion of colouring principles which are summarised within the account below.

Figure 34 illustrates the major areas of light and shade of the face under typical stage lighting. It is a good idea to study each puppet head under your own lighting conditions before proceeding to paint it. As a rule, forward facing and protruding parts of the face appear lightest, side areas are lightly shaded and recesses are in heavy shadow. Therefore, painting the protruding parts too dark or the shaded areas too light will neutralise the effect of the modelling and detract from the puppet's character.

Fettig suggests the use of four main shades: an overall application of a fairly light shade of the basic colour; a darker shade (of the same colour or

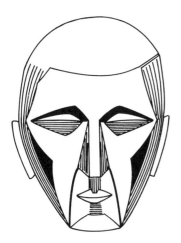

Figure 34 The main areas of light and shade on the face under typical stage lighting

Figure 35 Father, Hansel and Gretel in The Gingerbread House *by Playboard Puppets*

appropriate other colour) applied to the areas of light shadow; a darker shade again for the recesses; a very light shade for the frontal areas and protruding highlights.

One has to take account also of the space values and intensities of different colours. That is, warm colours appear nearer than cold colours, and stronger colours draw attention to themselves with a foreground appearance; pale colours and those mixed with white, black or grey tend to have a background quality.

Consideration of these principles enables one to paint with good dramatic effect and to modify somewhat the apparent structure of a face, which is particularly useful for disguising modelling weaknesses or creating different appearances from identical moulded faces.

Some painting tips

There are no rules for face colours. Anything is possible with puppets, but normal flesh hues can be mixed from varying quantities of white, yellow, red and brown. Ready-mixed flesh colours are seldom satisfactory but they can provide a useful base with which to mix other colours.

Pure white eyeballs sometimes tend to look bare and starey, in which case mix a slightly creamy colour. Remember that generally the more the white of the eye is showing, the less friendly the character can appear; large pupils help to suggest warmer character. It can be very effective to paint the whole eyeball a dark colour such as blue, black, purple or green.

Eyebrows can be painted or made from the same material as the hair. With very fair hair, the eybrows tend to be a little darker.

Hair

Hair is sometimes modelled with the head and painted but it is usually more effective to glue on suitable materials, either directly to the head or by creating a wig and attaching this securely.

A wide variety of materials may be used, such as knitting wool, rug wool, fur fabric, embroidery silks, rope or string (dyed if necessary), curled card, wood shavings, strips of felt fabric, etc. About the only definitely unsuitable material is real hair; real fur too may be inappropriate for many uses.

7 The glove puppet and hand puppet

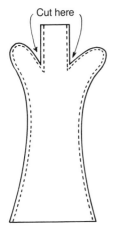

Figure 1/1 Making a paper pattern

Figure 1/2 The body shape

Construction

The distinction made here between 'glove' and 'hand' puppets is that between the puppet whose body is the more traditional glove style and those which are essentially a sleeve of material, the whole hand fitting inside the puppet's head.

Glove puppet heads are made as described in Chapter 6.

A 'glove' for the body

It is recommended that the basic glove is made from curtain lining or a jersey material and the costume then sewn or glued onto it. This makes it easier to achieve a good fit and makes the costume longer wearing.

First make a paper pattern: fold a sheet of paper in half (longways), lay one hand on the paper as illustrated (figure 1/1) and draw round the outline, but not too close to the hand.

Ensure that the neck will be wide enough after it is stitched to go over the puppet's neck, the body is wide enough to get your hand in and out easily and the glove long enough to reach almost to your elbow (your wrist is the puppet's waist). Short glove bodies will reveal your wrist or arm during the performance and fast access with one hand, while still manipulating with the other, is essential.

Lay the pattern onto a double thickness of material, wrong side to wrong side, and mark out the body shape (figure 1/2). (If a small tuck is pinned in the material for the back before marking out, it will be a little wider than the front, to permit the hand to move freely; remove the pins

Figure 1/3 The loop and hook bent from a piece of wire

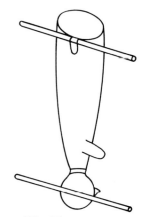

Figure 1/4 The loop of wire fixed in the hem

Figure 1/5 The puppet hanging in the booth ready for use

Figure 2/1   Mitten-type hand

Figure 2/2   Shaped hand with seams inside

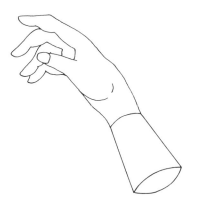

Figure 2/3   Modelled hand with a cardboard cuff

after the glove is stitched.) Stitch around the outline, leaving the neck and the bottom open.

Try the glove for comfort on both hands; if necessary, unpick and restitch. Cut out the glove within ¼ in of the stitching and snip into the corners between neck and arms (figure 1/2). Cut right up to the stitching or the glove will pull at these points when reversed. Reverse the glove so that the seams are inside.

Glue the glove to the puppet's neck, securing it with a strong draw thread.

Bend a length of galvanised wire (12 – 14 gauge) into a loop with a portion of it forming a hook (figure 1/3). Place the loop in the bottom of the glove and stitch up the hem so that it contains the loop (figure 1/4). The hook enables you to hang up the puppet in the booth and the loop holds the bottom open for speedy insertion of your hand during a show (figure 1/5).

Finally, fit the costume over the glove.

Hands

Hands may be made as an integral part of the glove, as described above. Alternatively, they may be made separately in a different colour fabric, or sculptured, modelled or moulded as described in Chapter 9.

To make a cloth hand, first cut out two shapes, mitten-shaped or with fingers (figures 2/1 and 2/2). Stitch the two shapes together inside out and then reverse. Where appropriate, stuff the fingers with foam rubber. Glue or stitch the hands to the glove body.

When hands are made by a more complicated technique, glue a strong cardboard 'cuff' to the hand (figure 2/3) and cover the card with whatever material is used for the hand. (With rubber hands, the cuff can be moulded with the hand and, if necessary, lined with card to stiffen it.) Glue the cuff inside the puppet's cloth arm and, for manipulation, slip your finger inside

Figure 3   Granny, by Ian Allen

Figure 4   Timmo Tarin, by Violet Philpott

Figure 5   Clown, by John Thirtle

Figure 6   Robber, by Frieder Simon

the cuff. This method permits greater character in the shape of the hands but more practice may be neeeded to achieve expressive gesture and effective handling of props.

Glove puppets with legs

If legs are required, they may be made simply as cloth tubes stuffed with cloth or foam rubber. Stitch the legs to the 'glove', inside the jacket (figure 7). Cut the feet from a chunk of foam rubber then cover them with glued-on material (such as felt). Glue and stitch the feet on to the legs.

However, a much more satisfactory method is to carve, mould or model the foot and lower leg as for a rod puppet or marionette (which helps considerably in controlling the movement). Glue securely to it a tube of material stuffed with foam rubber or fabric scraps for the upper leg and stitch the tops of the legs onto the glove body.

In order to conceal your arm when you manipulate a glove puppet with legs, make the glove long enough to reach your elbow. Use of a dark material helps it to recede (figure 7).

Such legs swing freely, controlled only by the overall movement of the body. It is possible, with a slight modification, to control them directly, but remember that this will require two-handed operation. Make the upper legs from strong hollow tubes which will accommodate your first two fingers. Cut and tidily finish holes in the covering fabric below where they join onto the body. Insert the fingers of your free hand into the tubes to operate the legs; your hand will need to be gloved and your arm covered with a sleeve to disguise it.

If desired, the lower part of the thigh can be solid, with a proper knee joint as described for rod puppets and marionettes.

Animal puppets

You can make a simple glove with an animal head, covering the glove with a human costume, fur or fur fabric. Alternatively, a complete animal body that rests on your wrist and forearm may be made of cloth and stitched to the glove (figure 8).

Stuff the body and hind legs with fabric or foam rubber.

A puppet required to maintain a particular body shape (such as a fish) may be made by covering a framework made from card (stuck or stapled into shape), or by covering a framework of wire netting padded with foam rubber (figure 9).

Figure 7 A glove puppet with legs

Figure 8 A glove puppet that sits on the arm

Figure 9 An animal puppet made from cardboard

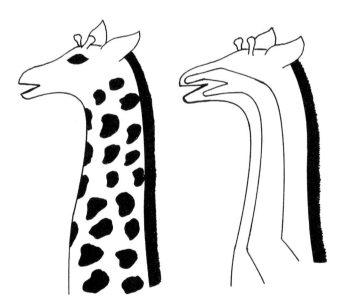

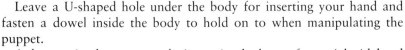

Figure 10 (Left) A sleeve puppet

Leave a U-shaped hole under the body for inserting your hand and fasten a dowel inside the body to hold on to when manipulating the puppet.

A sleeve animal puppet may be just a simple sleeve of material with head attached. Often the head has a moving mouth (figure 10). A stuffed body and dangling legs may be attached to the sleeve.

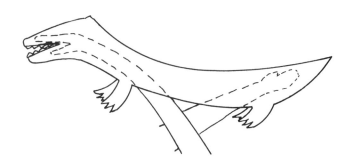

Figure 11 A two-handed glove puppet

Two-handed glove puppets are made on the same principle as sleeve puppets, leaving underneath a hole large enough to insert your crossed arms (figure 11). The body is often stiffened by lining it with buckram, foam rubber or even newspaper.

Moving mouths for animal puppets A moving mouth, which is employed at the expense of leg movement, may be made by one of the following methods:

A folded paper plate or an egg box makes an excellent pair of jaws. Glue a strip of stepped cardboard (figure 15) on top of, and underneath, the jaws. Slip your fingers and thumb under these strips to move the mouth. Glue the jaws into the material head.

Figure 12 Ferdy, by Julie Gosling

Figure 13 Moose and Mouse, by John Thirtle

108

Figure 14   Bandicoot and the Cro-codile from The Birthday Cake *by Violet Philpott*

Cut out two pieces of plywood for the jaws. Glue and tack a cloth hinge to the plywood. Tack strips of canvas to the plywood to slip your fingers into to hold the puppet and control the jaws (figure 16). This is a stronger method of construction, particularly suitable for use with a cardboard, or wire and foam rubber, body.

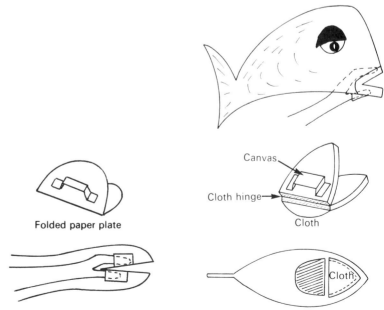

Folded paper plate

Figure 15   A simple moving mouth

Figure 16   A moving mouth made of wood

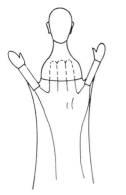

Figure 17 *A Catalan glove puppet*

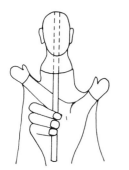

Figure 18 *A rod-hand puppet*

Catalan glove puppets

This type of puppet (figure 17) is now rarely used as it is heavier and more difficult to manipulate than an ordinary glove puppet. Traditionally the head, neck and shoulders are carved from one piece of wood, but a head may be made by one of the methods described in Chapter 6 and attached to a separate wooden shoulder block. Drill holes in the shoulder block for the first three fingers and use your thumb and little finger to control the arms. These are made from cardboard tubes glued to the hands (see page 105).

The rod-hand puppet

Made on exactly the same principles as a glove puppet, the head of this puppet is moved by a rod inserted in the neck. The thumb and index finger move the hands and the other three fingers grasp the rod (figure 18).

Muppet-type hand puppets

These are often a cross between hand puppets and rod puppets, usually with moving mouths. They depend upon the hand for head, mouth and body movements; the hands and arms are controlled in one of three ways: by a rod (figure 19), as described for rod puppets; by a human hand inserted into a hollow arm and hand which is part of the costume or by a human hand wearing a separate glove (or mitten) and sleeve (figure 20).

It is common practice for such puppet hands to have only three fingers (fit two of your fingers into one of the puppet's) which looks quite natural on the puppet.

These puppets tend to be larger than glove puppets, so the heads need to be made of a very light material: foam rubber or polystyrene, covered with fabric or fur fabric, are the usual materials. If foam rubber is used, the head and lower jaw are often cut in one piece. Otherwise the head is made in two parts, often hinged together with strong fabric glued on securely. The mouth and head movement is achieved with four fingers in the upper jaw and the thumb in the lower jaw (figure 21).

A slim tube of material would detract from the puppet's character, so make the body suitably full. Very often the whole puppet is created in foam rubber, the head and limbs from blocks and the body from a sheet of the material. It is quite common for the limbs not to be manipulated: they are held in suitable positions by wire inserted through their entire length and permitting a slight springiness.

Unfortunately some performers create second-rate imitations of the Muppet characters; the comparison this invites only highlights their own shortcomings. By all means use the technical method to develop *your own characters in your own style* but leave the Muppets and their style to those who do it best.

Note: a popular version of this type of puppet has a disproportionately large head and features a moving mouth, which is such a dominant characteristic that these figures are now termed 'mouth puppets'.

Figure 19 *Frank Oz operating Miss Piggy from* The Muppet Show

Figure 20 George and Zippy from Rainbow (Thames Television)

Figure 21 Operating a Muppet-type head

Control

Basically, the method of controlling a glove puppet is very simple although it needs a considerable amount of practice to achieve convincing movements. The glove type of body is usually manipulated with the hand in one of the three positions illustrated (figures 22/1, 22/2, 22/3), the first two of which are preferred by most people. Manipulation technique is discussed further in Chapter 14.

Figure 22/1 The recommended form of operation

Figure 22/1 illustrates the recommended method, which is more comfortable than it appears and gives the most definite control of the head. To turn the head, press your first two fingers apart inside the neck, moving them backwards and forwards to rotate the head. Manipulation with one finger in the neck (figure 22/2) requires your whole hand (and therefore the whole of the puppet's body) to turn if the head is to turn. The two fingers tucked into the palm also account for some well known television puppets appearing rather pregnant at times! Most people find the method illustrated in figure 22/3 uncomfortable and the least satisfactory for convincing movement.

Animal puppets with moving mouths are held by the puppeteer's whole hand in the head, with the thumb moving the lower jaw (figure 21).

Figure 22/2 A common manipulation technique but at the expense of some control and the puppet can appear pregnant!

Figure 22/3 A method best avoided

8   The rod puppet

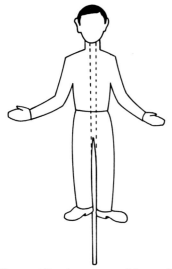

Figure 1/1   The short central rod allows more scope for movement

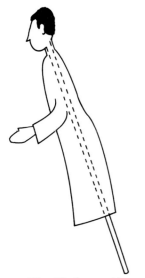

Figure 1/2   A puppet with legs will need a longer rod

Figure 1/3   The long rod limits waist movement

Construction

There is some overlap between the principles and techniques of rod puppet and marionette construction; such differences as do exist for the most part relate to the method of control. The present chapter, therefore, elaborates those techniques specific to the rod puppet and simply identifies the uses of those common to both types of puppet, for which the reader is referred to Chapter 9.

The body is constructed so that it can be supported by a central rod which may be free to turn within the body or may be fixed. It is increasingly common to use a short, central rod (figure 1/1) to give more scope for movement (your wrist becomes the puppet's waist). The advantage of the long rod is the height at which the puppet may be held and the facility for having puppets with legs (figure 1/2), but at the expense of the puppet's waist movement (figure 1/3) and general loss of flexibility. In its simplest forms, the rod puppet is just a 'marot', (the 'Fool's stick' carried by a jester in medieval times, figure 2/1) or a head and a robe fixed to a rod with no body or limbs (figure 2/2). The latter has neither shoulders, arms, nor legs but is surprisingly effective. The material of the robe plays a very important part: for example, a stiff satin material will give a very different movement from a soft, cotton fabric. The type of rod puppet which consists of a shoulder piece and flowing robes but no body or legs (figure 3) is said to be a development of the marot. However, it is often good practice

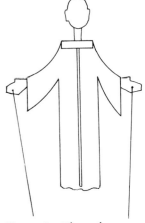

Figure 2/1   A marot

Figure 2/2   The simplest rod puppet

Figure 3   The rod puppet that developed from the marot

Rod free to turn

Figure 4/1 A puppet with the rod free to turn in the body

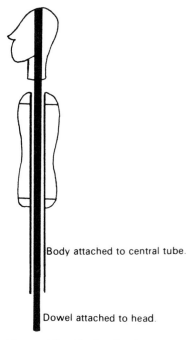

Body attached to central tube.

Dowel attached to head.

Figure 4/2 The head rod turns inside the body tube

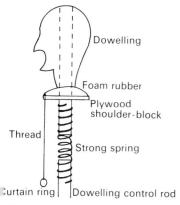

Dowelling

Foam rubber

Plywood shoulder-block

Thread

Strong spring

Curtain ring | Dowelling control rod

Figure 5 A simple nodding puppet

to have a body, or at least appropriate padding under the costume, to achieve the unity of characterisation discussed in Chapter 4.

The head

Rod puppet heads can be made as described in Chapter 6. Before progressing with its construction, read the next few pages. The considerations here will have a bearing on whether you make it with or without a neck.

A turning head If the rod were fixed rigidly in the head and the body (or shoulders), the head would not be able to turn, of course. Most rod puppets are constructed therefore *either* with the rod secured in the head, free to turn in the body, and with some form of block or 'collar' (made from wood, a strip of cardboard wound around or one of the modelling materials) fixed under the shoulders to hold them in place (figure 4/1), *or* with a rod secured in the head and strong tubing (e.g. aluminium, thick cardboard or rigid and strong plastic) fixed in the body. The head rod turns inside the tube which supports the body (figure 4/2).

A nodding head Two basic possibilities are available. The first method, with a spring, is more easily constructed in terms of the controlling mechanism but does not permit a turning action as well. The second method is recommended as it allows both a nodding and turning control.

A simple nodding puppet First glue a long dowel in the head. Then cut out a plywood shoulder block (with a coping saw) and drill a hole in the plywood to accommodate the dowel. Glue the shoulders on to the dowel and pad them with foam rubber (figure 5).

Fasten one end of a strong spring (e.g. a coil of spring steel) on to the dowel and the other end on to the control rod.

Attach a length of thread to the front of the shoulder block. Tie a large curtain ring on to the end of the thread. Pull the thread to make the puppet nod. (Hold the rod and slip the ring over your index finger for one-handed operation.)

A head that can nod and turn The head is made with no neck; it has an elongated hole in the base (figure 6/1) and pivots on the top of the central control rod. A hole is drilled across the top of the rod; a length of strong galvanised wire (coathanger wire) through the hole is attached securely in

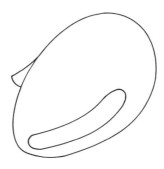

Figure 6/1 An elongated hole cut in the head

113

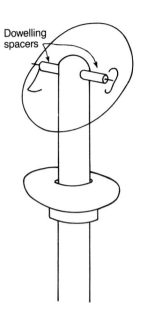

Dowelling spacers

Figure 6/2 The head secured to permit nodding and turning

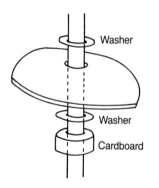

Washer

Washer

Cardboard

Figure 7 Supporting the shoulder block

the sides of the head (figure 6/2). Short lengths of dowel, with holes drilled through the centre, are used as 'spacers' to hold the head and neck in position.

Whilst the head is free to nod on top of the rod, it does not prevent the rod turning in the body as discussed above. The means of operating this type of head are detailed in the section on control later in this chapter.

Construction of the body

A shoulder block With a coping saw, cut the shoulder block from a piece of plywood. Drill a hole through to accommodate the central rod; ensure it moves freely if the head is to turn. Pad the plywood with foam rubber; glue it on, then trim to shape. Glue a long strip of card around the rod below the plywood (figure 7).

To ensure that the shoulders do not grip on this supporting block, make a washer to insert between the two; the plastic lids and bases of cream cheese or margarine containers are ideal. If the head and neck are built in one piece, you will need another washer between the bottom of the neck and the foam rubber shoulder padding; ensure that the neck cannot touch any part of the foam rubber.

The shoulder block may also be used to attach sheet foam rubber padding to give more shape to the body.

A plywood and canvas body The body is made from two plywood shapes joined by a tube of canvas, or some other strong material. Drill a hole in the centre of each piece of plywood to accommodate a rod or tube. Secure the rod or tube in the shoulder piece with strips of glued card (figure 8).

Tack the body on to both pieces of plywood and gather in the waist with a draw thread.

Glue foam rubber on to the shoulder piece to give it more shape; a washer will be needed between body and neck, as described above.

A buckram or cardboard body The body is constructed from strong pieces of cardboard or buckram, glued together (figure 9). Build the shape on a wooden shoulder block. Fasten the central rod or tube to the shoulders with strips of glued paper or card, as described above.

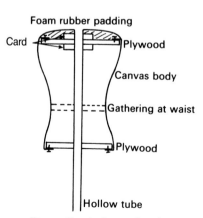

Foam rubber padding

Card

Plywood

Canvas body

Gathering at waist

Plywood

Hollow tube

Figure 8 A plywood and canvas body

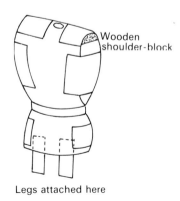

Wooden shoulder-block

Legs attached here

Figure 9 A buckram or cardboard body

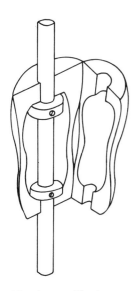

Figure 10   A carved body

A carved body   Although it is not very common practice to do so today, the body may be carved (see Chapter 6 for carving techniques). To reduce the weight, cut open the body and hollow out the centre with a chisel.

If it is to have a central rod, this is secured (but free to turn) with glued strips of card or wooden blocks screwed in place (figure 10). Insert washers on the rods, between the body and these securing collars. They are effectively made from pieces of plastic cartons. A central tube in which a head rod turns should be glued very firmly in place; card or blocks may be used for reinforcement.

A modelled or moulded body   The techniques used for modelling and moulding heads (see Chapter 6) may be used for bodies too. They are attached to the central tube or rod by whichever of the methods detailed above is appropriate for the chosen material. You may, or course, make just a thorax, or the whole body in one piece, or thorax and pelvis separately.

Figure 11   Rod puppets designed by John Blundall for use with 'black light' technique in Pinocchio *at the Cannon Hill Puppet Theatre*

Construction of arms and hands

The techniques described for making marionette arms and hands (see pages 133 – 136) are suitable for rod puppets, or the hands may be cut from a large sponge or a block of foam rubber. Arms may also be made of rope (figure 11). This gives a desirable firmness in the arm yet allows total flexibility of movement. Corrugated cardboard may be glued and wound around the rope, or foam rubber used, to give more shape to the arms. Puppeteers have a variety of preferences for wrist or elbow joints. It is usually preferable that rod puppets should have somewhat more restricted joints than marionettes for purposes of control.

Joints   A leather joint permits considerable flexibility whilst maintaining good control. This is a neat method for a bare arm. The wrist has sideways movement and the elbow vertical movement (figure 12).

Figure 12   Leather joints

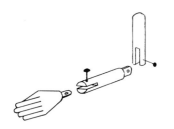

Figure 13/1 Wooden 'tongues' in slots

Figure 13/2 Screw-eyes pivoted in slots

Figure 14/1 Interlocked screw-eyes

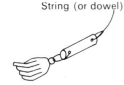

Figure 14/2 Screw-eye and thread

An open mortise and tenon joint, which tends to restrict a marionette's arms, is a useful joint for rod puppets (figure 13/1). A variation on this joint uses screw-eyes instead of the wooden 'tongues' (figure 13/2).

Although there seems to be general agreement that a more restricted joint gives greater control over the rod puppet, some puppeteers still prefer interlocked screw-eyes (figure 14/1), or simple string joints (figure 14/2). The screw-eye joint is not recommended, however, because it rattles and the arms can become caught in an odd position.

Occasionally, hands are built on to the arms without any flexible wrist joint. In this case, the fingers must be in an interesting position to compensate for the lack of wrist movement. The control rod for such hands is usually attached at the wrist.

Construction of legs and feet

It is not essential for the rod puppet to be given legs, especially if it is a large figure. Rod puppets are often visible only to waist or hip level, as noted earlier.

Figure 15 The Canterville Ghost by Playboard Puppets

116

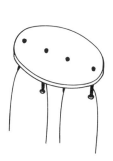

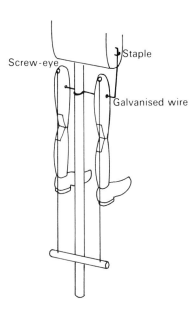

Screw-eye

Staple

Galvanised wire

Figure 16   A hip joint using strong cord

Figure 17   A leather, or canvas, hip joint. The leather thong is pushed through the slot, glued and tacked down.

Figure 18   A hip joint for legs controlled by strings

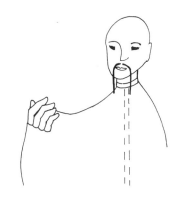

Figure 19   A rod-hand puppet

If the puppet is to have legs and feet, they may be made in the same way as those of a marionette (see pages 137 – 139). Cord (figure 16), leather or canvas joints (figure 17) are particularly useful for the hip joints. The ankle joints must be restricted sufficiently to prevent the toes pointing downwards all the time.

Usually the legs dangle freely; occasionally, they are controlled by strings from below. In the latter case, suspend them from a length of 12 gauge galvanised wire (figure 18). Allow a fair length of leg above the wire to facilitate good leverage for moving the legs.

The rod-hand puppet

There are a number of variations on rod-hand puppets (see also Chapter 7), but the example given here is the most common (figure 19). This type of puppet is also used for two-man operation, with one puppeteer controlling the head and the other providing the hands. The puppet may have a central rod but no body, only a robe. The puppeteer holds the rod in one hand and slips his other hand, usually gloved, through a slit in the puppet's robe. The slit may be elasticated if desired. Alternatively, it may be a rod puppet with human hands as described for the Muppet-type hand puppets in Chapter 7.

Animals

Animals can be made from a wide variety of materials. Two common techniques are described below.

A standard animal rod puppet   The head may be built with the body, all in one piece, or it may be made separately by one of the methods described

117

Figure 20 A character from Cannon Hill Puppet Theatre's production of The Tales of Hoffmann

Figure 21 (Above) Princess Shari from The Arabian Nights *by the Polka Children's Theatre*

Figure 22 (Below) Peter and the Bird from the Caricature Theatre's production of Peter and the Wolf

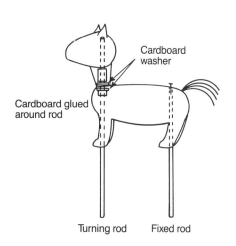

Cardboard washer

Cardboard glued around rod

Turning rod Fixed rod

Dowel glued into block of polystyrene

Head rod raised to extend the neck

Figure 23/1 (Far left) An animal puppet with turning head

Figure 23/2 (Left) This head can be turned and extended

118

Figure 24/1 An animal with a flexible body

Figure 24/2 An alternative form of the flexible body method

in Chapter 6. Sometimes it is painted but it is usually covered with the same material as the body.

If the head is to move, the head rod is inserted through the bottom of the body and is used to turn the head (figure 23/1) and raise or lower it by lengthening the neck (figure 23/2). Its movement may be restricted by a block or collar around the rod as detailed for other rod puppets. A nodding head may be achieved in the same way as for a 'human' rod puppet.

Carve, model or mould the body in the same way as a puppet head, then paint it or cover it with fabric, fur fabric or other materials as appropriate.

Make the legs in the same way as animal marionette legs (see pages 139,142). Glue the supporting rod into the body at the point where the body is well balanced on the rod.

An animal puppet with flexible body This alternative construction is based on a central rope or cord, one end of which is glued and tied to the head and head rod (figure 24/1). Graduated sized discs of foam rubber, with smaller pieces as spacers, are threaded and glued to the rope to create the body. A second rod attached near the tail facilitates a considerable degree of flexibility and control. The body may be covered or used just as it is, with or without dangling legs and feet of foam rubber. Figure 24/2 illustrates a variation on this method.

Control

The main feature of a rod puppet control is the central rod which supports the figure. Additional controls are added to move the head, hands and, occasionally, legs.

Moving the head

Two sorts of central rod have been described in the constructional section (page 113, figures 4/1 and 4/2).

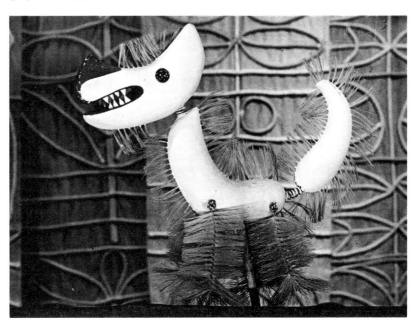

Figure 25 A dog from Happy Bunny *by the Pinokio Puppet Theatre, Łodź, Poland*

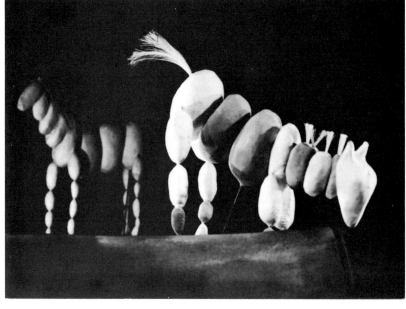

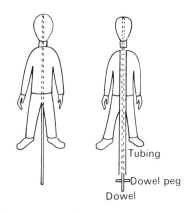

Figure 27/1   The central rod fixed to head and body

Figure 27/2   The central rod turns inside a tube

A rod passed through the body is attached to the head (figure 27/1). This requires only one-handed control and the head may move independently of the body, if so constructed.

A tube is incorporated in the body inside which turns a rod fixed to the head (figure 27/2). The head can be moved using two- or one-handed control. A short dowel glued into the end of the head rod will prevent the rod coming out of the tube.

Two-handed control   Hold the central tube with one hand and turn or raise the head rod with the other.

One-handed control   Cut a rectangular shape from the tube where your thumb would rest (figure 28/1).

Through the rectangular hole drill a hole in the dowelling head rod. Bend a length of 12 gauge galvanised wire into a thumb rest and glue the ends of the wire into the hole in the dowel. Hold the tubing below the thumb rest and use your thumb to effect all the head movements (figure 28/2).

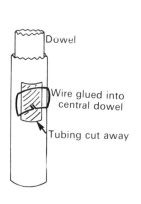

Figure 28/1   The control

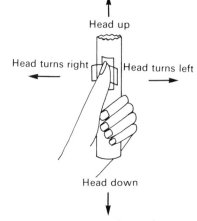

Figure 28/2   Manipulating the control

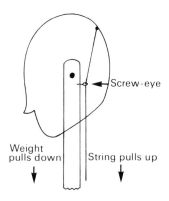

Figure 29/1

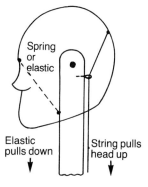

Figure 29/2

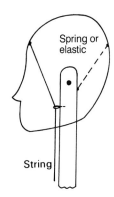

Figure 29/3

Figure 29 Three ways of using a pull-string to effect nodding

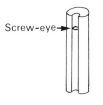

Figure 30 A central dowel grooved for the control string

Nodding controls   Two main techniques are common for controlling a nodding head: the use of a pull-string, counter-balanced by the weight of the puppet's head, a spring or a piece of elastic or the use of a wire lever.

A pull-string may be used in two ways: *either* pivot the head so that its weight pulls it forwards, and attach a string inside the back of the head to lift it (figure 29/1) *or*, pivot the head so that it balances on the rod. Attach a string to the back of the head and the control rod and provide a counter-pull to nod the head (figure 29/2). Alternatively, you may attach the string to the front of the head and the counter-pull to the back (figure 29/3).

Whichever control technique is used, it is advisable to groove the head rod for the string (figure 30). Used with a dowel alone as the central rod, the string runs through small screw-eyes in the groove to a small lever made of galvanised wire, fixed in the back or front of the dowel, as appropriate (figure 31). Press the lever to move the head.

The pull-string method is not recommended when the dowel turns inside a tube, but it is possible with this method for the head to turn as well, provided that the central rod turns inside the body or shoulder block as detailed earlier (figure 32). (The thread may need replacing more often because of rubbing.)

Figure 31   (Left) A lever control for nodding

Figure 32   (Right) A nodding and turning head

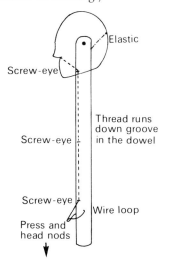

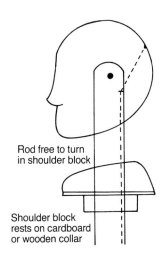

121

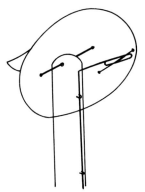

Figure 33/1   Securing a wire lever in the head

A wire lever does not need a counter-pull as the lever is used to hold the head in any position required. It is made from strong, galvanised wire and runs in the grooved rod like the string previously. It is secured to the rod by staples.

The top of the wire is angled and the end made into an elongated loop (figure 33/1). Another length of galvanised wire passes through this loop and is secured near the back of the head. By moving the wire up and down, the nodding movement is effected; some adjustment will be necessary to achieve the appropriate angle for the wire so that it moves smoothly and the head does not stick at certain points.

The other end of the wire is bent into a thumb rest (figure 33/2) or a wooden ball may be glued onto it (figure 33/3) to facilitate control.

Two possible controls for all head movements   When the dowel turns inside a central tube, it is possible to modify the above one-handed nodding control to effect all head movements.

Take a piece of 12 gauge galvanised wire, longer than the central rod, and bend one end into a thumb rest (figure 34/1).

Cut a slot in the central dowel to accommodate the short end of the wire (figure 34/2).

Put the dowel inside the tube and push the long end of the wire through the opening in the tubing and up the groove in the dowel. The short end of the wire fits into the slot in the dowel (figure 34/3).

Bend the top of the wire into an elongated loop and attach it inside the head as described above.

Turn the head by moving the lever from side to side with your thumb; raise and lower the lever to raise or lower the head.

An alternative method not using a rod in a tube is illustrated in figure 34/4, based upon a very successful design used by John Thirtle (Playboard Puppets). The head is joined to the neck and the control wire as described above (figure 33/1).

The head pivots on a short 'neck' rod which has a hole drilled through its entire length to accommodate the control wire. (You might need to drill into the centre from each end and, if necessary, jiggle about with the drilling until the two holes line up.) Saw a slot in the top of this rod to allow the angled top of the wire to move up and down: this effects the nodding

Figure 33/2   A thumb rest

Figure 33/3   An alternative means of facilitating control

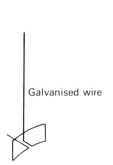

Galvanised wire

Figure 34/1   Galvanised wire bent into a thumb rest

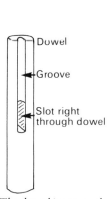

Dowel

Groove

Slot right through dowel

Figure 34/2   The dowel is grooved and slotted to take the wire

Figure 34/3   The control assembled

122

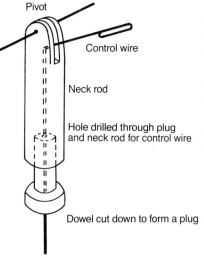

Head pivots on rod by
means of galvanised wire

Loop in
end of
control wire

Screw

Shoulder block

Dowelling plug

Dowel peg

main supporting rod

Wire bent into
thumb rest

*Figure 34/4 An alternative method
for controlling head movements*

Pivot

Control wire

Neck rod

Hole drilled through plug
and neck rod for control wire

Dowel cut down to form a plug

*Figure 34/5 The neck dowel and
the securing plug*

action. By turning the wire, the neck (and therefore the head) is forced to turn.

To join the neck to the shoulder-block use another length of dowel-rod, cut down to form the plug shape illustrated (figure 34/5). Drill a hole through this plug for the control wire and a wide hole in the neck to accept the plug: it must be a tight fit. In the shoulder block drill a wide hole in which the plug may turn freely without wobbling about. Insert the plug through the block and glue the end into the neck. Ensure that it does not become glued to the shoulder-block.

The shoulder-block is screwed to a supporting rod just in front of the neck (figure 34/4). Short dowels, glued into holes drilled into this rod, are themselves drilled to carry the control wire, the end of which is bent into a thumb-rest to raise, lower and turn the wire.

Controlling the hands and legs

Constructing the control for hands The hands are controlled by two lengths of thick (12 gauge) galvanised wire or, preferably, steel wire. It is advisable to drill a hole in a length of dowelling and glue the wire into the hole. The dowel is easier to grip than the wire.

To attach the wire to the hand, make a small loop in the end of the galvanised wire (figure 35/1) or, with steel wire, beat the end flat and drill a hole in it (figure 35/2). Then attach the wires to the hands by means of a thread or screw-eyes. With some hands (e.g. foam rubber) it will be necessary to attach the thread to some strong fixture such as a button in order to prevent it pulling back through the hand.

To restrict rod movement and achieve more direct control of the wrist action, make a slot in the side of the hand, insert the rod and secure it with a nail through the hand (figure 35/3).

If the hand is attached to the arm without a flexible wrist joint, an alternative method is to drill a hole through the arm, push the wire through, and bend the end over (figure 35/4).

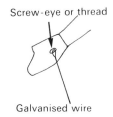

Screw-eye or thread

Galvanised wire

Figure 35/1 Galvanised wire

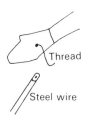

Thread

Steel wire

Figure 35/2 Steel wire

*Figure 35/3 Wire secured in a slot
in the hand*

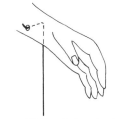

*Figure 35/4 Galvanised wire
attached to the wrist*

Wire 'hooks'

Figure 36/1 Galvanised wire bent into the hook shape to hold the hand wires

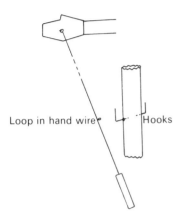

Loop in hand wire — Hooks

Figure 36/2 Hooks screwed into dowelling

A useful device for holding one hand wire whilst manipulating the other is a small hook on each side of the central rod, level with the puppet's feet. If it is a dowel rod, screw hooks into it. If it is a tube, bend a strong piece of galvanised wire into the shape shown (figure 36/1), then glue and bind it to the tube. Make a small loop in each hand wire (figure 36/2); this fits onto the hook and holds up the hand, permitting it to swing slightly, when it is not being manipulated.

Using the control It is quite common practice to allow one arm to hang limp whilst the other is being manipulated, but this is not a recommended technique (figure 37/1). *Either* hold the central rod with one hand and the two hand wires with the other (figure 37/2), *or* hold one of the wires with the little finger of the hand that holds the central rod (figure 37/3). This leaves your other hand free to control the other hand wire. If the hooks described above (figure 36) are attached to the control, these may be used to hold the hand wires as necessary.

Controlling the legs Very often the legs are allowed to dangle loosely. If, however, a leg control is required, attach screw-eyes to the tops of the legs (pivoted on a wire as described on page 117) and tie thread to the screw-eyes. Attach the other ends of the strings to a dowel rod which is 'paddled' to produce a walking movement (figure 38).

A much wider range of leg movements can be achieved with two-man puppets; a dowel-rod, usually painted black, is glued into each foot (figure 39) and the second operator effects leg movement by holding these. This is more common with ultra violet lighting techniques (see Black Theatre).

Figure 37/1 Simple two-handed operation

Figure 37/2 Jan King demonstrates the re-commended operating technique

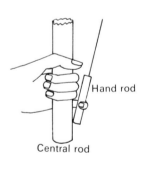

Hand rod

Central rod

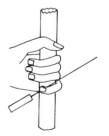

Figure 37/3 Holding the hand rod for simple gestures

124

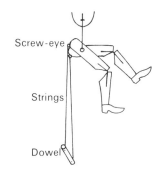

Figure 38   A leg control

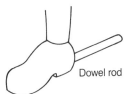

Figure 39   A dowel rod control for legs

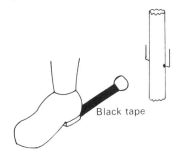

Figure 40   Restricting leg movements

Figure 41   Operating a Sicilian puppet

Figure 42   A variation of the Sicilian technique was used by Stefan Fichert for this bear in the Puppet Centre Collection

Alternatively, use the method described for Bunraku-type puppets (figure 44).

There may be times when dangling legs need to be prevented from swinging. The hooks for hand wires on the central rod (figures 36/1, 36/2) can also be used for this purpose. Glue and tack a strip of black tape to each heel of the puppet; stitch a small ring on to the end of each tape (figure 40). Slip the rings over the hooks to restrict leg movement. You may also move the legs individually by holding the tape.

Related rod puppet techniques

Sicilian style puppets

The traditional Sicilian puppets described in Chapter 2 are sometimes referred to as marionettes, at other times rod puppets. Though operated from above, the main means of control are strong metal rods to the head and the sword arm, with a cord to the shield arm (figure 41), the puppet itself being carved in wood, with armour beaten from brass. Recent explorations with this type of control have led to a number of variations, an example of which is illustrated (figure 42). The bear has head and body

Figure 43 The Pomegranate Princess by *Cannon Hill Puppet Theatre*

rods through which total control is effected. When standing upright, the puppet's momentum and gentle swaying of the body causes the legs to walk; when on all fours, walking is achieved by alternatively lifting front and rear legs and using the momentum of the body. The rods for the bear are constructed from aluminium tube, and the bear itself is modelled and hollow, so it is much lighter to operate than a Sicilian figure.

A similar style of puppet is suspended on strings attached to a cloth-bound ring on the puppeteer's head. It is operated by the puppeteer's head movement and hand rods (figure 43). Occasionally the puppeteer's shoes are attached to the puppet's feet too. This is, of course, part rod puppet and part marionette, but commonly called a 'body puppet'.

Bunraku-style puppets

The term *Bunraku* strictly refers to a unique style of Japanese performance comprising a blend of the arts of puppet theatre, *samisen* music and *tayu* narration. Increasingly the term 'Bunraku-style' is used to describe a similar type of puppet for which no other precise generic term has emerged.

The head of a true Bunraku puppet (figure 44) is carved and hollowed, sometimes with a range of moving features. It is mounted on a headgrip which fits into a wooden shoulder board with padded ends. Two strips of material hang from the shoulders at the front and back; to the bottom of these is attached a bamboo hoop for the hips. The limbs are carved, sometimes with shaped and stuffed upper parts; strings from the arms and legs are tied to the ends of the shoulder board. The padded costume itself creates the real body shape and character.

The chief operator inserts his left hand through a slit in the back of the costume and holds the headgrip to control head and body. With his right hand he moves the right arm. A toggle with strings attached, built into the

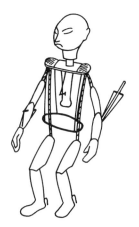

Figure 44 *A Bunraku-style puppet*

126

Figure 45 Bottom *by Graeme Galvin for the Puppet Centre*

Figure 46 The Sorcerer's Apprentice, *carved by Joyce Wren for Theatre of Puppets and operated in the manner of the Japanese Bunraku*

arm, is used to effect hand movements. The second operator uses his right hand to move the puppet's left arm, by means of a rod about 15 in long which is joined to the arm near the elbow. This also has toggles for hand control. The legs are moved by a third operator using inverted L-shaped rods fixed at the back of the ankles.

This technique has been adapted to a range of practices with one, two or three-man operation. Examples are illustrated (figures 45 and 46). The neck is often angled somewhat (figure 47) and the basic headgrip made from a strong strip of plywood. One end is built into the neck and the other end is made into a pistol-grip handle by gluing on shaped pieces of wood.

It is not common to include the toggle hand controls. Usually the hand is built onto the arm without a flexible wrist joint and the control wire, operated from behind, is inserted into the arm at the elbow (figure 48). The weight of the wire and the wooden dowel handle acts as a partial counterbalance to the arm, so it does not hang lifeless by the puppet's side while not being operated.

To limit the movement of the hand wires and facilitate one-handed control of the arms, it is helpful to link the wires with a small metal ring, as illustrated (figure 48).

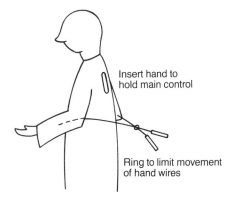

Insert hand to
hold main control

Ring to limit movement
of hand wires

Figure 47 *An angled neck attached to a pistol-grip control*

Figure 48 *Operating the arms from behind the puppet*

9   The Marionette

Figure 1   A marionette carved by John Wright for the Puppet Centre Collection

Construction

The essence of good marionette construction is balance and distribution of weight coupled with flexibility of movement, joints being restricted appropriately to allow adequate control. A well-made marionette will be able to move in a way which poorly constructed marionettes will never be capable of, regardless of their form of control or stringing.

It is important, therefore, to design the marionette as a whole, to ensure a suitable match of materials which will provide the balance required. This is why, for example, heavy wooden legs should not be attached to a light polystyrene body and why few marionettes work as well as a well-designed, carved wooden one.

Marionette heads can be made as described in Chapter 6.

The body

The body of a marionette is usually constructed in two parts with a joint at the waist. A body in one piece restricts the way a puppet moves, particularly its walk.

It may be made by any of the techniques described for puppet heads provided it is strongly made. The reader is referred to the note on necks (page 81); each design has its uses but the separate neck jointed inside the head and body is the best all-purpose method.

A cloth body   A cloth body is normally used with a sock head. To make a shoulder piece cut a hole in the centre of a cardboard disc. Make one cut from the perimeter to the centre (figure 2/1), then overlap and glue together the edges (figure 2/2).

Attach the head to the shoulder piece by pushing the loose end of the sock through the disc and sewing it to the cardboard, both near the centre and at the edge of the disc (figure 2/3).

Glue or stitch the edges of a piece of fabric together to make a tube for the body. Glue and stitch one end of the tube on to the cardboard shoulder piece.

Run two strong threads round the centre of the body and draw up to form a waist (figure 2/3).

Stuff the body with fabric, or foam rubber, and stitch across the bottom.

Stitch cloth arms and legs to the body.

Cardboard disc

Figure 2/1   The shoulders

Figure 2/2   Card overlapped and glued

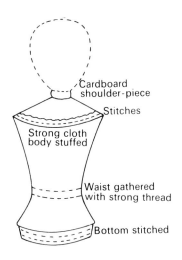

Figure 2/3   The body assembled

129

Figure 3/1 Plywood shape for thorax

Figure 3/2 Foam rubber glued to plywood

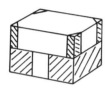

Figure 3/3 The shaded parts are cut from the block to form the pelvis

Figure 3/4 Two pieces joined for the pelvis

A wood and foam rubber body   Make the thorax by gluing foam rubber to a piece of plywood, or hardboard, cut to the shape illustrated in figure 3/1.

With scissors, snip the foam rubber into the required three-dimensional form (figure 3/2).

To make the pelvis, saw two sections from a block of wood (figure 3/3), leaving a T shape. Round off the sharp corners and pad with foam rubber. Alternatively, glue and screw together two pieces of wood in the T shape (figure 3/4) and pad.

A moulded body   Model the two parts of the body in plasticine on dowels and take a plaster cast as described on pages 93–95. Figure 4/1 shows where to divide the plasticine model when making the plaster cast. When the dowels in the body are removed from the casts, they will leave holes in the plaster through which latex rubber can be poured and this will also leave holes in the body parts that can later be used for joining them.

Cast the body in one of the materials described on pages 90–97. If rubber is used, allow it to form a fairly thick layer. If it is too flexible, it will need strengthening before attaching neck, arms and pelvis (cut open the thorax and glue into the centre a thin plywood shape with four holes drilled in it as illustrated in figure 4/2; stuff the body with foam rubber and seal the slit with glue).

A modelled body   Model the body according to the techniques described in Chapter 6. For extra strength, it may be made on a basic shape of balsa wood or polystyrene, which then remains inside the body.

A carved body   The techniques for woodcarving (Chapter 6) may be employed but it will be necessary to hollow out the thorax to reduce its weight (work from underneath, cutting up into the thorax). Before carving, design the whole puppet and determine the waist joint (see figures 1 and 8). It is not uncommon for beginners to carve the parts without allowing for the method of jointing.

Waist joints

Screw-eye joints   This joint can be used with wooden bodies, but tends to rattle.

Fasten a screw-eye in each section. Open up one of the screw-eyes with a pair of pliers, interlock it in the other and close the link again (figure 5). Alternatively, join the screw-eyes with string.

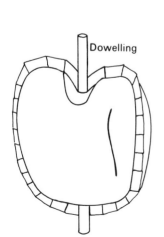

Dowelling

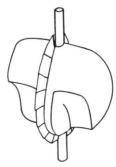

Figure 4/1 Where to divide the plasticine models for casting in plaster

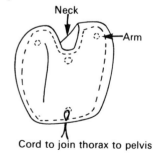

Neck

Arm

Cord to join thorax to pelvis

Figure 4/2 A hardboard or plywood shape glued into the rubber body

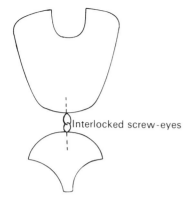

Figure 5   A screw-eye waist joint

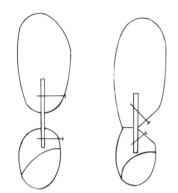

Figure 6/1   Leather waist joint prevents turning at waist

Figure 6/2   This restricted joint allows forward movement only

Leather joints   Leather may be used with bodies modelled on a solid base, with solid wooden bodies, and those laminated from layers of plywood and foam rubber.

Cut slots in each section. Glue the ends of the strip of leather and insert them in the slots. Secure the leather further with nails (figure 6/1).

If you want a restricted joint, permitting movement in only one direction, make the joint so that the thorax and pelvis are in contact. Cut away part of the thorax and pelvis (figure 6/2) to facilitate movement in the direction required.

Cord joints   These joints can be used with wood and foam rubber or moulded bodies. For the former, drill a hole in the plywood base of the thorax, insert a screw-eye in the top of the pelvis, and thread through cord (figure 7/1).

To join flexible rubber body parts, tie a strong cord to the hardboard or plywood in the thorax. Knot the ends and push them through the hole in the top of the rubber pelvis (figure 7/2). Pour plaster of Paris into the pelvis. This secures the cord and weights the body. (It is wise to join the legs to the pelvis at the same time. See hip joints on page 138.)

Ball joints   These joints allow excellent movement. They are frequently used for unclothed bodies but are recommended for most purposes.

For carved and modelled bodies, make the body with holes in the pelvis and thorax to accommodate a wooden ball (figure 8/1).

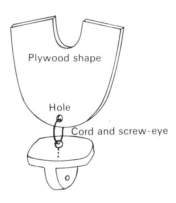

Figure 7/1   Cord joint for a wooden body

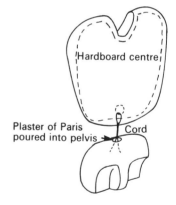

Figure 7/2   Cord joint for a flexible rubber body

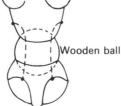

Figure 8/1   A ball joint

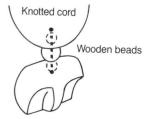

Figure 8/2   A ball joint suitable for rubber bodies

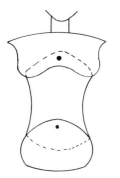

Figure 9 A body in three sections

Drill two parallel holes through the ball and through the thorax and pelvis as illustrated. On each side of the body thread a cord through all three sections and knot the ends where they emerge from the body. Sink the knots in the body, seal them with glue and cover with plastic wood or other modelling material.

Latex rubber tends to cling to the ball and not permit flowing movement, but the following method permits the body to roll on the ball. (This method can be used with other materials too.) Thread two beads and a central wooden ball onto a length of cord; knot and glue the ends. Before assembling the body parts, glue one bead into the thorax and the other into the pelvis, with the wooden ball as a spacer in the waist (figure 8/2).

A body in three parts This joint allows only sideways movement.

Make the body in three sections, leaving the chest and pelvis hollow to take the shaped centre piece (figure 9).

Insert the ends of the centre piece into the chest and pelvis and join the three sections with two large nails so that they are free to pivot sideways.

Neck joints

Joints used when the neck is built onto the head How to join a sock head to a cloth body is described on page 129. All other types of body and head can be joined by using any one of the following: interlocked screw-eyes (figure 10/1); screw-eyes joined by string (figure 10/2); a string through a hole in the body and a screw-eye in the neck (figure 10/3). All these methods presuppose a dowel built into the neck.

Joints used when the neck is built onto the body Fasten a screw-eye in the top of the neck (figure 11/1) or drill a hole from side to side through the neck (figure 11/2).

Drill a hole in either side of the head, just behind the ears.

Take a length of strong galvanised wire and pass it through the screw-eye or the hole in the neck and through the holes in the head (figure

Figure 10/1 Interlocked screw-eyes

Figure 10/2 Two screw-eyes joined by string

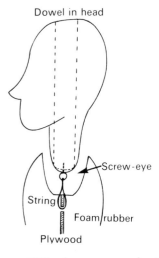

Figure 10/3 A screw-eye and string

132

Figure 11/1   Screw-eye in neck and wire through the head

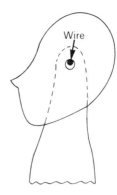

Figure 11/2   Hole through neck and wire through the head

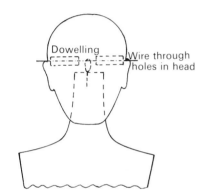

Figure 11/3   Full-face view of the screw-eye method

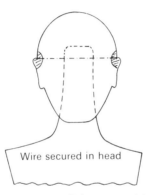

Figure 11/4   Full-face view of the wire through the neck, secured in the head

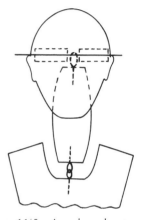

Figure 11/5   A neck made separate from head and body

11/3). With the screw-eye method, to prevent the screw-eye sliding too far on the wire, it might be necessary to drill holes through two short dowels and slip these on to the wire on each side of the screw-eye (figure 11/3).

Cut off the ends of the wire and secure the wire in the head with glue and more of the material used for the head (applied inside and outside the head as shown in figure 11/4).

Using a screw-eye allows the head to turn and nod, whereas the hole drilled through the neck restricts head movement to nodding.

Joints used when the neck is a separate piece   The neck piece is usually carved from a thick dowel or built up around a dowel. Any of the appropriate joints described above may be used to join it to the head and body (figure 11/5).

Construction of the hands

The shape of the hands is important in helping to create character. Characterless hands may spoil an otherwise exciting puppet. They can be simply shaped – detailed modelling is quite unnecessary – or indeed stylised, but the fingers should be held in an expressive manner. It is not uncommon for puppets to have only *three* fingers and a thumb.

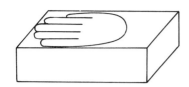

Figure 12/1 The first stage in carving a hand

Figure 12/2 The fingers are shaped and the palm hollowed out

Figure 12/3 The thumb in a different plane from the fingers

Figure 12/4 A hand shaped with only a surform rasp by a nine year old

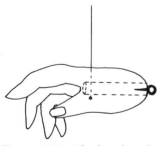

Figure 12/5 The dowel in a foam rubber hand provides fixtures for wrist joint and hand string

Cloth hands Cloth hands may be used with any sort of marionette. They are described on page 105.

Carved or foam rubber hands Hands may be carved from wood, following the same principles as for carving a head. Begin by marking out the hand shape and making saw cuts between the fingers (figure 12/1). Then carefully pare away at the fingers individually and hollow out the palm of the hand (figure 12/2).

Remember that hands held naturally are not flat and stiff, nor are the fingers all held in the same plane. The thumb also is set in a different plane from the fingers (figure 12/3).

The basic hand illustrated in figure 12/4 was made by a nine year old boy with two surform rasps and no other tools.

Foam rubber hands are cut with sharp scissors following the same principles of shaping as those sculpted in wood. Make a hole into the hand from the wrist to accommodate a dowel which is glued securely in place. This provides a strong fixture for the wrist joint and for attaching a controlling string (figure 12/5).

Plastic wood hands Plastic wood is an ideal material for modelling hands. When it is hard it can be cut away, carved, filed, sanded or built up with more plastic wood until the required shape is obtained.

To model the hand, intertwine three pipe cleaners and bend them into the required position (figure 13).

Cover the pipe cleaners with glue (Bostik No. 1, Sobo or another suitable, all-purpose adhesive) and add plastic wood in fairly large pieces. Do not try to attach it to the fingers individually. Snip between the fingers with a pair of scissors and then model the shape of the fingers. Use of acetone as a solvent (see section on modelling a plastic wood head, page 90) enables you to achieve as much shaping and detail as required.

When hard, build up or cut away the plastic wood as necessary, sand the hands smooth and attach a screw-eye or leather loop or strap for the wrist joint. It is possible for the leather to be built into the hand when it is modelled but care must be exercised not to damage the leather when smoothing and finishing the hand.

Celastic hands First make a pipe-cleaner frame as described above. Then soak a piece of Celastic in acetone (see page 92) and lay it over the back of the pipe-cleaner hand; lay a similar piece over the front and press the two layers firmly together. Trim between the fingers and shape as necessary; the wire will hold the fingers in any position. Use this as a basic shape upon which to build the hand required.

Depending on the wrist joint selected, it is a good idea to build into the hand a dowel, strip of leather, etc., as appropriate.

Rubber hands Rubber hands are moulded in the same way as rubber heads. Figure 14 shows where to place the metal strips in the plasticine model to make the plaster cast.

When the hand is made, glue a dowel into it. This provides a strong fixture for a screw-eye for the wrist joint and for attaching a hand string later. Alternatively, with a strong hand, you may glue into it a bead carrying a knotted cord as described for wrist joints.

Figure 13   A pipe-cleaner base for a plastic wood hand

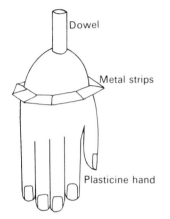

Figure 14/1   Preparing to make a cast for a rubber hand

Arms and arm joints

Cloth arms   Make cloth arms from tubes of material stuffed with stockings or foam rubber. Stitch across the arms at the elbows to help them bend.

Rope arms   Strong rope, tied to the body, is used more often when the rope is going to show and where this is a part of the design feature, rather than as a normal construction technique. It should be glued securely into the hand rather than having a wrist joint as such.

Foam rubber arms   Foam rubber may be trimmed to shape and threaded and glued onto a cord (figure 15). Make a loop in the end of a piece of coathanger wire and use this like a needle to thread the cord through the arms.

The ends of the cord are used to tie the arms onto the body and to the hands.

Carved or dowelling arms   Arms may be carved from wood or made from two pieces of dowelling built up with plastic wood or shaped down as necessary. Do not use thin dowel with no bulk for the arms.

Interlocked screw-eyes are *not recommended* for the elbow joint as they tend to lock in awkward positions. The best joints are an open mortise and tenon joint (figure 16/1) or a leather joint (figure 16/2) which are described more fully for the legs.

It is not uncommon, if one of these joints is too restrictive for particular purposes, to use string for the upper arm, sometimes weighted with lead, and dowelling for the forearm (figure 16/3).

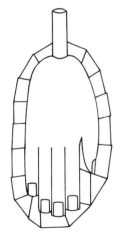

Figure 14/2   An alternative method of dividing the hand for casting

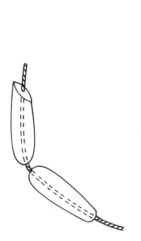

Figure 15   A foam rubber arm

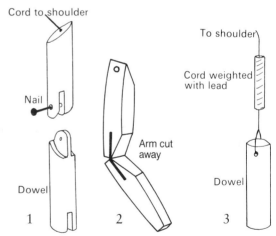

Figure 16/1   An open mortise and tenon elbow joint
Figure 16/2   A leather elbow joint
Figure 16/3   A dowelling and cord arm

Rubber arms   Arms may be moulded in rubber, as for the head; figure 17/1 shows where to divide the plasticine model for casting.

In order to permit the arm to bend, it will be necessary when the arm is dry to cut through the strip of rubber at the back of the elbow joint, leaving the front intact.

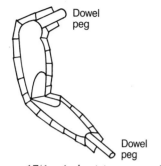

Figure 17/1   A plasticine arm ready for casting

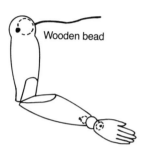

Figure 17/2   Shoulder and wrist joints for rubber arms and hands

A wooden bead with cord attached may be glued into the top of the arm to facilitate the shoulder joint (figure 17/2). Cut open the arm and reseal aferwards with glue to effect this.

Flexible wrist joints   The following joints are suitable for the wrist. The choice will depend on the degree of restriction required and the materials used for hand and arm:

A strip of leather may be glued and nailed into slots cut in the arm and hand (figure 18/1); this restricts movement to one direction.

An alternative and more flexible leather joint, popular for carved puppets, is made by gluing and pinning into a slot cut in the hand the ends of a ¼ in wide loop of leather. The loop fits into a hole drilled into the forearm and is secured with a nail (figure 18/2).

Glue the end of a rope arm directly into a hole in the hand (figure 18/3).

A screw-eye in the hand may be attached by a thread through a hole in the arm (figure 18/4) or by securing it with a nail, either in a slot in the arm or in a hole (figure 18/5).

Rubber arms and hands may be joined by gluing into them wooden beads joined by knotted cord (figure 17/2). A bead may be used between hand and arm to promote flowing movement but allow for this when making the arms or the hands will hang too low.

Cloth hands and arms are stitched together.

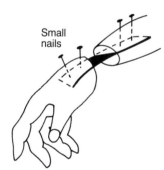

Figure 18/1   A leather strap wrist joint

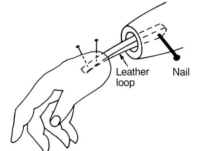

Figure 18/2   A leather loop wrist joint

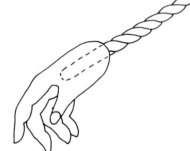

Figure 18/3   Rope glued into the hand

Figure 18/4   A screw-eye and string wrist joint

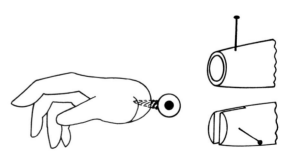

Figure 18/5   A screw-eye pivots in a hole or slot in the arm

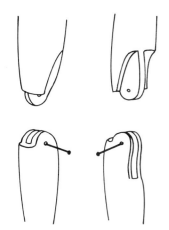

Figure 19   An open mortise and tenon joint for wooden legs

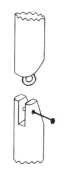

Figure 20   A screw-eye knee joint

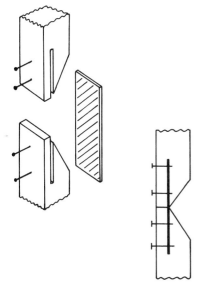

Figure 21/1   A leather knee joint: the slot cut for the leather and the rear corners cut away

Figure 21/2   Securing the leather

Legs and knee joints

Note that you must decide on your ankle joint before you make the legs.

Cloth legs   Cloth legs are made from stuffed tubes of material in the same way as cloth arms. They are sewn on to the cloth body.

Carved or dowelling legs   Legs may be carved or made from dowelling built up with plastic wood or shaped down. Two joints are suitable:

An open mortise and tenon joint which is made by cutting a slot in one part of the leg and a tongue in the other, shaping them as illustrated (figure 19) to allow the leg to bend one way. Leave a ridge on the front of the knee to prevent bending in the wrong direction.

Put the leg together and drill a hole across the joint; then enlarge the hole in the 'tongue' to allow it to pivot freely on the nail which is to secure the joint. Reassemble the leg, insert the nail and secure it with glue and plastic wood.

It is possible to use a screw-eye instead of the wooden 'tongue' (figure 20) but it is not so satisfactory: it is less secure, can rattle and the leg can twist out of line.

A leather strap joint which is made by cutting slots in each piece at the knee, then cutting or filing away a wedge shape behind the knee to permit bending (figure 21/1). Glue a piece of leather into the slots and secure with small nails (figure 21/2); the leather must be short enough to allow the leg pieces to touch, as illustrated (otherwise they will bend the wrong way), and should fit tightly into the slots.

It is a good idea to leave a little spare on the sides of the leather to enable you to pull it securely into the slots. Cut off the waste when the joint is completed.

Plywood and foam rubber legs   Legs laminated entirely from plywood strips can be rather heavy if the desired bulk is achieved and those made of foam rubber are too light to be controlled easily. However, a combination of the two provides a very satisfactory joint and good control without too much weight.

The basic shape is made from four plywood shapes which form an open mortise and tenon knee joint. With a coping saw or bandsaw, cut out the four leg shapes as illustrated in figure 22/1. Make the lower leg from *slightly* thinner plywood and leave sufficient on the bottom of it to slot into the foot for the ankle joint.

Glue together the three thigh sections, forming a slot to accommodate the 'tongue' on the lower leg. Insert the tongue into the groove and drill through the joint at the point indicated in figure 22/2. Enlarge the hole in the tongue, ensure the leg moves freely, rejoin the leg with a nail (figure 22/3) and secure the head with glue.

Glue foam rubber onto the plywood and trim to shape. Ensure that the foam rubber does not cover the parts of the lower leg that fit into the groove in the thigh.

Rubber legs   Rubber legs are moulded in one piece. The procedure is the same as for the rubber head. Figure 23 shows the shape of the plasticine model. When the rubber is dry, slit across the front of the knee joint to allow it to bend.

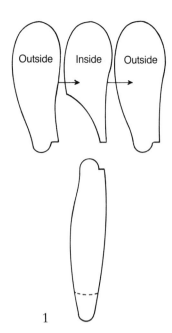

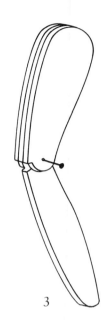

Figure 22/1   Plywood leg shapes

Figure 22/2   The position of the hole for jointing

Figure 22/3   The parts assembled

Figure 23   A plasticine model for rubber legs

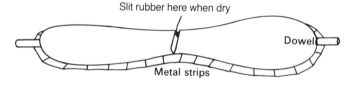

Slit rubber here when dry
Dowel
Metal strips

Hip joints

For wooden legs all of the following methods are possible; for other legs the leather method is not suitable. Your selection will depend also on what material is used for the pelvis.

A strip of leather may be looped and the ends glued and nailed in a slot in the top of the leg. The loop is suspended from a piece of galvanised wire (c. 12 gauge); the wire passes through a hole drilled in the leg-divider. With pliers, bend each end of the wire upwards and bend the tips again so that they fit into the holes drilled in the sides of the pelvis (figure 24). Secure the wire with glue and staples if necessary.

The legs may be suspended from the same wire by a hole drilled across the top of each thigh (figure 24). This is the recommended method.

Strong cord may be threaded through holes across the tops of the legs, and through holes drilled up through the pelvis. Knot and glue the ends on top (figure 25).

Feet and ankle joints

Carved and modelled feet   Feet may be carved or modelled by the techniques described previously. To remove plasticine from a modelled foot, cut off the sole, then replace when the foot is hollow. Some people glue pieces of felt onto the bottoms of the feet to prevent them making too much noise on the stage floor.

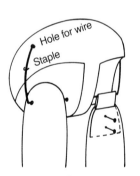

Figure 24   Two hip joints using wire

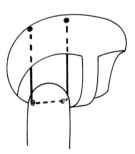

Figure 25   A cord hip joint

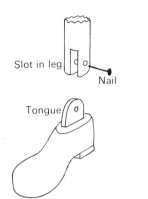

Slot in leg

Nail

Tongue

Figure 26   An ankle joint with the slot in the leg

Tongue on leg fits into slot in foot

Nail

Figure 27   The recommended ankle joint with a slot in the foot

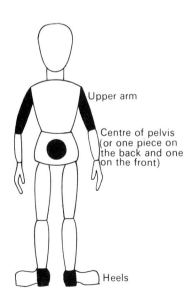

Upper arm

Centre of pelvis (or one piece on the back and one on the front)

Heels

Figure 29   Weighting the puppet

To make an effective ankle joint, *either* build a tongue onto the foot to fit into a slot in the leg (figure 26), *or* make a slot in the foot (by drilling a series of holes and cleaning out with a craft knife) to fit a tongue on the leg (figure 27). Insert the tongue into the slot and secure with a nail, ensuring that there is *some* ankle movement, but not enough to let the toes point downwards or drag when the leg is lifted.

The slot in the foot is recommended as it permits you to exercise control more easily over the degree of ankle movement. If a tongue is required on a modelled foot, build a piece of plywood into it for this purpose.

Rubber feet   Rubber feet are moulded in the same way as a rubber head (pages 93–97). When making the plaster cast, insert the metal strips around the sole.

If the bottom of the leg is moulded with the foot (figure 28/1), this may be glued over the actual leg when attaching the foot. Preferably, cast the

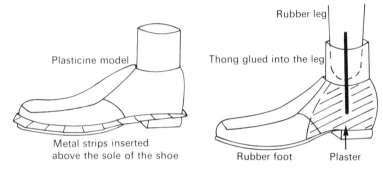

Plasticine model

Metal strips inserted above the sole of the shoe

Rubber leg

Thong glued into the leg

Rubber foot   Plaster

Figure 28/1   Preparing to make the plaster cast   *Figure 28/2   The ankle joint*

parts with a tongue on the leg and a slot in the foot; insert the tongue in the slot and secure with a nail or piece of wire as described previously. This will work only with fairly thick rubber; thin rubber will soon tear.

Alternatively, glue a rubber strip into a slot cut in the leg and insert the other end of the strip into the foot. Pour liquid plaster of Paris into the heel to hold the strip and weight the foot (figure 28/2).

Weighting the marionette

To give really precise control it may be necessary to weight a puppet, although a really well-made figure should not need it. Figure 29 shows points at which weight may be added. It is especially important that the pelvis is not too light as it will affect the puppet's walking action. If it is necessary to weight the foot, avoid making the toe too heavy or it will drag when the puppet walks.

The usual method for adding weight is to glue and, or, nail on a piece of lead. With moulded rubber parts, pour liquid plaster into the part to be weighted.

Animal puppets

The head can be made in any of the ways described in Chapter 6. Most leg shapes required cannot be carved from dowelling so they are usually made from plywood with open mortise and tenon joints (see figure 36 and

Figure 30 A Day at the Seaside: *marionettes by John Thirtle*

Figure 31 A scene from The Fisherman and his Soul *by the Little Angel Theatre*

140

Figures 32 and 33   Clown Percy, and the Chauffeur, by John Thirtle

Figure 34   Charlemagne from the Hogarth Puppets' production of Master Peter's Puppet Show

Figure 35   The King from Derek Francis' production of The Light Princess

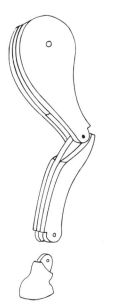

Figure 36 *Plywood legs for an animal marionette*

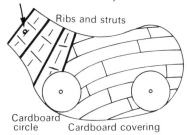

Hole for cord for neck joint

Ribs and struts

Cardboard circle   Cardboard covering

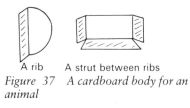

A rib   A strut between ribs

Figure 37 *A cardboard body for an animal*

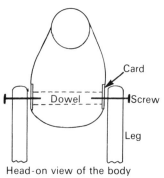

Card
Dowel   Screw
Leg

Head-on view of the body

Figure 38 *Attaching the legs*

Plywood legs, page 137). Occasionally rubber is used. Methods for making bodies are described below.

A cardboard body   A cardboard body is made in the same way as a cardboard head (see page 89) as a base for modelling.

Cut a basic shape from strong card. Make a hole in the neck for a cord from the head (for the neck joint). Make two holes in the card to accommodate ¾ in diameter dowels (for attaching the legs later) and glue the dowels into the holes. Glue 'ribs' and strengthening pieces to the basic shape then cover it with card (figure 37). Over the end of each dowel glue a circle of smooth card on which the legs may turn. Screw the legs to the ends of the dowels (figure 38).

Cover the cardboard body with plastic wood, nylon 'hair', fur fabric, knitting wool fluffed up, or cloth. If necessary, a plain cloth may be coloured with dye or paint. Acrylic colours mixed thinly with water can be used to paint on special markings.

Cover the neck joint with material and then colour it or cover it with fur etc.

A plywood and foam rubber body   Cut out a plywood body shape with a coping saw or bandsaw.

Drill two holes in the shape and glue dowels into them for attaching the legs (as described for a cardboard body). Glue blocks of foam rubber to each side of the plywood and trim the foam rubber to the shape of the body (figure 39).

Cover the body with material, wool, fur fabric, etc.

Control and manipulation

Strings attached to the puppet are joined to a wooden control which is constructed and manipulated in such a way as to produce movement of a particular part of the puppet. The actual stringing procedure is described on pages 148 to 149, and manipulation on pages 149 to 152. The marionette must be dressed before you start to string it.

Two kinds of marionette control are in common use: the upright control and the 'aeroplane', or 'paddle', control. The tendency in Britain is to use the upright control for human puppets and the aeroplane control for animals but in America the aeroplane control is used extensively for both. The determining factor must be the requirements of the individual puppet. For children's use, an aeroplane control is recommended.

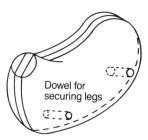

Dowel for securing legs

Figure 39 *A plywood body covered with foam rubber*

Figure 41 The Stork, by Albrecht Roser

Figure 40 The Elephant from the Mejandes Marionettes' Children's Show

Figure 43 Gigi, a giraffe with an extending neck, by the author

Figure 42 The Lion from the Lanche.

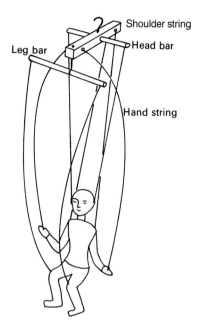

Figure 44 A simple aeroplane control

It is a mistake to make the control of a marionette too simple unless it has very few strings. Most strings support the puppet and tilting or turning the control achieves a wide range of movements; if the control is too simple, it becomes more difficult to operate the puppet as the puppeteer must then pull individual strings to effect such movements.

As a rule small holes are drilled in the control for the strings, the strings being threaded through and tied. (Some puppeteers prefer to fasten screw-eyes for the strings but this is not recommended as the screw-eyes tend to catch in the strings of other puppets.)

A simple aeroplane control The control consists of a main wooden bar (1 × 1 in and 8 in long) to which are attached the hand strings, shoulder strings and dowels for the head bar and leg bar (figure 44).

To attach the head bar, drill a hole through the main bar and glue the dowel into the hole.

To attach the leg bar, drill a hole down through the front of the main bar. Thread a strong cord through the hole and knot the top; tie the other end to the leg bar (preferably, thread it through a hole drilled in the bar).

To attach the hand strings, drill a hole across the main bar just behind the leg bar. The hands are controlled by one long running string threaded through the hole. A similar hole at the back of the bar accommodates a run-through shoulder string.

The standard aeroplane control This aeroplane control consists of an 8 in main bar (of 1 × 1 in wood) from which are suspended dowelling head and shoulder bars and a removable hand bar. A leg bar is firmly secured to the control, forming a T shape (figure 45). All dowels are approximately ¼ in diameter.

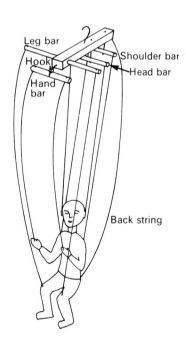

Figure 45/1 The standard aeroplane control and stringing

Figure 45/2 An alternative joint for the leg bar

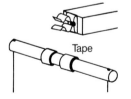

Figure 45/3 A spring clip used to hold the hand bar

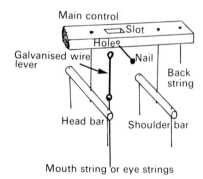

Figure 45/4 Controlling eye or mouth movements

144

To attach the head bar, drill a hole down through the main bar, approximately in the middle, and another through the centre of the dowel rod. Thread a cord through the holes and knot the ends (figure 45/4).

The shoulder bar is suspended from the back of the control in the same manner.

To attach the leg bar to the front of the control, *either* glue the dowel into a hole drilled across the main bar (figure 45/1), *or* glue and screw the dowel on to the top of the main bar (figure 45/2).

To attach the hand bar, tie a small curtain ring to the dowel. Screw a small hook into the front end of the main bar and hang the hand bar from it (figure 45/1). Alternatively use a screw-on spring clip to hold the bar (figure 45/3).

To attach a back string, drill a hole down through the rear end of the control.

If the puppet is to have a moving mouth (or eyes), the string for operating these is controlled by a wire lever attached to the main control. Make the lever from a piece of 12 or 14 gauge galvanised wire with each end bent into a loop. Cut a slot in the control just behind the head bar (an easy way is to drill a series of touching holes) and fix the lever in the slot by a nail through one of the loops (figure 45/4). The mouth or eye string(s) is tied to the other loop.

An aeroplane control for animals This control consists of a main wooden bar (1 × 1 in) of about the same length as the puppet, with a dowelling leg bar attached at the front as described for the previous control. A removable T-shaped head bar is suspended from the front of the main bar and a spring to control the tail is attached to the rear of the control. Back strings are attached directly to the main control bar (figure 46).

To make the head bar, drill a hole in the centre of a ½ in diameter dowel and glue into the hole a ¼ or 3/16 in diameter dowel. The main head strings are attached to the ends of the larger dowel. A string to the nose, or to a moving mouth, is attached to the end of the smaller dowel.

To attach the head bar to the control, screw a hook into the front of the main control and suspend the head bar from it by means of a small curtain ring tied to the bar.

To attach back strings, drill a small hole down through each end of the main bar. Thread the strings directly through these holes and knot them on the top.

To attach the tail control, drill a hole into the end of the main bar and glue the spring into the hole.

Add ear and eye strings if required. *Either* thread them through holes drilled in the head bar and knot them, *or* thread them through holes drilled across the front of the main control bar. If either of the strings is attached to the main bar, the ears will be raised or the eyes closed whenever the head bar is unhooked and lowered.

Note: For most animals each front leg is connected to the control at the same point as the opposite back leg, so that the puppet lifts these two legs together (i.e. front right and back left; front left and back right). Some animals, however, (e.g. giraffes and camels) move their near and offside legs together, which produces a rather rolling gait.

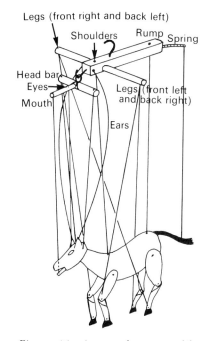

Figure 46 An aeroplane control for animal puppets

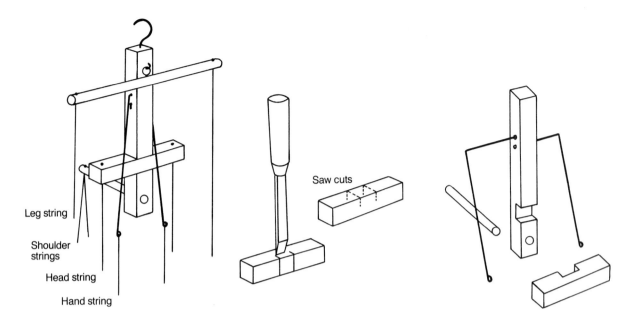

Figure 47/1 The basic upright control and stringing

Figure 47/2 Making the cross halving joint

Figure 47/3 An exploded view of the main control

Leg string

Shoulder strings

Head string

Hand string

Saw cuts

The upright control   The upright control consists of a vertical 9 in length of wood, to which a head bar is fixed forming an inverted cross shape. To the back of the control is secured a shoulder bar. A detachable leg bar is suspended near the top of the control and wires to control the hands are attached to the main control just below the leg bar (figure 47/1).

The main cross is made from 1 × 1 in wood, the leg and shoulder bars from dowelling (of c. 5/16 in diameter) and the hand control from galvanised wire (coathanger wire).

Attach the head bar (which should be a little longer than the width of the puppet's head), with a cross-halving joint. Make two saw cuts halfway through each piece of wood and then chisel out the waste (figure 47/2) so that the two pieces can be glued, interlocked and screwed together (figure 47/3). Alternatively, the head bar may be made from a piece of dowelling; drill a hole through the control, glue the dowel into it and secure with a small nail (figure 47/4).

To attach the dowelling shoulder-bar, drill a hole in the control (from back to front) below the head bar and glue the dowel (c. 5 in long) into the hole so that it sticks out at the back (figures 47/3 and 47/4). Further secure with a small nail. This dowel must be a tight fit and long enough to hold the shoulder strings away from the head so that its movement is not restricted.

As an alternative to making the shoulder bar of wood it can be made of galvanised wire, which has the advantage that it can be folded for packing. To attach the wire to the control, first drill a hole through the main bar just below the head bar. Loop the wire through the hole, bend the ends together and glue and bind together the two halves of the wire with strong thread (figure 47/5). Bend the ends of the wire into a loop for attaching the shoulder strings. If necessary, to keep the shoulder strings well clear of the head, attach them to the ends of a separate dowel and suspend the dowel by a curtain ring from the loop in the end of the wire (figure 47/6).

To attach the leg bar, screw a screw-eye into the centre of a dowel

146

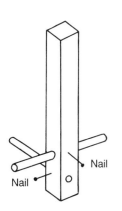

Figure 47/4 A dowelling head bar and the shoulder bar

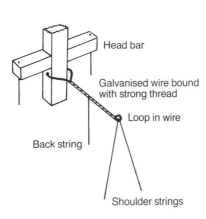

Figure 47/5 A shoulder bar that folds up for packing

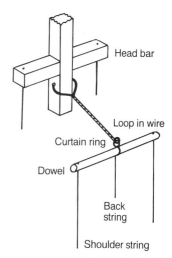

Figure 47/6 Holding the shoulder strings away from the head

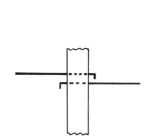

Figure 47/7 The ends of the hand wires

Figure 47/8 The hand wires bent into position

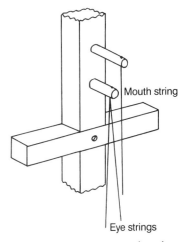

Figure 47/9 Fixing mouth and eye strings to the control

(which will need to be about 8 in long) and suspend this from the top of the control by a small hook (figure 47/1).

Drill two holes, one about ⅜ in above the other, across the control for the hand wires (just sufficiently below the leg bar not to interfere with it). To attach the hand wires, first bend one end of each wire into a right angle using pliers (figure 47/7). Insert the long straight pieces of the wire through the holes in opposite directions, then carefully bend them over with pliers (figure 47/8). Do not make them too tight to the upright or they will not turn freely; make the angles as sharp as possible as wide curves will let them wobble. (To obtain a sharp angle, while bending the wire down, keep a firm pressure upwards on the wire across the control. This takes a little practice to achieve.) Cut the wires to the same length and make loops in the ends for attaching hand strings (seal the closures of the loops with glue).

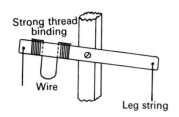

Figure 48/1 A wooden rocking bar with a wire thumb loop

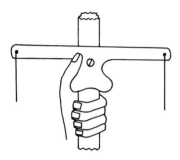

Figure 48/2 A shaped wooden rocking bar

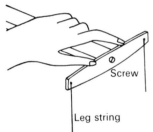

Figure 49 A rocking bar for the aeroplane control

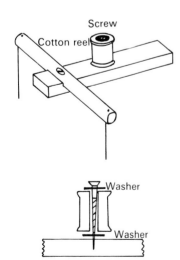

Figure 50 A rotating control

These wires must be at least long enough to rest on the head bar and usually need to be about level with the bottom of the control.

If fixtures are required for mouth and eye strings, attach them to the ends of short dowels. To attach the dowels to the control, drill two holes in the front of the control above the head bar and glue the dowels into the holes (figure 47/9).

Any back string may be attached to some part of the shoulder bar (figures 47/5 and 47/6).

Variations on controls

Rocking bars A rocking bar is a wooden leg bar which is screwed to the main control. It permits the control to be held and the puppet walked with one hand, leaving the other hand free. The disadvantage is that the leg action is not usually as good as when a separate leg bar is used, except in the hands of a very skilled operator.

The upright control Drill two holes through the leg bar and push the ends of a loop of wire through the holes (figure 48/1). Bend over the ends of the wire, then glue and bind them with strong thread. Slip your thumb into this wire loop to move the bar. Alternatively, use an all-wooden leg bar (cut from strong plywood) with two large notches cut out for your thumb (figure 48/2).

The aeroplane control Screw the rocking bar onto the front end of the control and move it with your thumb and index finger whilst holding the control with your other fingers (figure 49).

Rotating controls A rotating control allows the puppet to be spun round. Screw a cotton reel (empty spool of thread) to the top of the control (figure 50). Use washers on top of, and underneath, the cotton reel and ensure that the screw is secure, or it will unscrew when you turn the control. Hold the reel with one hand whilst turning the control with the other.

Stringing the marionette

To string the puppet use No 18 carpet thread (dark green or black), or a comparable substitute. Rub the thread with beeswax from time to time to prevent it becoming brittle and fraying. Nylon thread is not recommended as it has a tendency to stretch, glistens under stage lighting, and retains crinkles after being wound up for packing.

The strings should be long enough to allow the control to be held comfortably over the back cloth (usually about elbow height) when the puppet is standing on the stage. If the stage has a bridge, the strings must, of course, be longer.

With any removable control bars, such as a leg bar, make the strings just long enough to allow the bar to be unhooked without moving the puppet.

It is easiest to string a puppet when it is supported in a standing position. The best way of achieving this is to stand the puppet on a table or a work bench and suspend it from a gallows.

To make a gallows Screw a 12 in length of wood to a length of about 5 or 6 ft to form a right angle. Strengthen the joint with a shelf bracket. Attach the upright to the table or work bench with another bracket (figure 51/1) or, for added firmness, three brackets (figure 51/2). Screw a hook into the

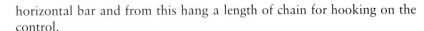

horizontal bar and from this hang a length of chain for hooking on the control.

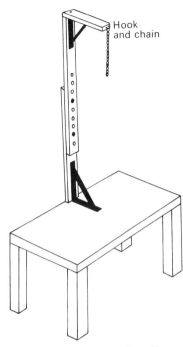

Figure 51/1 Securing the gallows

Attaching the strings All strings must be attached securely to the puppet, not to the costume or body padding. When attaching the strings to the control, knot them loosely at first so that adjustments can be made. The procedure for stringing the puppet is as follows.

1 Attach the head strings (with an animal, the back strings) so that the control is the required height.

    To attach the head strings *either* drill holes for the strings through the tops of the ears if they are strong enough, *or* fasten screw-eyes into a dowel built into the head just behind the ears, as described in Chapter 6.

2 Attach the shoulder strings and back strings *either* to screw-eyes fastened in solid bodies, *or* thread the strings directly through holes drilled in the body. For bodies with a plywood centre, attach the strings to this; for hollow bodies, tie the string to a button inside the body. (With an animal, attach the head strings.)

    Adjust the tension of the head and shoulder strings so that it is approximately the same for each but with the shoulder strings just taking the weight. Slacken the head strings to create a stoop.

Figure 51/2 A more secure fixture

3 Attach hand and leg strings. To do this, drill holes in the hands or the thumbs and in the legs just above the knees. Thread the strings directly through the holes and knot the ends of the strings. (Countersink the holes in the hands so that the knots do not show.) The hand strings are usually just long enough to let the puppet's hands hang loosely by its sides and the leg strings long enough to allow the puppet to stand straight. None of these strings should be slack. Take great care over where you attach strings to the hands or their movement may appear very awkward.

4 Having attached the main strings, attach any other strings that may be required and seal all knots with Bostik No 1 glue, Elmer's Glue All or some other all-purpose glue.

Note: When stringing a cloth marionette it will be sufficient to sew securely on to the material any strings that bear little weight.

Manipulation

If a marionette is dropped, the golden rule is, do not just pick it up as any loose tangles will be pulled tight into knots. Lift the control (not the puppet) gently, undoing the loose tangles carefully. If there *are* any tangles, trace the strings up from the body in a systematic manner, twisting or turning the control. Following this procedure will avoid most problems.

    To prevent tangling when transporting marionettes, it is advisable to wind the strings round 'winders', i.e. pieces of hardboard or plywood in which two slots have been cut to take the string (figure 52).

    It is also a good idea to keep puppets when not in use in polythene bags (large enough to allow them to stand upright). Fasten the bag with a pipe cleaner.

The simple aeroplane control Hold the main control bar with one hand. To move the head, turn or tilt the control appropriately; to move the

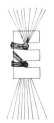

Figure 52 A 'winder'

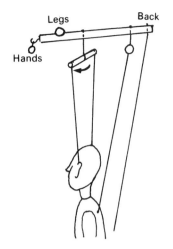

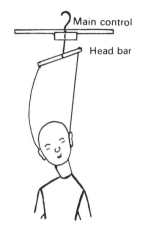

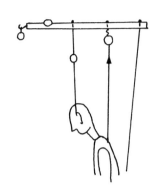

Figure 53/1   To turn the head: tilt control slightly and turn head bar

Figure 53/2   To incline the head: rock the head bar sideways

Figure 53/3   To nod or bow the head: lift the shoulder bar

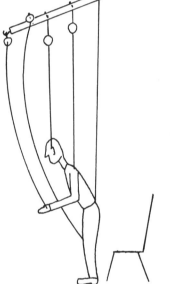

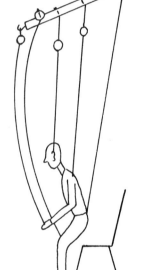

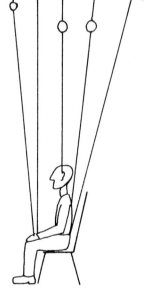

Figure 53/7   Walking: 'paddle' the control

Figure 53/8   To seat the puppet: tilt the control; bend the knees and lower the control; straighten up

hands, lift the strings with your free hand; to walk the puppet, rock the leg bar in a paddling motion.

The standard aeroplane control   Hold the control with one hand. To turn the head, tilt the control very slightly forwards to take the weight on the shoulders, and turn the head bar with your index finger and thumb or with your free hand (figure 53/1).

To incline the head to one side, tilt the head bar sideways (figure 53/2).

To nod or bow the head, lift the shoulder bar with your free hand, or pull the string by which it is suspended with one of the fingers with which

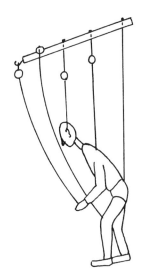

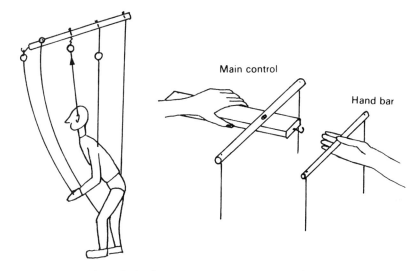

Figure 53/4 To bow the head and body: tilt the control

Figure 53/5 To bow the body, keeping the head upright: tilt the control and lift the head bar

Figure 53/6 Hand movements

Figure 54/1 To lower the head: un-hook and lower the head-bar. To turn the head: turn the head bar

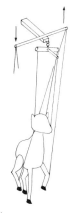

Figure 54/2 To walk the puppet: 'paddle' the control

you are holding the control. At the same time lower the control slightly, taking care to keep it level (figure 53/3).

To bow the body and the head, tilt the control forwards (figure 53/4).

To bow the body, keeping the head upright, tilt the control and lift the head bar (figure 53/5).

To move the hands, hold the hand bar in your free hand. Lift the whole bar to move both arms together or, to move just one, tilt the bar or lift individual strings (figure 53/6).

To walk the puppet, rock the main control from side to side in a paddling motion (figure 53/7). The head and shoulders will remain level as they are suspended from the control.

To make the puppet sit, first tilt the control so that it leans forward. Then bend the knees and lower the puppet to the chair. Finally, straighten the control so that the puppet sits up (figure 53/8). It is poor technique to stand the puppet and then simply lower the control so that it has a straight back throughout.

The aeroplane control for animals Hold the control with one hand. To move the head, unhook the head bar and move it with your free hand (figure 54/1).

To effect movements of the body, tilt and turn the main control.

To walk the puppet rock the control from side to side (figure 54/2).

The upright control Hold the main control with one hand. Take the weight of the control with the second, third and fourth fingers wrapped around the main control (figures 55 and 56/1) and with the little finger under the head bar, if this is comfortable.

To nod or bow the head, tilt the main control forwards (figure 56/2). The shoulder strings take the weight.

To incline the head to one side, tilt the control sideways (figure 56/3). This will not affect the movement of the shoulders.

151

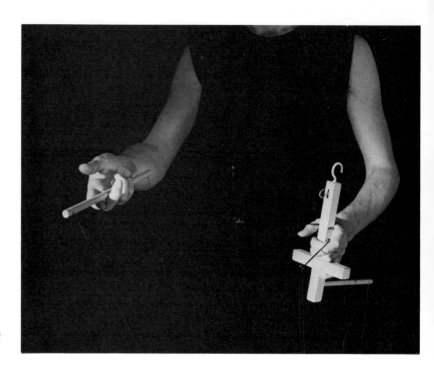

Figure 55   Manipulating an upright control

To turn the head, tilt the control very slightly forward to take the weight on the shoulder strings, at the same time turning the control in the appropriate direction (figure 56/4).

To close the eyes or open the mouth, pull the strings with your free hand or move the strings by flicking out one of the fingers that hold the control.

To bow the body and head, pull the back string taut to take the weight and tilt and lower the control (figure 56/5).

To bow the body whilst keeping the head upright, pull the back string taut and lower the control, keeping it upright so that the head strings are taut and the shoulder strings loose (figure 56/6).

To move the hand wires, use your index finger and thumb of the hand holding the control (figure 55). You can also lift the individual strings with your free hand.

To walk the puppet, unhook the leg bar and move it in a paddling motion with your free hand (figure 55).

To make the marionette sit convincingly, first tilt the control slightly forward. If the puppet has a back string, pull this taut and lower the control a little, as well as tilting it. Keeping the body bent forwards, bend the knees and lower the body on to the chair. Finally, straighten up the control (figure 56/7). To make it stand up again, lean the body forwards before raising the puppet (observe humans as they sit down and stand up).

Specialised marionettes

The term 'specialised' is used to cover a wide variety of techniques from the simple addition of a few carefully positioned strings to something far more complex. The techniques described illustrate the basic principles involved and show the sort of effects that may be achieved without special tools or

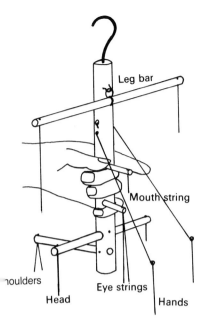

Figure 56/1 Holding the control to effect head/body, hand, mouth and eye movements

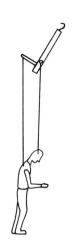

Figure 56/2 To bow or nod the head: tilt the control forwards

Figure 56/3 To incline the head: tilt the control sideways

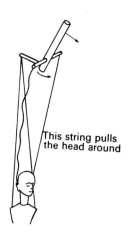

Figure 56/4 To turn the head: tilt and turn the control

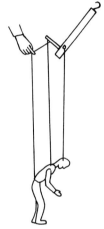

Figure 56/5 To bow the body: tilt the control and pull the back-string

Figure 56/6 To bow the body, keeping the head upright: pull the back-string and lower the control slightly

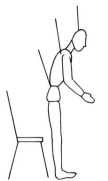

Tilt the control forwards and pull the back string

Bend the knees and lower the puppet with the control still tilted

Straighten up

Figure 56/7 Sitting the puppet

153

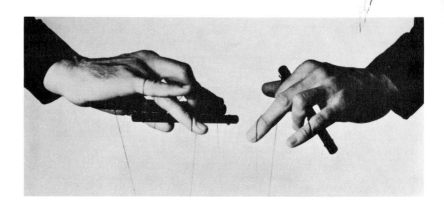

To the control

Figure 58 Raising a hand to the mouth

Head strings pass through brim of hat

Extra string to hand through brim

Figure 59 Raising a hat

facilities. Most of them can be used in situations other than those described.

For the best results, keep mechanisms and stringing as simple as possible.

Raising an object to the mouth Attach a string to the object; thread the string through a hole drilled in the mouth and out through another in the top of the head. (It is helpful to glue a plastic drinking straw in the head for the string to run through.) Pull the string to raise the object (e.g. a bottle) to the mouth (figure 58).

Raising a hat Thread the head strings through holes drilled in the brim of the hat. Attach an extra string to one hand and thread it through another hole drilled in the brim (figure 59). Pull the string to raise the hand to the hat; continue to pull it to lift the hat.

Picking up an object Attach a string to the object. Drill a hole through the hand, thread the string through the hole and then attach it to the control (figure 60/1). To pick up the object, first rest the hand on it, then pull the string taut. As the object is lifted the hand will be lifted with it. The same technique is used to bring the hands together (figure 60/2).

It is not always feasible to pick up an object in the way described as the puppet may then be required to put it down and leave it. In such a case a wire hook or button-magnet built into the hand is useful (figures 60/3 and 60/4). If a magnet is used, it is necessary to put the object down on a stronger magnet than the one used to pick it up. (With non-metallic objects, glue a strip of tin to the surface.) If the object does not need to be put down on the stage but extra stringing is impractical, glue strips of 'Velcro' into the hand and on to the object (figure 60/5) so that they cling together when the hand is placed on the object.

Stringing for a pianist's hands Fasten a string to the back of each hand and another to each forearm.

Make the hand control from three pieces of dowelling fixed in an H shape. Attach the strings to the corners of the H (figure 62).

Rock and tilt the bar to produce a simulation of a pianist's hand action. Tie a small curtain ring to the centre of this control and hang it from a hook screwed into the main control.

Stringing for dual control Dual control (figure 63) is used when two or more marionettes are required to perform the same actions side by side.

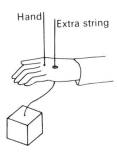

Figure 60/1 *Using an extra string to pick up an object*

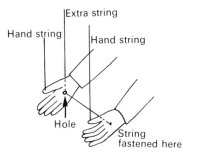

Figure 60/2 *Using an extra string to bring the hands together*

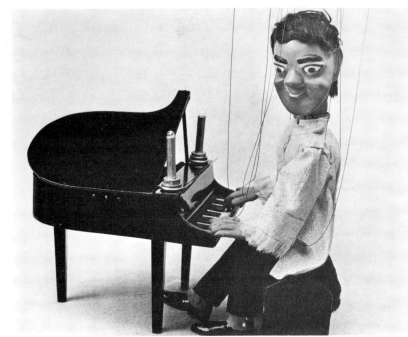

Figure 61 *Toski, the author's pianist*

Figure 60/3 *Hook in palm of hand*

Figure 60/4 *Button magnet*

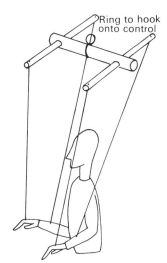

Figure 62 *Stringing for a pianist's hands*

Figure 60/5 *'Velcro' fastening*

Glue and nail the shoulder bar into a hole drilled in the head bar; this allows the heads to be tilted forward. Alternatively, attach the shoulder strings to the head bar on either side of the head strings.

Join the head and leg bars with a length of string tied to the centre of each bar.

Fix the right hand and right leg strings of both puppets together on the right-hand side of the leg bar and the left hand and left leg strings on to the left of the bar.

Now the puppets will move or dance together.

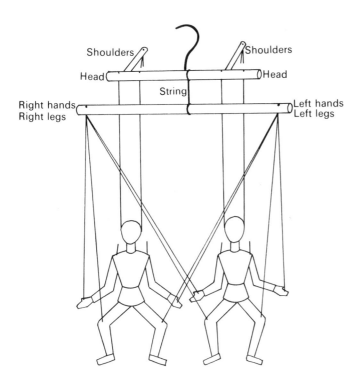

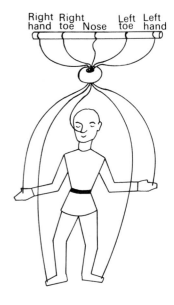

Figure 63 *(Left) Dual control*

Figure 64 *A juggler puppet*

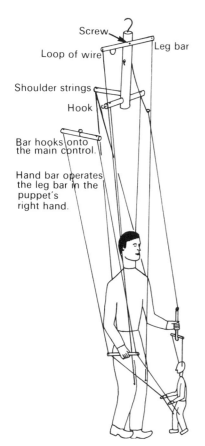

A simple juggling puppet It is possible to create the effect of juggling by threading a ball onto each hand string. Jerking each hand string will bounce each ball. Skilfully done, this mere suggestion of juggling can be as effective as the real thing. Indian puppeteers have perfected such techniques to an amazing degree.

Extra stringing for a juggler To achieve this effect extra strings are attached to a special bar. They have nothing to do with the puppet's support or any of its movements apart from those involved in juggling.

Attach a string to each part of the body to be involved. Thread these strings through a hole in the object to be juggled and attach them to the juggling bar (figure 64).

To juggle the object, simply take the tension on each of the strings in turn. Pulling the string to the end of the nose, *whilst leaving all the others slack*, takes the object to the nose. Releasing the nose string and pulling a hand string transfers the object to the hand. Each of the strings must be long enough to let the object bounce to any part of the puppet (if, for example the nose string is too short, the object will not be able to drop to the toe).

A puppet puppeteer The two puppets are made by any of the methods described earlier. Only the stringing differs from the usual (figure 65).

Attach the head and shoulder strings of the large puppet to the upright control as usual and use a rocking bar for the leg control. Only one hand wire is needed on the control of the larger puppet; use this to raise and lower the small control, held in the puppet's left hand.

In one end of the head bar fix a small hook and from it hang another

Figure 65 *The control and stringing for a puppet puppeteer*

156

Figure 66 (Left) Jerome, the author's puppet-puppeteer, manipulating Frederick

Figure 67 (Right) Gordon Staight's Uncle Gordon operates Herbert Jnr watched by Mr. Herbert

dowel rod. This rod controls the hand/leg bar held in the large puppet's right hand. Attach the hand and knee on each side of the small puppet by a short cord, so that when a hand is raised the corresponding leg is raised too.

Creating a stoop Tension on a back string attached to the pelvis will create a stoop, but the effect will be much enhanced if the puppet is made with the head set lower on the body than usual (figure 68).

Figure 68 Scrooge from Derek Francis' production of A Christmas Carol

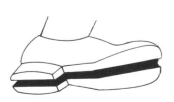

Figure 69/1 The feet

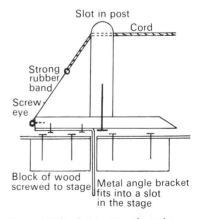

Figure 69/2 Supporting the tight-rope

157

A tight-rope walker This requires no special features except a slot cut along each foot (figure 69/1). Make the tight-rope (figure 69/2) as follows.

Screw two pieces of wood at right angles to the bottom of two uprights (dowelling) to make bases. Cut a slot in the top of each upright to accommodate the tight-rope.

Fasten metal angle brackets to the bases and fit them into slots in the stage. To help to hold them securely, screw blocks of wood under the stage on each side of the slots.

Fasten the tight-rope between the upright posts. Secure the ends to screw-eyes in the bases. To maintain the tension of the cord, attach a strong rubber band (such as a Meccano 'driving band') between one end of the cord and the screw-eye.

A tumbler puppet This can be an extremely effective transformation. The puppet consists of two heads and two bodies joined together at the waist. The lower body is hidden by a large 'full' skirt, which may need to be weighted around the hem (figure 70). Make the skirt from a reversible material which looks attractive when turned inside-out or use two pieces of material joined at waist and hem.

Raise the strings attached to the lower head, whilst releasing the tension of the upper head strings, to make the puppet 'tumble', or turn over, and reveal the hidden puppet. The skirt drops to cover the other puppet.

The two heads must face in opposite directions, so that when it tumbles, the hidden puppet will rise facing the same way as the other.

Figure 70   A tumbler puppet

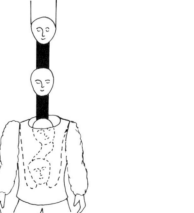

Figure 71/1   Heads inside the body

Figure 71/2   (Right) Heads 'nested' inside each other

Scaramouche There is more than one version of this type of puppet. One has a number of heads which are hidden in a hollow body and which emerge one above the other (figure 71/1). Another has hollow heads which fit inside each other (figure 71/2).

A collapsible (or extending) puppet Make the body from three pieces of hardboard joined by thread at the front, rear and sides (figure 72/1). Make the legs from a series of wooden discs cut from a large dowel rod and joined in the same way as the body (figures 72/1 and 72/2).

On each side of the legs and body pieces drill small holes. The strings which raise and lower the legs and body pass through these holes (figure 72/1). The strings run freely through the whole puppet, being attached only to the feet and to the control.

158

These strings run through holes in the body and in the legs

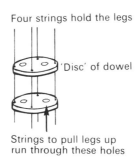

Four strings hold the legs

'Disc' of dowel

Strings to pull legs up run through these holes

Figure 72/2   The leg sections

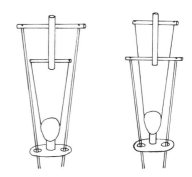

Figure 72/3   The control for an extending puppet

Figure 72/4   The control for a collapsible puppet

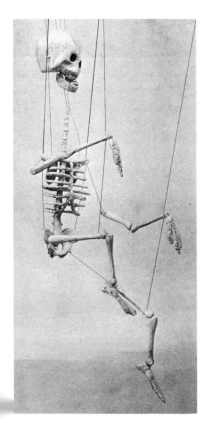

A string is also fixed at the back and front of each leg section

Figure 72/1   Construction of the puppet

Figure 72/3 shows the stringing for the extending puppet. The legs and body are contracted when normal; to lower them, tilt the control forward.

Figure 72/4 shows the collapsible puppet. When the control is held upright, the legs and body are at their maximum length; to raise them tilt the control, raising the bottom.

The dissecting skeleton   Figure 73/1 shows the skeleton complete.

Make the head from plastic wood or a similar material. Fasten a dowel across the head with Bostik No 1 glue and plastic wood. Screw a screw-eye into each end of the dowel, through the sides of the head (figure 73/2).

Make the ribs, breast bone, shoulder blades and pelvis from plastic wood over a cardboard shape smeared with Bostik No 1 glue. It is best to have eight ribs. (If the proper number is used, the body will appear too long and thin.)

The first five ribs are made as a closed loop and the bottom three open in the front (figure 73/3) to join on to the breast bone which is glued on to the top five ribs.

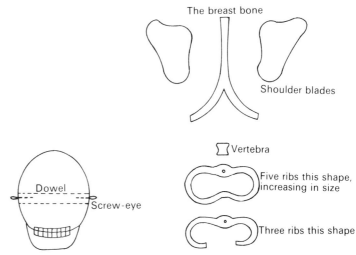

The breast bone

Shoulder blades

Vertebra

Five ribs this shape, increasing in size

Three ribs this shape

Dowel

Screw-eye

Figure 73/1   Georgina, the author's dissecting skeleton

Figure 73/2   The head, showing the dowel, and screw-eyes fastened in place

Figure 73/3   The parts of the rib-cage

159

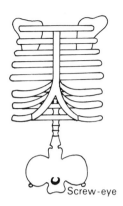

Screw-eye

Figure 73/4   The body assembled

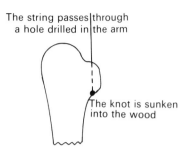

For the elbow, ankle and knee, one side is built up to restrict the joint.

Nail

Strip of aluminium glued and nailed in leg

Figure 73/5   The wrist, elbow, knee and ankle joint (an open mortise and tenon joint)

The string passes through a hole drilled in the arm

The knot is sunken into the wood

Figure 73/6   Fastening a string to the top of the arm

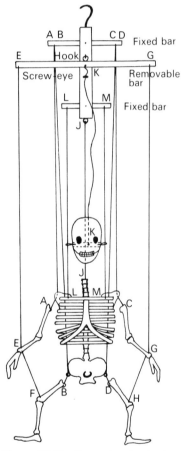

A B   C D   Fixed bar

E   Hook   G

Screw eye   K   Removable bar

L   M   Fixed bar

J

K

J

L   M

A   C

E   G

F   B   D   H

Figure 73/7   Control and stringing

File, or carve, grooves in small pieces of dowelling for the vertebrae.

The body is assembled on a length of strong galvanised wire which is glued in the pelvis and runs through the whole backbone.

When all the parts are glued together (figure 73/4), cover and strengthen the joints with plastic wood.

Model the hands and feet with plastic wood on pipe cleaners smeared with Bostik No 1 glue, as described on page 134.

Roughly carve the arms and legs from dowelling and build up details in plastic wood.

The wrist, elbow, knee and ankle joints are open mortise and tenon joints (see page 137). The 'tongue' is a strip of aluminium, glued and nailed in one part, and pivoted on a nail in the other part (figure 73/5).

The head, arms and legs are joined to the body by strings which form part of the control (see below). Figure 73/6 shows how to attach the strings to the arms and legs.

String the puppet so that when the control is held upright with the leg bar hooked on to it, the parts are all close together and not dissected (figure 73/7).

The puppet is supported by the body strings, L and M, and the centre string J. Attach strings L and M to each side of the top pair of ribs; they run through the screw-eyes in the head to the control and *must be parallel*. Attach J to the top of the neck; thread the other end through a hole in the dowel fixed in the head, and through the top of the skull to the control.

Fasten another string, K, to the dowel in the head; this runs through a screw-eye in the centre of the control to the centre of the arm-and-leg bar. Pull this bar forward to raise the head. (The head returns to its normal position when the bar is replaced.)

Attach the hand strings, E and G, to the arm-and-leg bar. F and H join the wrists to the knees. By paddling the bar the arms and legs are moved together.

Fasten the strings, A and C, which support the arms, and B and D, which support the legs, to the top cross bar of the control. A and C run through the shoulder blades; B and D run through screw-eyes on each side of the pelvis, up through the rib cage and through a hole in the top rib. The arms and legs are detached from the body by tilting the control forwards.

Figure 74 Twonky Feathers, a dissecting marionette by Gordon Staight

Figure 75 John Thirtle's unicyclist

Figure 1/1 Magic Shadows *by Pol-ka Children's Theatre*

Figure 1/2 A figure cut partly in profile, partly turned

162

10   The shadow puppet

The most underestimated and neglected of the main types of puppet, shadow puppets are normally flat, cut-out figures that are held by a rod or wire against a translucent screen whilst some form of light is shone on to them. As the puppets move, the audience on the other side of the screen watches the shadows of the figures. Shadow puppets were traditionally made of parchment or hide but they are now usually made of strong card or, sometimes, translucent acetate. They are not difficult to make or to operate and, even if only roughly cut, look surprisingly delicate and intricate on the shadow screen. Modern materials and methods have brought increased interest in full-colour figures. Strictly, of course, these are 'translucencies' rather than shadows but they are always classed together.

Shadow puppets are controlled from below or behind, usually by means of wires or rods and occasionally from above by strings. It is most common to support and move the figure by one main wire. Extra wires or strings are added, if required, to control the movement of the limbs and head.

The puppet figures are represented by convention partly in profile, partly straight on. The Javanese *wayang kulit* figures, for example, are designed with the head and legs depicted as a side view whilst the body is viewed from the front. Although this sounds strange, it is acceptable on the shadow screen. It can also help towards characterisation to employ this technique, as shown in figures 1/1 and 1/2 where the head, legs and feet are in profile and the shoulders and body slightly turned.

When designing shadow puppets, plan their size in relation to the screen on which they will be used; try to avoid very narrow parts, such as skinny waists, or the puppets will soon fall in two.

Lighting for the shadow screen is discussed in Chapter 13 Lighting and Sound.

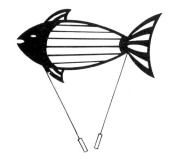

Figure 2   A mixture of materials: head and tail are made of cardboard, and body of a jersey fabric

Construction

For black silhouette puppets, any fairly strong card will do; it need not be black – a cereal box will do and is about the right thickness. Some puppeteers strengthen their card by coating it with the PVA medium. A figure may be made from a number of different materials. For example, imagine an animal with head and tail made of a rigid material, such as cardboard, but the body in between made of a stretchy fabric (figure 2). Such puppets allow a variety of movements and also present the opportunity to experiment with the shadow created by different textures.

Figure 3   A simple shadow puppet

To make simple shadow puppets, draw the shape of the figure (usually in profile or part-profile) on a piece of cardboard. Cut out the shape with scissors (figure 3) and add one of the controls described below (pages 172 – 175).

Articulated shadow puppets

Draw on cardboard the parts of the figure. The pieces that are to move must be designed to overlap for joining. There are no restrictions on where to make the joints – e.g. waist, head and shoulders to torso, etc. as well as those illustrated. It depends simply on what you want to achieve and what is possible in practice. However, remember your limitations in using controls; parts that move naturally without an extra control are fine, but take care about those that need their own control.

Cut out the shapes (figure 4/1) and join the separate parts, either with cord threaded through holes in the card and knotted on either side (figure 4/2), or with rivet-type paper fasteners (figure 4/3). If using cord, simply make the holes with a needle; with paper-fasteners, use a paper punch (the holes must be large enough to permit free movement). The pieces must be joined in layers, one on top of the other as shown in figure 4/4. If joined as shown in figure 4/5, they will lock together. To restrict the movement of joints, tie the moving parts (figure 4/6).

Washers between the moving parts are sometimes thought to give greater flexibility. (Make the washer from the same material as the figure.) However, provided reasonably smooth card and good quality thread (e.g. No 18 carpet thread) is used, a washer will not usually be needed. It is better to avoid anything that will prevent the puppet being held tightly against the screen.

Shadow figures made of fairly stiff card do not as a rule need any special weighting. On the other hand, the puppeteer who is developing his skill may find that he can improve the control of his figures by gluing a thin

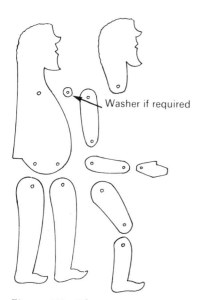

Washer if required

Figure 4/1   The separate parts

Figure 4/3   A paper-fastener joint

Figure 4/5   Incorrect method for joining the parts

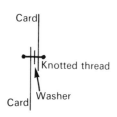

Card

Knotted thread

Card   Washer

Figure 4/2   A string joint

Figure 4/4   Correct method for joining the parts

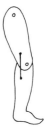

Figure 4/6   String used to restrict leg movement

strip of lead to certain parts. These will vary depending on the particular needs of the situation but will usually be the feet, the forearm and/or the hand.

Moving mouths It is usually unnecessary – even undesirable – for shadow puppets to have moving mouths. This will take your attention away from the overall movement of the puppet and shadows are generally better used with narration anyway. However, in particular circumstances it might be required. Two methods are described: the first is used with profile views, the second lends itself best to comic use with full-face views and can be extended to include opening and closing eyes.

1 Cut out the figure with the upper part of the head separate and the lower jaw attached to the body. Join the separate piece to the main figure so that, as it moves, the mouth appears to open (figure 5).

2 Cut out the eyes and mouth, both wide open, from a figure viewed full face (figure 6/1). Cut a strip of card so that it can be used to cover part of the eyes whilst uncovering part of the mouth (figure 6/2).

   Attach the card to the head with cardboard strips (about 1 in wide) glued at the ends and further secured with rivet-type paper fasteners (figure 6/3).

   Raise and lower the strip of card to effect eye and mouth movement (figures 6/3, 6/4 and 6/5).

Decoration

Shadow puppets can be decorated by cutting small slits or other shapes or by punching holes in them. The Javanese *wayang kulit* shadow figures, the Indian shadows and the beautiful, intricate, Chinese shadow puppets all use these methods and it will help to study these (figure 7/1). The amount of cutting away that is possible depends on the material used.

If a design is cut in an articulated figure it is advisable to cut away as much as possible of one of the overlapping parts to allow the design in the

Figure 5   A moving mouth (profile view)

Figure 6/1   The shapes cut from the head

Figure 6/2   The cardboard shape which produces the effect

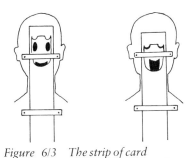

Figure 6/3   The strip of card attached: eyes open, mouth closed

Figure 6/4   The strip of card attached: eyes closed, mouth open

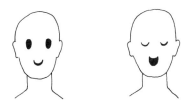

Figure 6/5   The effect achieved

Figure 7/1   Chinese shadow puppets from the collection of Jan Bussell and Ann Hogarth

A cut-away
design

The overlapping
part

*Figure 7/2 Decorating overlapping
parts. The shaded parts are cut away*

other part to show (figure 7/2). Leave sufficient material in both parts to
allow the usual joint to be made.

It is possible to strengthen figures with cut-away decoration by gluing a
piece of clear acetate over the weak part. Alternatively, cut out the entire
puppet in card, spray it with glue and press it onto a strong acetate sheet.
Then cut out the acetate around the outline of the figure.

As an alternative to cutting an intricate design, you may cut away an
entire area and cover it with an appropriate loose-weave, textured
material such as lace, net, paper doilies, etc.

*Figure 8 Shadow puppets at the
Little Angel Marionette Theatre,
London*

166

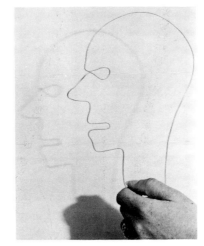

Figure 9   Varying shapes and expressions are obtained with this wire shadow puppet, made by the author

Wire puppets

Wire is becoming more widely used for making shadow puppets. Bend the wire to the outline of the required shape; whilst it retains the basic shape, it will also give a certain amount of spring. This offers interesting possibilities for shadow play. The head illustrated (figure 9) can change in shape, character or mood.

Three-dimensional puppets

There have been many recent experiments with three-dimensional objects and figures, exploring the possibilities of the 'puppets' as seen from various angles. Solid objects with perspex or acetate parts have interesting properties to explore but one of the most fascinating forms of three-dimensional shadow play is that which uses wire puppets.

Make the figures from chicken wire or by bending galvanised wire to the required shapes. Join separate parts by interlocking small loops made in the wire (figure 10). Control the figures with wires in the same way as a rod puppet.

Solid, three-dimensional puppets with strong designs can be used to good effect to cast two-dimensional shadows; Theatre of Puppets used this technique most effectively in their production of *Starchild*, where certain characters appeared at one time as rod puppets and at another simply as shadows.

Three-dimensional figures can be illuminated in one of the ways described below to create two or three-dimensional shadows.

Two-dimensional shadows As the three-dimensional puppet cannot be held flat against the screen, a strong, single source of light, such as a projector, is needed.

Three-dimensional shadows Two lights are required, one with a green filter, the other with a red filter.

Cut glasses frames from card. Tape to the inside of the frames two pieces of coloured acetate, one green, one red, for the lenses. Arrange the lights behind the screen on the left and right to correspond with the lenses in the

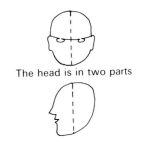

The head is in two parts

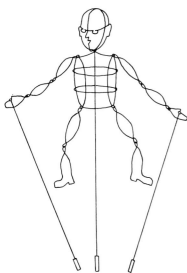

Figure 10   A three-dimensional wire-sculpture shadow puppet

167

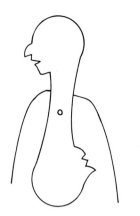

Figure 11/1 A transformation shadow puppet

glasses. The positioning of the lights will require careful adjustment to produce a good three-dimensional image.

This technique has many possibilities and can be extremely effective but it relies entirely upon the audience wearing special glasses so its importance in the shadow theatre is limited.

Tricks and transformations

Solid black figures make it possible to 'hide' things – such as a puppet with two heads, one shielded by the body and which appears when there is a change of character (figure 11/1). 'Madame Souhami' has a splendid character which, with a rotation and the unfolding of a hidden part, transforms into a dragon.

Other techniques can be used with back-projection to transform scenery. The two interlocked scenes of a palace and an apartment block (figure 11/2) illustrate the method by which Theatre of Puppets has effectively changed their scene in silhouette. The structure, attached to a rod, must be held securely by some small shelf or other device in front of the projection box.

You may wish your shadow figure to have a variety of positions for his hand. To achieve this, cut out substitute hands and arms and mount them on a wire or strip of strong acetate (figure 12). The arm that is attached to the puppet must hang completely out of sight.

Figure 11/2 Transformation scenery

Extending shadow puppets You may want the body of the puppet to extend and contract, in which case use either a concertina body or a scissor control. To make a concertina body, cut out a figure in cardboard, making the body from arm to waist level about twice the normal length. Pleat the cardboard and attach one wire to the lower part of the body and another as a vertical rod running through the folds and attached to the head (figure 13).

The scissor control is made by cutting strips of strong card and joining them with rivet-type paper fasteners to form a trellis (figure 14).

Cut out a cardboard figure but make the body from arm to waist level from a long strip of material glued to the card.

Attach the 'scissor' control to the top and bottom of the body only. Operate the control-like scissors to extend and contract the body.

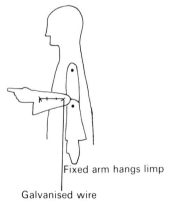

Fixed arm hangs limp

Galvanised wire

Figure 12 A substitute hand

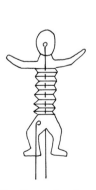

Figure 13 Operation from below

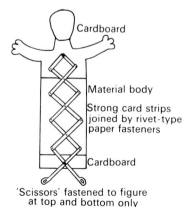

Cardboard

Material body

Strong card strips joined by rivet-type paper fasteners

Cardboard

'Scissors' fastened to figure at top and bottom only

Figure 14 A scissor control for an extending body

168

Figure 15 Hatziavatis who contends with Karaghiosis in the traditional Greek shadow show (here by E. Spatharis)

Figure 16 (Below, left) Mr Punch, designed and cut by Lotte Reiniger in less than two and a half minutes

Figures 17 and 18 (Below, right) The Eagle and the Owl, and Butterflies from Black Fantasy, *by the author*

Figure 19   Colour achieved with cellophane paper, tissue paper or acetate

Figure 20   Colour and textured materials used together in puppets created by Geraldine Bone

Colour with translucent materials

Colour can be introduced by covering cut-out shapes in cardboard figures or scenery with coloured acetate, tissue paper or cellophane paper (figure 19). Alternatively, the puppets and scenery may be cut from fairly thick plain or coloured acetate. Plain acetate may be coloured with glass painting colours or with Letrafilm shapes. (Letrafilm is a self-adhesive, translucent, coloured film.) The use of plain acetate permits many colours to be combined in the same figure. Join moving parts with strong thread or with nylon thread (seal the knots with a clear glue).

The coloured, translucent material can be used in conjunction with textured materials (described above) as illustrated in figure 20 and with black paint.

Full-colour puppets in the traditional style

Through the ingenuity and experimenting of Jessica Souhami in particular, it is possible to create full-colour puppets easily, using techniques akin to those of the traditional oriental puppets, but with modern materials.

The technique of making the puppet from lampshade parchment and tinting it with inks has been used to good effect for some time. Now you can also colour plain card and treat it to make it translucent. This is admirable for professional use, and it is also particularly suitable for young children who may not appreciate with silhouettes that any detail drawn on the puppet cannot be seen. This technique is, in effect, a cut-out drawing on a stick and whatever is drawn *will* be seen.

Draw the puppet lightly on thin white card (cartridge paper is too thin and floppy, and not suitable). The best card to use goes under various names such as Ivory Board, Ivorex, Ivortex (*ivory* is the quality), and the best weight to use is 335 gm/sq. metre.

Colour the puppet (and any parts to be articulated) with some form of transparent colouring. Felt tip pens are excellent: water-based pens are recommended as the colours are stable and will not merge. With spirit-based pens the colours drift together; for a few weeks the effect can

Figure 21 (Left) Sortir, en quelque sorte *by La Cit-rouille, France*

Figure 22 (Above) Translucent figures created by oiling card coloured with felt pens

be very subtle and beautiful but eventually they all merge and the effect is spoilt.

Water colour paints may also be used but transparent dyes, diluted and painted on, are best of all for the professional (though not suitable for young children). 'Dylon' is a possibility; Luma Water Colours or, preferably, Dr Martin's Radiant Concentrated Water Colours are recommended. With Dr Martin's a great deal can be achieved with just three colours, by diluting in different strengths and by mixing 8A Turquoise Blue; 15B Daffodil Yellow; 39C Tropic Pink.

Next, to make the card translucent, rub it with cooking oil or, preferably, clear liquid paraffin: lay the card on a piece of kitchen tissue and rub the coloured surface with another piece of tissue soaked in oil. Then turn over the card and rub the oil into the other side until the colours show through (the card will now be translucent and stronger).

Wipe any excess oil from the card and finally cut out the shape and any required detail. Do this last or you might damage the puppet whilst oiling it. If the puppet is articulated, use nylon thread (4½ lb fishing line is good) to join the parts; seal the knots in the thread with clear glue. Gluing the knot to an acetate washer on each side of the card joint prevents the knot pulling through the card (figure 23). As an alternative to tying a knot, the thread may be melted to a tiny bubble at each end with a lighted spill.

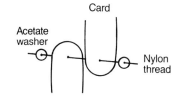

Figure 23 A nylon thread joint

171

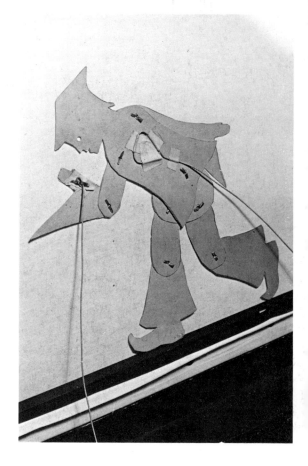

Figure 24 Effecting control over the whole puppet from one main rod

Small, rivet-type paper fasteners may be used for joints, but they will show just a little.

For repairs or strengthening, glue clear acetate to the puppet. Many glues will not adhere to the oiled surface but UHU, a clear contact adhesive, is very good.

Store the puppets in polythene bags to protect your clothing, to stop them sticking together and to prevent them drying out or they will need to be re-oiled.

Control

It is common practice to attach controls to the body (or head if it moves) and one arm if needed. The other arm and legs are allowed to swing freely. In fact, considerable control can be exercised indirectly over the puppet's legs from the one main control rod (figure 24).

For the control, use either c. 14 gauge galvanised wire (coathanger wire), which is strong but easily bent to the required shape, or $5/16$ in diameter dowel rod. Garden canes and the like are *not* suitable for most purposes. When using wire, it is useful to glue the end into a dowel rod or bamboo cane for easier handling (a long wire with a short rod or a short wire and a long rod).

172

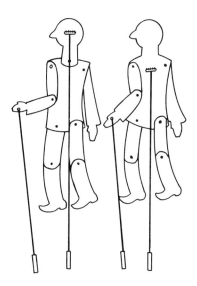

Figure 25/1 Control from below with wires attached to head or body

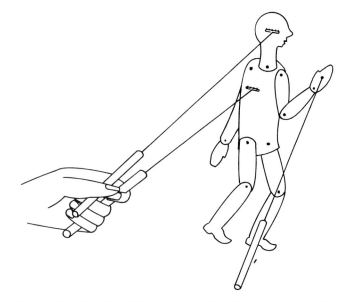

Figure 26 One-handed operation of head and body controls

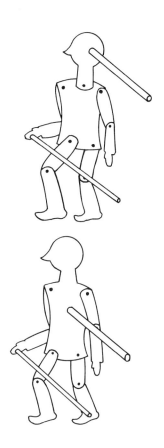

Figure 25/2 Control from behind: hand rods may be omitted if desired

The controls illustrated in figures 25/1 and 25/2 are sufficient for most purposes, whether the puppet is operated from below or behind. The puppet may have a head *and* body control (figure 26) but this is more difficult to operate; most additional techniques are included because the reader may have particular needs, but the golden rules are: do not try to do too much (certainly not more than you can hold) and let the puppet's natural movements and the audience's imagination supply the rest. The merest hint of movement is sufficient.

For ease and flexibility of movement, control from behind is favoured but the method of operation will depend on your individual purposes. This decision must take into account the mode of lighting to be used – and vice versa.

Methods of fixing main controls

If the puppet has a moving head, the main control must be fixed to the head. If it has not, attach the main control to the body, just above the point of balance so that there is *just a little* more weight below the control than there is above it. Then the puppet will keep itself upright rather than tending to 'somersault' as you operate it. Use one of the following techniques to attach the control:

1 Secure the rod to the puppet with a drawing pin (figure 27/1). It must be tapped in firmly or the puppet will turn on the rod. Alternatively secure the rod with Velcro tape (figure 27/2) glued to the rod and to the puppet (use UHU glue for oiled puppets). For extra security, staple the Velcro to the puppet. Velcro is suitable for puppets up to about 15 in high; if larger, they will be too heavy for the Velcro to grip. These methods are suitable only for control from behind.

2 Attach a wire to the puppet with masking tape (figure 27/3). This is suitable for control from below and, if you bend the wire out at right angles to the card, from behind too.

173

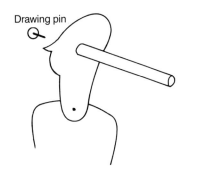

Figure 27/1 Rod secured with a drawing pin

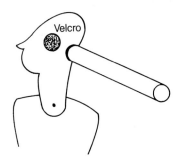

Figure 27/2 Rod secured with Velcro

Figure 27/3 Wire taped to puppet

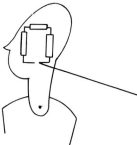

Figure 27/4 Wire joined by card (or acetate)

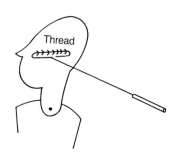

Figure 27/5 Wire sewn to puppet

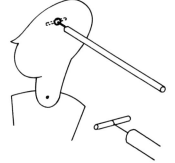

Figure 27/6 Eyelet and toggle fastening

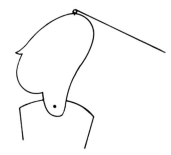

Figure 27/7 Loop in end of wire sewn to puppet

3 Wire with an elongated loop in the end may be secured by a strip of card (or acetate) glued to the puppet over the wire (figure 27/4), but not to the wire itself, so that the wire can be raised and lowered for control from any angle. Alternatively, stitch the wire to the card with strong thread (figure 27/5).

4 Fix a large eyelet in the puppet and attach the rod by a toggle pushed through the hole (figure 27/6). The toggle, made from a small piece of dowel, is attached to the rod by fairly thin but strong wire. This method permits control from any angle.

5 A small loop in the end of the wire may be sewn onto a suitable point at the edge of the figure (figure 27/7). This permits control from any angle and *also allows the puppet to be turned round to face the opposite direction.*

Note: Clearly, using only the last of these methods it is possible to turn the puppet to face the opposite way. However, with shadow puppets it is an easy task to make a duplicate facing the other way. When deciding on which side to attach the controls, take account of who has to talk to whom and what the action requires.

Other types of main control

The palette control The 'palette' control is an old method of both supporting and moving the puppet (figure 28). It is simply an extension of the figure. All strings controlling the figure are attached to the palette and pulled to move the limbs. It is limiting in that the figure cannot leave the ground, for the palette would show on the screen and it does not permit the flexibility of movement achieved with other methods of control.

Control from above Shadow puppets can be hung on threads like a marionette and suspended from one or two control bars (figure 29). (Nylon threads will be scarcely visible on the screen.) The control bar is simply a length of dowelling.

If one bar is used, hold it in one hand and move individual strings with the other. If the limbs are attached to a separate bar, join the head and limb bars with string. Hold the head bar with one hand and use the other hand for the limb bar and for moving individual strings.

In order to obtain the sharpest possible image, the puppet must hang flat against the screen or a very strong light source must be used.

Controlling moving heads and mouths

A moving head is often manipulated by attaching the main control to it rather than to the body, and quite a lot of control may be exercised over the body with a little practice. Alternatively, the puppet may have the main control attached to the body and a second rod or wire attached to the head to effect head and/or mouth movements (figure 30).

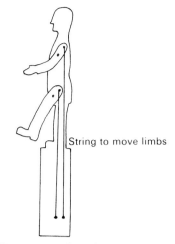

String to move limbs

Figure 28   The palette control

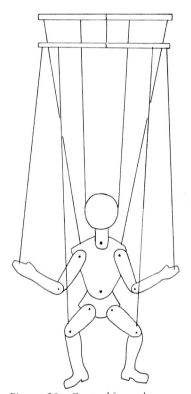

Figure 29   Control from above

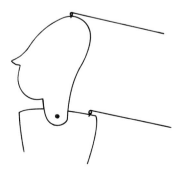

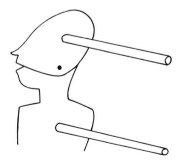

Figure 30   Effecting head and mouth movements from behind

175

Figure 31 A head controlled from below

If operated from below, the moving part is controlled by a piece of stiff wire attached where good leverage can be achieved (figure 31). A main control to the body is also required.

Arm controls

It is possible not to have any arm controls but to let the arms hang and move freely. With the very large Indian figures, it is common practice for the puppeteer to pick up the hand and simply hold it against the screen.

A variety of methods for controlling arms is described; the first is the best all-purpose method.

1 Join a wire to one hand with strong thread (figure 32/1) by making a loop in the end of the wire (seal the closure of the loop with glue). Umbrella spokes are useful for this control.

2 Attach a dowel rod to the hand by means of a drawing pin (figure 32/2). Unlike the main control, ensure the hand can turn on the end of the rod or the card will soon tear. This may be used only for control from behind.

3 A strip of strong, clear acetate may be attached to the hand by thread, knotted at each end, as for arm and leg joints (figure 32/3). This may be used only for control from below.

4 Extend the top of the arm to give a little leverage and attach a string (figure 32/4). Pull the string to raise the arm. Attach a piece of elastic to the arm and the body to provide a counter-pull to the string for better arm control (from below only).

5 Make the arm in two parts, with an elbow joint. Two strings control its movement. Attach one to the top of the arm and the other to the forearm. The latter string passes through a loop of thin wire fixed in the upper arm (figure 32/5) and is used to raise and lower the forearm from below. This technique is unnecessarily complicated and not recommended, but it might meet certain specialised requirements.

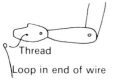

Figure 32/1 A wire control for the arm

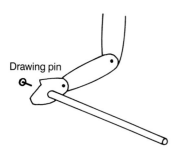

Figure 32/2 A dowelling control

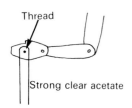

Figure 32/3 An acetate control

Figure 32/4 A string control for arm movement

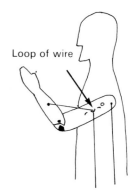

Figure 32/5 A string control for an arm with an elbow joint

Figure 33/1   Galvanised wire leg control

Figure 33/2   Leg control of strong, clear acetate

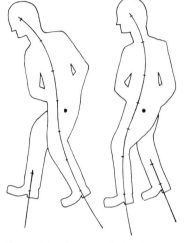

Figure 34   A controlled walking action

Leg control

The best advice on leg controls is not to use any. Movement is invariably better when the legs hang and move freely. The Chinese and Turkish method involves only slight pressure downwards with the main control rod.

If it is essential to move a leg in a particular way, attach a piece of galvanised wire (figure 33/1) or a strip of strong, clear acetate (figure 33/2), joined to the foot with thread.

If a controlled walking action is required, cut out the figure with one leg articulated as shown in figure 34. Attach the main control wire to the figure and an extra wire to the articulated leg. The puppet stoops forward slightly and then straightens up as it walks along.

Figure 1 Aladdin, *performed with a toy theatre by the author*

Figure 2 *Characters from* The Miller and His Men

11 Related puppetry techniques

The toy theatre

The term 'toy theatre' refers to a small table-top theatre in which cut-out figures are moved on 'slides' projecting from the sides of the stage. The terms 'toy theatre' and 'model theatre' have become almost synonymous but, strictly, a model theatre is a scale model of a real theatre. Toy theatre performances, known as the Juvenile Drama, date from the early nineteenth century and are thought to have their origin in the contemporary fashion for caricatures. Not only caricatures of the famous and infamous were published, but also portraits of actors and actresses in poses from their plays. These became extremely popular as souvenirs and to supply the demand they were soon printed not as large single figures but in sets of sheets with six figures on each. Soon it was possible to buy all the characters of a play in all their different costumes *and* in a variety of attitudes. By 1812 scenery was being published too, then proscenia and orchestra strips.

These souvenir prints were sold for a penny a sheet or for twopence, hand coloured (hence the famous term 'penny plain, twopence coloured'). It was the young boys of the day who were the great enthusiasts for these theatrical souvenirs and they were soon animating the figures cut from the sheets and performing their favourite scenes or plays. This was the start of the Juvenile Drama, a young man's pastime rather than a child's toy.

The characters and scenery were cut from the sheets and mounted on card. To manipulate the figures they were held in slots cut in wooden 'slides' which were moved in grooves in the stage floor. Between 1830 and 1840, tin slides with long wires attached were introduced, which allowed considerably more movement. The Juvenile Drama was essentially drawing-room entertainment, taking its life and inspiration from the theatre of the day.

Originally home made, the earliest manufactured toy theatre was advertised in 1829, probably made by the shop that sold it rather than the publishers of the figures. In America the toy theatre never really became popular although some of the English toy theatre sheets and plays were published there about 1825.

The toy theatre suffered a decline in the second half of the century. One of the publishers who continued in business was the firm of J. K. Green which in 1860 was taken over by John Redington. Redington was himself succeeded by his son-in-law, Benjamin Pollock, whose last new sheet was published in 1883. After this he contented himself with reprinting old sheets. Pollock managed the business from 1876 until his death in 1937.

Claudine. Ravina. Count Friberg.

Figures 3 and 4   More characters
from The Miller and His Men

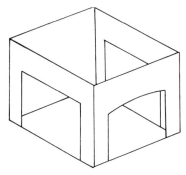

Figure 5/1   Box with proscenium
arch cut out and sides partly cut away

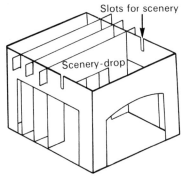

Figure 5/2   The theatre with scenery
drops

The business subsequently changed hands and premises a number of times and at one stage was forced to close down. However, the demands of the enthusiasts led to Pollock's being bought and re-opened by Mrs Marguerite Fawdry as a toy theatre shop and toy museum, which is now situated in Scala Street in the heart of London under the name of 'Pollock's Toy Museum'.

Although the toy theatre trade was declining, there was formed in 1925 an organisation known as the British Model Theatre Guild, later called the British Puppet and Model Theatre Guild. The Guild was formed by H. W. Whanslaw ('Whanny') and Gerald Morice, following the considerable interest that had been aroused by the publication of Whanny's book, Everybody's Theatre. They originally aimed at reviving interest in the Juvenile Drama and developing model theatre technique. Through exhibitions the Guild played a part in promoting the interests of the toy theatre makers and various Guild publications on the toy theatre are of particular interest. Although its scope has widened and other types of puppetry are now the main interest of most Guild members, the toy theatre enthusiasts continue to play an active part, exhibitions still contain toy theatres, and toy theatre performances draw good audiences at the Guild meetings.

Theatres may still be purchased from Pollock's Toy Museum (see Appendices) but suggestions are offered here for those who wish to construct their own. It is advisable to limit the size of the theatre so that a solo manipulator can operate the figures from both sides of the stage at once and see from above what he is doing.

Constructing a toy theatre from a cardboard box   Remove the top of the cardboard box and cut a proscenium opening in one side (figure 5/1). Partly cut away two sides to allow the figures to be operated from the wings. Cut slits in the sides to hold the scenery (figure 5/2), and then make scenery drops and a back drop from cardboard.

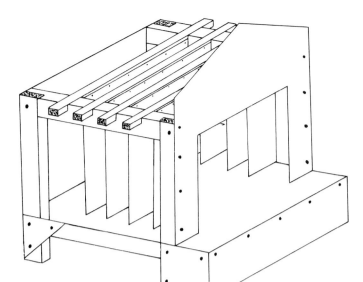

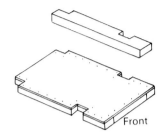

Figure 6/2   The stage floor

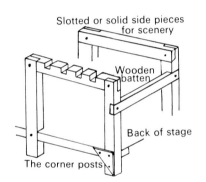

Figure 6/3   The framework attached to the stage floor

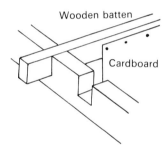

Figure 6/4   Supporting the scenery: scenery battens fit into slots in the framework

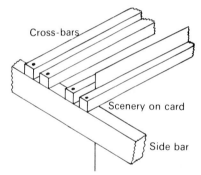

Figure 6/5   Supporting scenery: scenes on card stand between cross-bars fixed to the framework

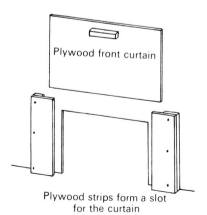

Figure 6/6   The front curtain

A plywood theatre   Figure 6/1 shows the completed theatre. Make the stage floor from plywood with four pieces cut out to accommodate the uprights. Tack, or screw, strips of wood to three sides of the plywood (figure 6/2). Screw the four corner uprights to these strips of wood. Secure the back corner posts by triangular plywood plates (figure 6/3).

Screw two other side pieces to the tops of the uprights with angle halved joints (figure 6/3). These side strips may be slotted or not, depending on the type of scenery grid to be used (see below). Fix a batten between the back corner posts, near the top, to hold them firm (figure 6/3).

To make back drops and wings; *either* tack cardboard scenery drops to cross-battens which fit into slots in the side pieces (figure 6/4), *or* make a scenery grid with small strips of wood tacked to the side pieces (not slotted). The scenes, mounted on card, stand between the cross bars (figure 6/5).

The proscenium arch is made of plywood. Glue and screw or nail it to the front uprights. Mask the front of the stage with three strips of plywood tacked to the wooden battens under the stage floor. The plywood tacked to the sides helps to secure the front uprights.

The 'front curtain' is made of plywood. It is held in place by double strips of plywood, glued, screwed or tacked to the inside of the proscenium arch (figure 6/6). Glue and screw a small block of wood to the inside of the 'curtain' so that it may be lifted easily and removed for the performance.

It is best to paint the stage floor matt black to help to show up the characters and scenery. They are not so clear against a light floor colour.

Lighting for the theatre   The following are the two most useful types of light in the toy theatre.

1 A striplight attached to a small wooden batten and connected to the electricity supply.

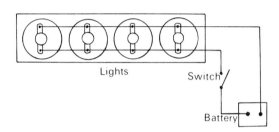

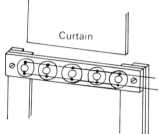

Figure 7/1   (Left) Connecting the lights, switch and battery

Figure 7/2   Mounting the lights in the theatre

2 Flashlight bulbs (or coloured lights) screwed into bulb-holders and fastened to small wooden battens. The bulbs are connected in parallel in a circuit with a battery and switch (figure 7/1).

The batten is fastened to the wooden strips which form the slots for the front curtain (figure 7/2).

For extra illumination of the back drop, another batten may be held above the stage by *either* slotting it into the side strips that hold the scenery *or* attaching the batten to the scenery grid. The method used depends upon the type of scenery construction employed.

Footlights will impede the audience's view unless a small section is cut from the front of the stage floor to make a well to accommodate them. All lights must be adequately shielded so that they do not shine in the eyes of the audience.

The characters   For the toy theatre proper, the 'Penny Plain, Twopence Coloured' type of sheet is still supplied by Pollock's with the printed plays. The characters printed on these are mounted on card and cut out. For the sort of original performances that children might engage in, the characters may be drawn on card, then coloured or painted, and cut out.

A slide will be required to support the cut-out figure so that it can stand without being held, and to move the figure. The following types of slide are in general use. (It is advisable to paint slides matt black.)

1 The traditional tin slide has been replaced by a plastic one but the tin version may still be made by the performer himself if he has the facilities (figure 8/1).

2 A wooden strip with an end slit to hold the cardboard figure (figure 8/2).

3 The slide made entirely of wire, bent to shape, went through a popular period but was never as popular as the tin slide. It is, however, the easiest type to make, galvanised wire being used (figure 8/3).

Figure 8/1   Traditional tin slide

Figure 8/2   Wood and wire slide

Figure 8/3   Wire slides

Figure 9 George Speaight giving a toy theatre performance

The performance The first consideration is the manipulation of the figures. The Juvenile Drama requires swift action so there is no time during a performance to change the characters in the slides. It is therefore necessary to have a slide for each character.

The obvious difficulty in the toy theatre is in showing clearly which character is speaking. This can be achieved by moving the slide with a slight shaking motion, more accentuated movement accompanying stronger speech.

The Juvenile Drama seems to benefit from having a solo operator as this brings greater unity to the performance, but this is not a hard and fast rule. When considering the number of manipulators, one must also consider the number of speakers. A solo performer may be able to provide all the voices himself or he may rely upon a number of speakers back stage. It is

183

preferable that the manipulator(s) speaks for the characters so that movement and speech are synchronised, but if the manipulator is to speak, he must know his play by heart. It is impossible to read the play and operate the figures successfully.

Three other factors help to keep the play moving at a steady pace and minimise the length of scene changes. The first is to have only the bare essentials in terms of effects as these divert the attention of the manipulator from the main business of speaking and operating the characters. Secondly, he should be able to recognise each character from the back, by its attitude or outline shape. The characters stand beside the theatre on each side, ready to be used, so they must be immediately recognisable in a restricted light. Finally, to speed up scene changes it is advisable to arrange the scenery systematically. As far as possible, place all the scenery drops in order on the stage, the first at the front. Then, as each scene ends, remove the scenery to reveal the next. Alternatively, insert them as required, working from the back to the front of the stage.

Music aids the peformance but great care should be exercised in selecting the piece or pieces to be used. Old musical boxes are ideal, the quality of the music being in keeping with the atmosphere of the performance.

The operator may be screened so that he is not visible to the audience, but for many it is part of the enjoyment of the performance to see the manipulator furiously at work back stage. Remember that the toy theatre was a drawing-room entertainment and is not suited to large audiences. Between twenty and thirty people is a workable proposition, being enough to make a good atmosphere but not to preclude anyone seeing.

There are two further essential elements in a toy theatre performance if it is to be played in the conventional manner: there must *always* be movement on stage and the audience must be involved in the performance. As George Speaight writes: 'They must co-operate; they must applaud the heroic and moral passages, and they must hiss the villain'.*

Puppets in film and television

The Dark Crystal

The film of *The Dark Crystal*, created by the Henson Organisation, which also brought us the Muppets, merits a section to itself as a landmark in the advancement of puppet film technique. It has been described as 'an alchemy of acting, puppetry and electronics', the project really evolving its own technology based on puppetry, painting, mime, make-up, costume, modelcraft, electronics and hydraulics.

The starting point for the film was Jim Henson's concept of a reptilian race assuming control over some splendid past society. Reversing the usual development procedure, he invited Brian Froud, whose books of supernatural paintings had won wide acclaim, to become Conceptual Designer and create the characters and their environment. These were then woven into a story by Henson and later developed into the screenplay.

The History of the English Toy Theatre, Studio Vista, London/Plays Inc. Boston, 1969

Figure 10 Jen the Gelfling talking with urZah, the urRu Ritual-Master; both parts are played by Jim Henson in the film of The Dark Crystal

Figure 11 SkekOk, the Scroll-Keeper from The Dark Crystal

The specifications for the characters brought many demands in craftmanship and technology. After two years of development, Jim Henson was invited to help bring to life Yoda, who was to become such a prominent feature of the film *The Empire Strikes Back*. The Dark Crystal technology was applied to Yoda, with Henson's close associate Frank Oz playing the role. Gary Kurtz, producer of *Star Wars* and *The Empire Strikes Back* now agreed to co-produce *The Dark Crystal* and Yoda served as a working prototype for further Dark Crystal developments.

A very impressive production team was thus assembled working with a total of four hundred craftsmen, technicians, actors, acrobats, etc. and the attention to detail was meticulous. For example, the effect of the eyes was considered so critical it took two years to meet Froud's specification of red irises with a defined depth of focus and the strength to contain the necessary micro-mechanisms.

The creatures are largely complete masks and costumes which contain a puppeteer-actor-acrobat-mime. Heads, faces, hands and feet were moulded in latex foam. Fabrics were specially woven, embossed and dyed. Each puppet had internal mechanisms with as many as twenty exterior pneumatic control cables, plus remote controlled servo-mechanisms implanted in eyelids and elsewhere, activated by radio signals. Four or five technicians were needed for each puppet.

There was also a dual camera system which allowed the action to be filmed and simultaneously transmitted to television monitors throughout the studio. Miniature screens were also built into some of the characters.

Yet, despite all of these 'animatronics', the core of each puppet's performance is still the puppeteer. As Frank Oz so clearly states: 'You can never let the technical side take over. Before anything else, you have to know your character, how he thinks, behaves, moves, walks, the smallest facial tic.' Ultimately, it is the acting that makes the creatures so wonderfully convincing, even though with some characters this had to be achieved while operating for long periods in a crouching position, knees bent, back curved, with one arm stretched straight forward and carrying a costume weighing some seventy pounds.

The Dark Crystal, released early in 1983, is a magnificent achievement, a blend of technology, crafts and performance skills which sets new standards in puppet film artistry.

The Muppets

Jim Henson's first television show, *Sam and Friends* – five minutes a night on a local Washington D.C. television station in 1957 – starred a puppet created from a sleeve of his mother's old green coat and a couple of ping-pong balls. This was the original of Kermit. The show, which was aimed at adult audiences, ran for eight years and brought him an Emmy Award and regular appearances on major national shows.

He then moved to New York and made a series of commercials with the early Muppets, a style of puppet for which the name 'Muppet' has become the generic term. When the Children's Television Workshop launched *Sesame Street* in 1969, Muppet creatures like Cookie Monster, Bert and Ernie and Big Bird were regular features of the show.

Six years later, the Henson Organisation in association with Lord Lew

Figure 12 The Muppet Show: *Jim Henson operating Kermit*

Grade's organisation, created the half-hour series, *The Muppet Show*, which reached an audience of 235 million in over a hundred countries and led to two Muppet feature films. *Time* magazine calls it 'almost certainly the most popular entertainment produced on earth' and the roll-call of stars who have taken part is most impressive – Rudolf Nureyev, Danny Kaye, Elton John, George Burns, Liza Minelli, Charles Aznavour, Peter Ustinov, Raquel Welch, Diana Ross, Peter Sellers, John Cleese, Liberace, Spike Milligan, Bob Hope are just a selection. The zany humour, inventiveness and sheer delight of the characters and the show reflect the talents of Jim Henson, Frank Oz (Creative Consultant and actor behind many characters, including Miss Piggy) and the other members of the Muppet team. The contribution of the Muppets to the acceptance of puppets as a television entertainment for adults cannot be over-estimated. Now a new series, *Fraggle Rock*, featuring Muppet-type characters known as Fraggles, Doozers and Gorgs has been filmed in Canada and is also being seen around the world.

The making of *The Muppet Show* is entertainingly detailed in

Figure 13 Kyrano servant to Jeff Tracy from a Thunderbirds *supermarionation television film*

Christopher Finch's book *Of Muppets and Men* (Muppet Press/Michael Joseph Ltd, 1982).

Supermarionation

This term was coined to describe the elaborate marionette films made for television by Gerry and Sylvia Anderson. The series which paved the way for the development of this technique was *Four Feather Falls*. Within three and a half years of this series starting, its successor, *Supercar*, the first of the 'space-age' puppet programmes, was being viewed in a dozen countries, and in Britain yet another series, *Fireball XL5*, had made its impact and was drawing four million viewers every week. More series, such as *Stingray*, *Thunderbirds*, *Captain Scarlet and the Mysterons* and *Joe 90* were to follow, each one a technical advance on its predecessor.

The characters have interchangeable eyes for blinking and swivelling movements with pre-recorded speech. The effects, too, have become increasingly impressive with each series.

Figure 14 The Adventures of Prince Achmed, *a Lotte Reiniger silhouette film*

Recently, a new generation of supermarionation programmes has emerged but the striving after realism has resulted in some rather unconvincing characters. This is highlighted by the evil characters which still have bold, even grotesque, modelling and which are so much more successful as puppets.

Silhouette (or shadow) films

The art of making this type of film owes an immeasurable debt to the late Lotte Reiniger who began her career in Germany but lived for many years in Britain. One of her films, *The Adventures of Prince Achmed*, was the first animated full-length feature film in the history of the cinema.

For silhouette films, the usual technique is to lay the articulated figures on a transparent glass surface, illuminated from below, then take a picture of it with an overhead camera. The figure is then moved very slightly and another picture taken; in this way a series of 'frames' is built up which, when projected at the correct speed on to a screen, results in animation. Apart from the design and construction of figures and sets, Lotte Reiniger's unique talent is evident in her ability to analyse and visualise the components of each movement. Without her appreciation of this aspect of the art her films would undoubtedly lack the charm and grace that help to make them the masterpieces that they are.

The developments on cine-cameras and accessories in recent years have made possible the making of such films by the amateur as well as the professional. It is also possible to suggest three dimensional movement with silhouettes; by increasing or decreasing the size of a figure *very slightly* every few frames, it appears to be either approaching the foreground or receding into the distance. For details of the finer points of this technique, see Lotte Reiniger's book *Shadow Theatres and Shadow Films* (Batsford, 1970).

189

Figure 15   A scene from the phase puppet series Trumpton by Gordon Murray

Figure 16   On the set of a Clangers television film. The Clangers are knitted puppets with friction-tight, jointed skeletons

Phase puppet films

These films use three-dimensional figures and sets. The technique is related to that of silhouette films in that it uses the 'stop motion' method of putting separate frames together to make an animated or 'phased' film. The puppets are often made of wood and friction-jointed or like the rubber 'Bendy' toys that stay in whatever shape they are put.

Phase puppet films have been made in many countries for young children's television programmes. The leading figure in this field was Jiří Trnka, a Czechoslovak puppeteer and artist whose work has been internationally acclaimed. He died in 1969. Today there is an increasing

190

Figure 17 Prominent British politicians (Roy Jenkins, Norman Tebbit and Margaret Thatcher) fall prey to the humour of Spitting Image

number of film-makers demonstrating a mastery of the medium in productions for children and adults.

Both phase puppetry filming and silhouette filming require considerable patience, as can be seen from the fact that twenty-four frames are needed to make one second of film time.

Other television and video techniques

Television utilises a wealth of technology in its puppet creations, technology which permits blue-garbed operators to disappear from sight, which can superimpose images and even turn them inside out. Yet, some of the most successful television puppetry relies heavily upon good puppet technique coupled with sympathetic camera work and direction.

This was particularly evident in the first series of the adult satirical television programme *Spitting Image*. The caricatures of the Royal Family, politicians, etc. were created superbly in latex by Fluck and Law and were operated by accomplished puppeteers. Yet the first few programmes were a great disappointment – then suddenly it all came together very successfully. It is difficult to identify exactly how it changed but certainly the scripts improved considerably: experienced writers were used but the early programmes suggested a lack of understanding of what is needed in writing for puppets (see Chapters 14 and 15). Directors, camera crew and lighting technicians all need experience with puppets and in all these areas improvement was evident too.

In the end the programme was sharper, funnier and altogether more entertaining. The programme also highlighted the wide degree of tolerance afforded the puppet in terms of rudeness, bad taste, etc; nobody was spared and few, if any, taboos were evident. It now has a wide cult following that spans all generations.

One of the fundamental problems for the puppeteer in a television studio is the strict lines of demarcation. He knows about puppets but he cannot tell the lighting crew about lighting puppets, nor the cameraman about shooting them – and particularly not the director about directing them. So they spend many hours asking for the puppets to do very inappropriate things or discovering the principles for themselves. The puppeteer knows that you do not light most puppets from behind or the operators will be seen, but the lighting crew know how to light subjects for television and they will press on regardless. It took one crew three days of work on a single item before they 'discovered' this principle, which the puppeteers had been arguing from the outset. It seems unbelievable but this is what working in television *can* be like.

The boom in home video equipment now means that the recording of remarkably good quality tapes for educational or home entertainment purposes is within the reach of many people (though broadcast quality equipment is a very different matter). One can make do with surprisingly little space and, of course, all that appears is that which is within the frame of the camera shot, so there is considerable scope for ideas not possible in a live theatre setting. A stage is not necessary – indeed, undesirable – but low stools on castors can be very useful for the performers.

It is important to discover the nuances of puppets in television compared with live theatre, to discover the things that work well and build around these rather than trying to fit a live show into the video format; often it will not work. One also has to learn the technique of working with a television monitor; for example, the image is the very opposite of that achieved with a mirror (i.e. instead of moving *with* you, it moves in the *opposite* direction).

A monitor is necessary because of the need to be constantly aware of how the puppet looks on the screen and the need to stay in frame. The close-up nature of the medium requires considerable precision in this way and, in particular, with eye focus and lip-synchronisation to the voice.

Video is particularly useful too for rehearsal purposes for live shows, for it is the only way in which a puppeteer can really see and study his own work in detail. When used for this purpose, it is advisable to use only one fixed camera and not to use clever mixing, close-up shots, zooming facilities etc., as this can spruce up a boring show and give a false impression of its dramatic effectiveness.

Black theatre*

The term 'black theatre' in the puppetry context refers to the form of presentation which was developed with great success by the Black Theatre of Prague and is now used by many puppet companies, sometimes for special effects, sometimes for a whole production.

Basically, black theatre involves holding puppets in carefully directed beams of light (a curtain of light across the stage, illuminated from the sides), or the use of ultra-violet lighting with the puppets painted and dressed with fluorescent materials. The rest of the stage, which has a black

*Strictly, some people would distinguish between 'black theatre' (a curtain of light) and 'black light theatre' (ultra violet lighting with fluorescent colours) but, in practice, the term 'black theatre' is widely used for both techniques. Indeed, as is clear in the text, companies specialising in black theatre may use both together in the same production so it would seem unnecessarily pedantic to treat them separately here.

Figure 18 Smash and Grab *by Polka Children's Theatre using 'black theatre' technique*

Figure 19 The Dragon Who Loved Music, *a 'black theatre' production by the Caricature Theatre*

background and floor covering, remains completely dark, and the operators, usually dressed in loose black velvet clothes and hoods (with black gauze fronts), are not visible to the audience.

With black theatre the performers have to be careful not to let their bodies or limbs get in front of the puppets as they move about the stage so the choreography is very important. Of course UV lighting may be used to enhance puppets presented in a more conventional stage, but one of the advantages of black light is the way in which the performers are released from the confines of a booth and able to utilise a larger area without themselves being visible.

It also makes possible a variety of effects facilitated by extra, invisible pairs of hands; black-backed objects can disappear just by being turned; black shapes cut out as stencils allow background colours to show through and objects can be mounted on black boards without the mounting showing. Scenery created on a black fabric base and rolled up can suddenly appear as if by magic, just by unfurling the roll. Tricks and transformations are easily arranged and a colourful world of fantasy can be brought to life.

More complicated effects can also be achieved. For example, paint a figure or piece of scenery with an ordinary – but not dark – paint and then paint over it with invisible, transparent, fluorescent colours. By changing from ordinary lighting to ultra-violet lighting, the paint underneath 'disappears' and the fluorescent paint glows, and vice versa. It is essential to test both the ordinary and fluorescent paints under both types of lighting to ensure that they all fulfil the requirements to produce the desired effect.

Several technical points are worthy of note: ultra-violet rays are invisible but they cause certain materials to emit cold light or to 'fluoresce'. This shows most clearly when the room or hall is totally blacked out. For this reason, the puppeteer should not rely too heavily upon ultra-violet lighting for his show as he may have to perform in places that cannot be blacked out, but large black plastic garbage bags and masking tape often provide the solution. Companies which specialise in black theatre have to take great care about the venues in which they agree to perform.

There are different kinds of fluorescent colours: some are visible only under black light and invisible under any other type of lighting; others are visible under all kinds of lighting but much stronger under ultra-violet lights. To produce a stronger glow, it is best to have a light-coloured base upon which to paint the fluorescent colours. The colours can be mixed but they do not produce the same colours as ordinary paints. To illustrate the point, blue and yellow, which would normally produce green, give an off-white glow with fluorescent paints. It is therefore wise to experiment with the fluorescent colours under ultra-violet lighting. It is useful to see how the colours look under ordinary lighting too.

Recently, UV materials and others with similar fluorescent properties have become much more widely available; one can buy felt pens with fluorescent colours, 'Dayglo' papers and self-adhesive labels, and paints which are applied with a brush or using a spray-can. Actual UV fabrics are not so common; they are obtainable from theatrical fabric specialists but the range of colours is quite limited and some of these are not as effective as one would wish. However, experimenting is the answer for fabrics; you will find a substantial range of soft fabrics and nets that meet your needs. Explore the off-cuts of friends' dressmaking activities and collect small samples from shops to test at home.

There is also a number of materials that will glow under black lighting, such as corn starch, mentholatum and petroleum jelly. Similarly, washing powders which contain a 'blue' ingredient may be used on a fabric (but take care not to rinse it out). These materials transmit a bluish-white light and may be used for some effects if fluorescent paint is not available.

Some companies use very little colour on their puppets, keeping the clothes and faces mostly white and using UV paint only to accentuate the form (e.g. shading in the features). Props similarly would be mainly white with outlines in UV paint. Where colour is used, it is spotlit by a hand-held spot, so it need not necessarily be painted with UV colours; some operators dim this light simply by holding a hand over it with open fingers. All UV lights are situated in front of the acting area but white spots for cross-lighting may be fixed in the wings and supplemented by hand-held spots when necessary. The 'experts' say that the white light does not negate the UV effect as it has a different wave length.

Operators who have to perform very close to their audience, as in some cabaret shows, sometimes employ small, 'pygmy' 15 watt lights as 'blinders'. These are placed around the stage area at about 12 inch intervals and shielded from the operators; whilst they appear somewhat decorative, their effect is to make the audience's pupils contract slightly in order to prevent them seeing the puppeteers.

Finally, whilst it is easy to be seduced by the colourful appeal of ultra-violet lighting and fluorescent colours, remember that these may have limitations in performance. It is splendid for bright spectacle and special effects but some people find it tiring on the eyes to watch or perform by for long periods and the colour is rarely subtle. So do remember the alternative form of black theatre presentation, which tends to be more suitable than UV technique for serious drama.

Masks

George Speaight refers to the puppet as 'the complete mask – the mask from which the human actor has withdrawn'.* There is, indeed, a close relationship between the puppet and the mask. Actors who use masks have been known to say: 'When I put on a mask, I become a puppet', referring to the way in which the actor can become depersonalised. It is this that many people of the theatre have sought to achieve by using masks – to free the actor from those aspects of his personality which interfere with the performance.

Edward Gordon Craig, largely unsympathetically received by actors of his day, saw the masked actor – the 'Übermarionette' – as a way of freeing the actor to *create* rather than imitating, for 'while impersonation is in the theatre, the theatre can never become free'.* He believed that the mask, having separated the work from direct representation, permitted the artist to create a consistent unity based upon the inter-relationships of the theatrical elements:

The History of the English Puppet Theatre (Harrap, London 1955)

Masks carry conviction when he who creates them is an artist, for the artist limits the statements which he places upon these masks. The face of the actor carries no such conviction; it is over-full of fleeting expression ... frail, restless; disturbed and disturbing, and ... on this account not material with which to make a work of art.

Edward Gordon Craig: *A Note on Masks*

There has been an upsurge of interest in the use of masks in recent years, both for performances entirely by masked actors and for those which use masked actors and puppets. The decision to use masks with puppets is usually based upon considerations of scale and the theatrical nature of the performance. But there is no point in having a mask if you cannot use it sucessfully; that would be like having a fabulous costume that restricts movement. The mask, of course, could be a whole costume; it need not stop at the face.

For speech a half-mask is better; it does not cover the mouth or chin and therefore does not distort the voice. The full-mask tends to be more widely used for silent characters and for dance/movement type productions. Sometimes the full-mask is given a big mouth to permit clear speech, but it is thick enough to create deep shadows which will disguise the actor's

Figure 21 Wide elastic is used to secure the mask

mouth. If you need a wide range of vision but there are only small eye apertures, make pin-pricks all around the apertures; they allow a great deal of vision but remain invisible. One of the factors that help to make some masks very mysterious is their absolute symmetry, so unlike the human face.

One performance filled the stage with famous characters by cutting large pictures of faces from magazines, mounting them on card and turning them into masks. Modelling on a balloon-base is a common technique in schools: the balloon is blown up to head size, smeared with petroleum jelly and covered with up to seven or eight layers of paper and wallpaper paste; when it is dry, the balloon is burst and the mask cut out. Professionals tend to cast in rubber or to model on a plasticine/clay base or on a wig-stand. Techniques for using a variety of suitable materials are described in Chapter 6, but do ensure that the inside of the mask is appropriately finished.

For a comfortable fit, some performers glue strips of foam rubber (plastic foam) inside the mask at forehead, cheekbones and chin. The mask is held securely on the head by two wide strips of elastic, one around the back of the head and one over the top of the skull to the mid-point of the other piece (figure 21). Many mask makers cover the back of the head with a head-dress or materials suggestive of hair, rather than attempting to achieve a realistic hair effect.

Other techniques

Finger puppets

Figure 22/1 Single-finger puppets

The simplest form of finger puppet is the type which fits over one finger. These may be used to particularly good effect in telling stories to young children. The characters in the story can be made very quickly and slipped on to fingers to show the characters speaking. One quick method of construction is to use two strips of card (or one small cylinder of card) for the piece into which the finger fits and to build a felt body around this (figure 22/1). This may be stuffed with foam rubber if required.

A more unusual type of finger puppet is a small figure with loose arms, the puppeteer's own fingers forming the legs. It may be just a cut-out cardboard shape with features, costume, etc., painted on, or it may be a figure modelled and dressed over a central piece of cardboard. The end of the card is folded backwards just below the waist and at right angles to the body. Two holes for the puppeteer's fingers are cut in this part of the card (figure 22/2). The fingers both support the puppet and form the legs. Small boots can be slipped over the tips of the two fingers and it is also possible to have loose trouser-legs attached to the body so that the fingers are covered. It is usual for operators to wear black gloves with the first two fingers cut off for manipulating the figure. If the body will not remain upright, attach a small loop of elastic to its back and slip your fingers through this before inserting them in the leg holes.

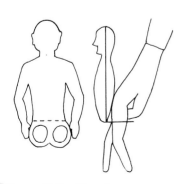

Figure 22/2 Two-finger puppets

Another variant of finger puppet has strings to the arms, manipulated by the puppeteer's free hand, which of course precludes using more than one puppet at a time.

Fist puppets

Figure 23 A fist puppet

A fist puppet is used most frequently by ventriloquists. It may be formed by simply painting the features on the hand with lipstick and other make-up. Alternatively a white glove or mitten may be used with felt features glued, or stitched on and hair (wool) added. In each case, the thumb becomes the lower jaw (figure 23).

Note: Some American authors have used the term 'fist puppet' as a synonym for 'glove puppet'.

Humanettes

Figure 24 A humanette

A humanette is a figure that is part human (head and hands) and part puppet (body and legs). Figures of this type are used sometimes with the actor's face masked.

There are many variations on the humanette: it may be used in 'black theatre' presentations (see above) with the operator's body remaining in the darkness, or on a table top with the operator hidden under a dark cape. Figure 24 shows a humanette performed on a table.

The stuffed puppet body hangs from the operator's neck. Sometimes, particularly when used in black theatre with the operator kneeling on the floor, the legs are moved by the operator's own hands. Alternatively, a large curtain ring may be fastened to a cord running from each shoulder to the knee. By slipping a finger into the ring and raising the hand, the leg can be moved.

The humanette can be extremely funny, even intriguing, but it may appear rather grotesque, though this may be the desired effect.

Jumping Jacks

The Jumping Jack (or *Pantin*) is a simple type of puppet that became popular in the eighteenth century. It is a flat cut-out figure which is best made from stiff cardboard, although thin plywood can be used. The costume and features are painted on the figure, or the card may be decorated with other materials – such as gold paper shapes (figures 25/1 and 25/2). It was once possible to buy printed paper sheets of the parts and mount them on card but these are rarely found today. (Try the Puppet Centre or Pollock's Toy Museum: see Appendices.)

To fasten the separate parts use knotted string or rivet-type paper fasteners (figure 25/3). Suspend the figure by a string attached to the head. Attach a control string to a string connecting the arms and to another connecting the legs. A downward pull induces movement of the limbs. Alternatively, use two control strings, one for the arms and another for the legs.

'Marionnettes à la planchette'

This type of puppet was common in Western Europe by the end of the

Figures 25/1, 25/2   A Jumping Jack

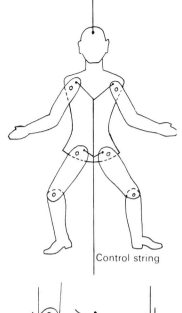

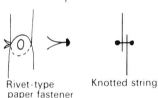

Control string

Rivet-type
paper fastener

Knotted string

Figure 25/3   Construction and control

fifteenth century. Little painted wooden figures with dangling limbs are suspended on a horizontal string which passes through a hole in each body. (The hole must be fairly high in the body or the figures will turn over and hang upside down.) Originally the supporting string was attached to a small post fastened to a plank, hence the name.

One end of the string is fastened to a post, a chair, a table leg or any other suitable fixture, whilst the other end is tied around the operator's leg, below the knee (figure 26/1). Slight movements of the leg make the puppets dance. Alternatively, one or two operators may hold the ends of the string to make the figures dance (figure 26/2). Originally the leg was used to leave the operator's hands free to play a musical instrument, such as bagpipes.

A slight variation is to have two strings, each one passing through both figures. These are operated by two people.

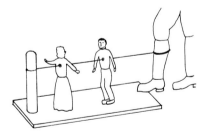
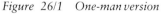

Figure 26/1   One-man version

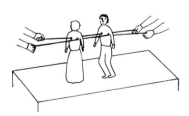

Figure 26/2   Two-man variation

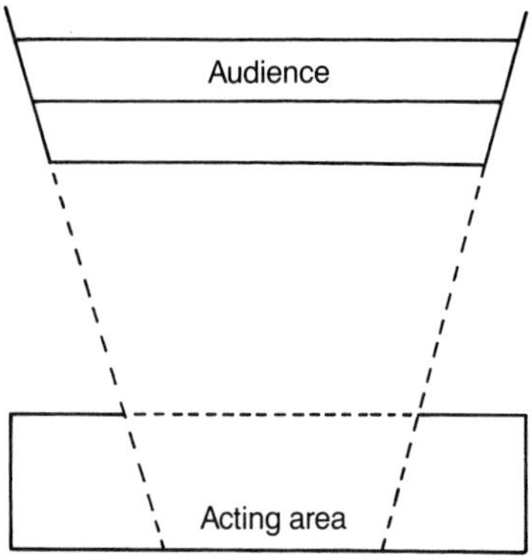

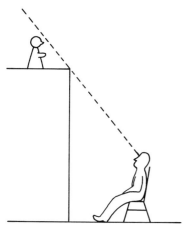

Figure 1 Visibility angles created by a proscenium arch

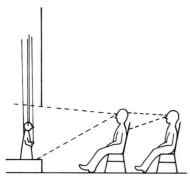

Figure 2 Glove or rod puppets disappear from view if the audience is too close

Figure 3 Sight-line problems occur if marionettes are too low

12   Staging techniques

It must be recognised from the start that no single puppet stage will suit all performances or all venues. If your need is for one stage which will be used for all performances, then some compromise will be necessary, both in your staging and your performances. However, it is possible to create a basic stage, or staging units, which may be adapted to some degree in accordance with particular needs.

In the following pages basic stage designs and units are described, together with details of suitable materials and construction techniques for those designs. Whilst these suggestions may be followed closely, it is recommended that you draw freely from the suggestions and develop your own individual structure, having first asked yourself 'What do I need it to be able to do?'

There are certain requirements that will apply to most stages: portability, lightness of weight coupled with strength and rigidity, ease of assembly and dismantling, suitable dimensions for your mode of transport, for the types of venue in which you are likely to perform and for the comfortable movement of the performers it has to contain – remember that three puppeteers take up more space than the three puppets they operate. It is also necessary, of course, for the overall design to meet the needs of the performance and for the staging to be as presentable as the puppets.

Flexibility is highly desirable whether it be a solo performer's booth which is to be used for all productions or one specifically designed for a single production. With the former, you obviously want as much scope as possible for varying presentation techniques, being able to introduce or omit wings or other pieces of scenery, achieve particular effects, etc. Even when the staging is constructed for a particular production, it is desirable to have some adjustment in width and height – and perhaps even depth – because of the idiosyncrasies of different venues. It is not uncommon to arrive at a studio theatre, arts centre, etc. to find that, whilst the quoted dimensions are correct, they did not mention the beam that supports the roof or the permanently fixed lighting bar.

Sight-lines are an important consideration, so it is useful to have some idea of the sort of audience you are aiming at: is it birthday parties in private houses and small halls, school performances, arts centres, theatres? This decision will help you to determine the size of audience and types of venue to expect so that you can design your stage accordingly. Some performers argue that open stages (i.e. those with no proscenium arch) permit a very wide viewing angle. Certainly, a proscenium arch imposes limitations on the spread of an audience and the amount of acting area you can use and still be visible (figure 1) but open stages do have their limitations too. Somebody sitting to the side of the stage might be able to

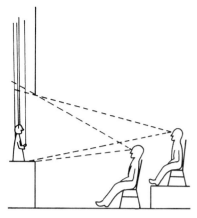

Figure 4 A raised stage with a raked auditorium or tiered seating

Figure 5 A backstage view of Play-board Puppets

see the puppets, but they will miss a great deal of the action.

Furthermore, a spectator who is too close to the fit-up (and parents *do* have a tendency to push their children right up to the front) will see little, if anything, of glove or rod puppets (figure 2) unless the puppets are hanging over the front of the booth; a few inches back from the playboard, the puppets disappear. This same feature applies when booths, which are designed to be set up on the same floor level as the audience, have to be used on a stage (such as in a school hall). The viewing angle for a good proportion of the front of the audience is at best uncomfortable. For comfortable manipulation, the top of the front screen should be just above the puppeteers' heads.

Similarly, if marionettes are too low, even the third and fourth rows will have difficulty seeing them (figure 3), especially if the front row is too close. Keep the marionette stage well above the floor level, do not seat the audience too close and keep them as well spread as possible. Ideally, one would have a raised stage floor and a raked auditorium or tiered seating (figure 4). Tiered seating *is* often possible to achieve, especially with rostra

Figure 6 The staging for the Hungarian State Puppet Theatre's production of Ligeti's Adventures

Figure 7 Pinocchio *at the Circus by Caricature Theatre, Cardiff*

blocks, or by sitting different rows on seats of different height. Raising the stage floor or working from a bridge are possible, of course, only where the headroom is sufficient.

Taking such considerations into account, you need to design a stage which will make the best possible use of the available space. Remember that your stage may have to contain not only the puppeteers, puppets, props and scenery, but lights, lighting control and sound system. Space needs to be considered also – and most importantly – in terms of the scope for acting. There is a tendency to restrict the size of the stage for purposes

Figure 8 A classroom 'shop' converted into a puppet theatre

Figure 9/1 A cardboard table-top screen

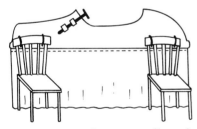

Figure 9/2 A larger cardboard screen

of transport, weight, etc. and, in doing so, to limit the acting area so much that the puppets are relegated to performing almost in a straight line along the front of the booth. Do allow sufficient depth in the acting area to permit the puppets to move within the stage.

Above all, whilst the units described may form the basis for many forms of presentation, do not conceive all staging simply in terms of a conventional booth. Wider possibilities are illustrated (figures 6 and 7).

Improvised stages

Improvised stages suit many classroom needs; the possibilities are endless and a selection are indicated below. However, one method that is frequently quoted in books is *not* recommended: pinning a curtain across a doorway. This can cause all sorts of problems; additionally, doorways are seldom suitably positioned for such use, they are too narrow for performing effectively and impose a narrow viewing angle.

Whatever method is adopted, it is important to ensure that the stage stands firmly. Little arms do get tired quite quickly and it is inevitable that they will rest against the staging, so take suitable measures to stabilise the framework. For example, just tying or taping the back of the stage to a chair or table leg is sufficient.

Simple stages for glove and rod puppets

Many items of free-standing school equipment make excellent stages – the classroom shop, the 'Wendy House' (holding the puppets over the top), low level screens for display or classroom dividers, peg boards for holding shelving, can be used without any preparation or with just a drape over them to establish them as puppet theatres for glove and rod puppets. Those methods which could contain a screen, like the shop illustrated (figure 8), can be used also for shadow puppets, detailed later.

A cut-out screen A screen cut in any shape from the side of a large cardboard box may be used on a table top by gluing supporting cardboard struts (figure 9/1) onto each side of the screen. Larger screens may be used with a masking curtain tacked to the bottom with strong thread. Tie the ends of the screen to the backs of chairs for support (figure 9/2).

A model booth A large model made from cardboard boxes serves as a puppet theatre (figure 10). The operators are hidden inside the model,

Figure 10 A large model used as a booth

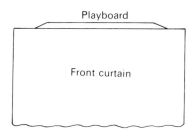

Figure 11/1 The booth set up

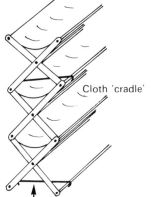

Figure 11/2 An airer with cloth cradles attached

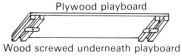

Figure 11/3 Securing the playboard to the airers

which permits 'theatre in the round' quite literally.

A booth made from collapsible clothes airers This is a useful fit-up which requires the minimum of construction and setting up. The main elements are two collapsible clothes airers which support a playboard and a front curtain (figure 11/1). To prevent the two airers collapsing, hook lengths of strong galvanised wire between the bars (figure 11/2). Use wires of different lengths to raise or lower the height of the fit-up.

Make the playboard from a piece of plywood of suitable dimensions. Screw two strips of wood to each end of it to prevent it from moving when placed on the airers. Screw a small piece of wood to one of the wooden strips at each end of the playboard, and turn it to secure the playboard to the airer (figure 11/3).

Support the front curtain rod (a long dowel rod) by hooks screwed into the tops of the airers (figure 11/4)/. Attach fabric between the bars of the airers to make cradles to hold equipment (figure 11/2).

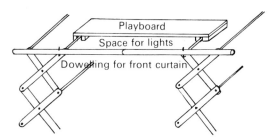

Figure 11/4 The playboard and front curtain rail

Simple staging for marionettes

Marionettes can be used, of course, in a totally open stage style (figure 12) though they will often need to be on a raised platform for comfortable viewing.

An apron backcloth is a simple form of back drop for open stage performances. To make one, suspend a curtain from a dowel rod and attach a long loop of cord to the rod. Hang this around your neck to that the curtain just touches the ground (figure 13).

A table turned on its side quickly makes an open stage (figure 14/1). A background scene painted on paper may be attached to the table top with masking tape. Alternatively, use the table upright as a 'bridge', with marionettes with long strings. A curtain draped over the table acts as a backcloth (figure 14/2).

Another form of backcloth is created by attaching a curtain or painted scene to a long rod (such as a window pole or the cross-bar from a jumping stand); this is supported by resting the ends on desks or chairs (figure 14/3).

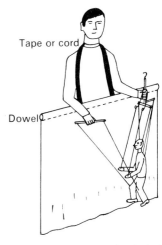

Figure 12 Albrecht Roser of Stuttgart performing in open-stage style

Tape or cord

Dowel

Figure 13 An 'apron' back cloth

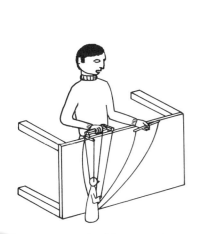

Figure 14/1 A table-top used as a
back-screen

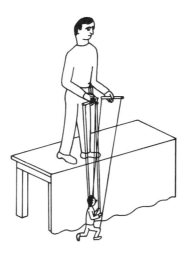

Figure 14/2 A table used as an
operating bridge

Figure 14/3 A backcloth suspended
between two tables

205

Simple staging for all types of puppet

A clothes-horse theatre   A three-sided clothes-horse, suitably draped, is very useful for all types of puppet (figure 15). Use a piece of cotton, or polyester-cotton, sheeting for the shadow screen; attach it with drawing pins (thumb tacks), pulling the screen taut.

 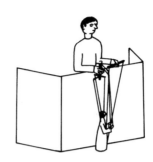 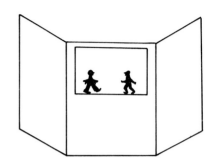

Figure 15   A clothes-horse used for each type of puppet

Glove and rod puppets are shown to better effect if they have a back-screen (figure 16/1). The back-curtain (or a background scene) is pinned or stitched over a long dowel rod. This is held by two vertical dowel rods (broom-handles) which are tied to the clothes-horse (figure 16/2). The joint between the horizontal and vertical rods is effected by long nails through holes drilled in the ends of the rods as illustrated (figure 16/3). The weight of the curtain holds it down.

 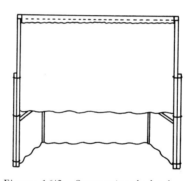 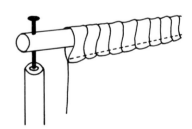

Figure 16/1   A clothes horse theatre with a back-screen

Figure 16/2   Supporting the back-screen

Figure 16/3   The joint for the horizontal and vertical rods

A cardboard table-top theatre   The theatre is made by cutting the top flaps and one side from a large cardboard box. Leave two of the bottom flaps turned inwards (figure 17/1) and bend the middle flap forwards to help steady the theatre. If necessary, stand something heavy on the inside flaps or secure them to the table with masking tape. Decorate the box as required.

Like the clothes-horse theatre, it can be used for all three-dimensional puppets and a screen can be added in the front section for shadow puppets, as detailed later. When used with marionettes, it can be used with the side pieces folded backwards (figure 17/2) or forwards (figure 17/3).

Figure 17/1 A cardboard-box theatre for glove and rod puppets

Figures 17/2 and 17/3 Two methods of using a box for marionettes

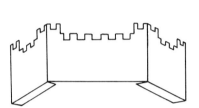

Figure 17/4 A shaped top to the booth

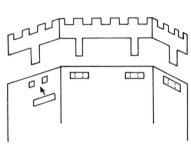

Figure 17/5 The use of a scene-setting piece

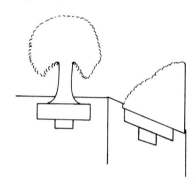

Figure 17/6 The scenery slots used for individual items of scenery

The top of the booth may be shaped (figure 17/4). Alternatively, keep the top plain and vary the scene by the use of large scene-setting pieces. These are held by scenery slots which are created by gluing three pieces of card onto the inside of the booth as illustrated (figure 17/5). This may be used also for individual items of scenery (figure 17/6).

Purpose-built stages: construction

The following pages detail appropriate materials, their construction techniques and design possibilities. Most puppet stages, for reasons of both weight and appearance, are constructed as a framework which is covered by drapes.

Materials

Strong cardboard boxes may be used for improvised staging for classroom use, but a strong wooden stage is recommended for the rigours of long-term use. Wood is the most commonly used material for stage construction, but it is essential that joints are secure and the whole structure suitably braced to prevent it wobbling. 2 in × 1 in timber is a suitable size for many requirements.

Dexion aluminium tube is comparatively expensive but very strong and light. It is square tubing (also available in steel as Dexion Speedframe but this is much heavier) which is easily cut to any length required and assembled with a selection of joining pieces of various shapes. It is, in fact,

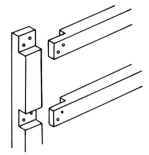

Figure 18/1 Half-lap joints

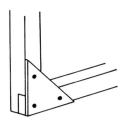

Figure 18/2 A plywood plate used for bracing

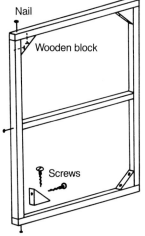

Figure 19 A framework nailed and screwed together with corner blocks for rigidity

cheaper than the comparable strength in wood and the variety of shapes that can be achieved with the same pieces of tubing is considerable.

Metal 'slotted angle', which is L-shaped in cross-section and bolts together, is very strong and suitable for constructions which have to bear the weight of puppeteers (such as bridges for marionette stages) but it is *very* heavy.

Scaffolding may be used for the basic structure of very large staging which has to bear heavy loads. It is assembled with specially manufactured joints. Very few companies indeed would be large enough to need such a structure and the transport needs for such a theatre would be substantial so, whilst the technique is acknowledged, it is not detailed further.

Methods of jointing

Wood Wood joints are best glued and screwed. Use a good quality woodworking glue. Half-lap joints (figure 18/1) are recommended; if carefully cut and securely fastened (using a try-square to ensure that right-angles are true), they should not need further bracing. If they do, use a triangular plywood plate (figure 18/2). An alternative method (figure 19) uses glue and nails and is held rigid by triangular wooden blocks glued and screwed into the corners.

Many parts of the structure may need to be joined for the performance but taken apart or folded up for packing. Bolts with wing nuts (figure 20) are popular but are fiddly and time-consuming when setting up and the nuts always seem to get lost. Nonetheless, it is a strong method. It is essential to drill out the holes thoroughly so that the bolts fit in easily, but without being too loose.

A hinged bar may be held rigid by a length of wood screwed to one half and bolted to the other (figure 21). Where thick dowel rods need to be joined, screw or nail half of a length of metal tubing to one dowel and insert the other dowel into the other half of the tube (figure 22). This dowel is secured by a removable metal pin or bolt.

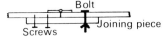

Figure 21 Securing a hinged bar

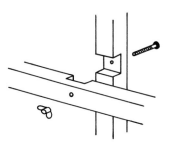

Figure 20 Joint secured with bolt and wing nut

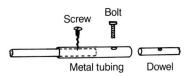

Figure 22 A metal tube used to join dowel rods

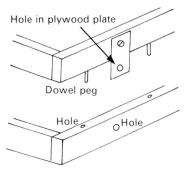

Figure 23/1   Joining two stage sections

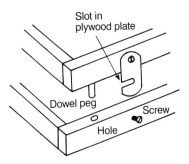

Figure 23/2   An alternative fastening device

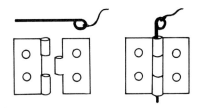

Figure 24/1   A pin-hinge

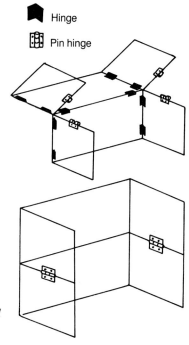

Figure 24/2   A staging unit secured with pin-hinges

When joining different staging units, one method is to use dowel pegs which are glued into holes drilled in one section and which fit into corresponding holes drilled in the other section. The units are fastened together by a plywood or metal plate which is screwed to one section and either bolted to the other (figure 23/1) or slotted over a screw in the other section (figure 23/2).

Pin-hinges (figure 24/1) are very useful for joining units quickly and easily. They can be purchased or made by knocking the joining rod out of a standard hinge and replacing it with a thick, galvanised wire 'pin'. Figure 24/2 illustrates an application of the pin-hinge; Charles MacDonald devised this folding stage unit, the flaps of which are lifted up and joined by two pin-hinges. By pulling the two pins, the whole structure can be dismantled.

Plywood shapes and other boards may be bolted to the structure; alternatively, they may be held by dowel pegs (as in figure 23/1) and depend on gravity to hold them down, or secured by strips of wood on the underside, which fit over the framework and which are fastened by a rotatable strip of plywood (figure 11/3), page 204.

To join dowelling rods to the main structure, towel rail holders are very useful (figure 25). Gravity also helps with some simple structures, as with the long nail through one rod dropped into the end of a second rod (figure 16/3) and held by the weight of the curtain it carries.

G-clamps (or C-clamps) are also very useful devices for temporarily securing parts of a fit-up.

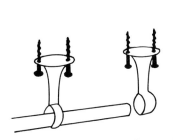

igure 25   Towel rail holders used ɔ carry dowels or metal tubing

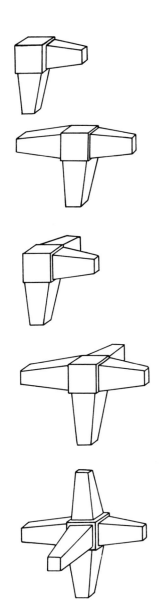

Dexion aluminium tube and Speedframe   Most joints with this square section tubing are made by using one of the various jointing pieces illustrated (figure 26). A plastic insert (figure 27) is dropped into the end of the tube and the joining piece is then inserted and tapped firmly into place with a mallet; the next length of tube is now joined in the same way (figure 28).

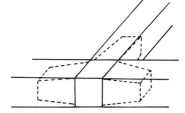

Figure 28   Sections of tubing joined together

To make joins in lengths of tubing so that they can be packed, use another square tube or a 'U' sectional length of aluminium, either of which must be the same size as the *internal* dimensions of the Dexion tube. Half of the internal tube fits into one section and is secured with self-tapping screws, whilst the other half slots into the other section (figure 29). With vertical tubes, gravity will hold them in place; horizontal tubes will require a bolt or some other metal pin to secure the internal tube.

Slotted angle   Metal slotted angle has holes and slots, which facilitate the alignment of bolt holes for sections that are to be joined (figure 30). It is necesary to secure the sections with large nuts and bolts, using a spanner. Triangular plates are bolted on to secure the structure.

Designing flexible staging units

Many of the stages described in this chapter can be designed on a unit structure. It is easier and quicker to assemble and dismantle units than to bolt together and brace lots of separate lengths of timber. However, for flexibility of stage design, a complete unit system is recommended.

Wood   The units are constructed in 1½ in × 1½ in or 1 in × 1 in wood in a variety of shapes and sizes (figure 31). Some may be left as single units whilst others are hinged together. Depending on the mode of transport available if they are to be toured, the units may conveniently be anything up to 8 feet high.

The units may be joined in any shape required (figure 32) by G-clamps or by drilling series of equally-spaced and carefully aligned holes which permit the units to be bolted together, but take care not to weaken the structure. Design the structure so that weight is well-distributed and it cannot topple over. Stage weights may be used if needed.

Screens for rear-projection or for shadow play may be built into the structure and a selection of arches, windows, turrets, etc. may be built up as they become needed for different productions; ³⁄₁₆ in or ¼ in plywood on a timber frame is useful for this.

For trying out ideas, tape sheets of kitchen paper or newspaper to the frames and paint the paper. For the actual productions, some performers

Figure 26   A selection of joining pieces for square-section tubing

Figure 27   A plastic insert used to secure the joints

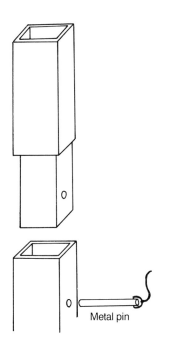

Figure 29   Joints in long bars to facilitate transportation

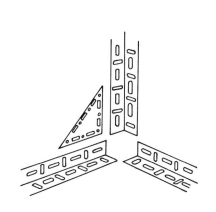

Figure 30   Metal slotted angle

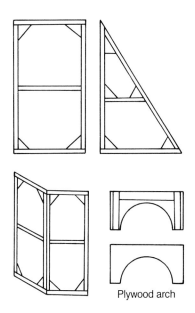

Plywood arch

Figure 31   A variety of flexible staging units

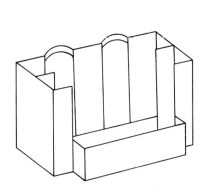

Figure 32   Two examples of possible structures

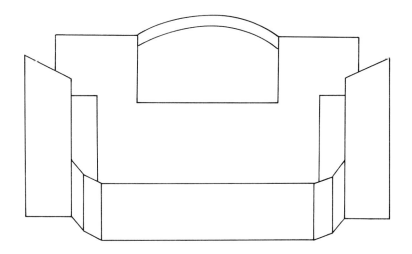

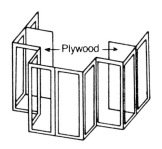

← Plywood →

Figure 33/1   The basic frame

use long drapes which tie onto the frame with strong, fabric tapes or one of the methods detailed on pages 228–229. Alternatively, you can cover the units with a suitable fabric stretched across one face and stapled to the sides of the frames. Fabrics used range from hessian (burlap) to velvet.

Hinged units may also be adapted easily to create boxes for carrying curtains, puppets, etc. The units are hinged in a zig-zag arrangement (figure 33/1 and 33/2) so that they fold flat. Glue and screw a sheet of plywood to the outer sections of the folded frame, to create the box, which is held together by a strap (figure 33/3).

Note: For some types of open stage performance, it is often useful to have a portable 'playboard', a surface on which to establish some of the action. A simple framework on castors supporting a plywood 'shelf' is all

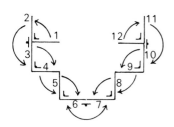

Figure 33/2 *Plan of the fit-up, showing how the sections fold up into a box for puppets, props or curtains*

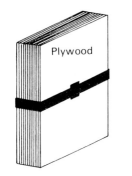

Plywood

Figure 33/3 *The basic framework folded up*

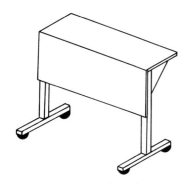

Figure 33/4 *A playboard on castors*

that is needed (figure 33/4). Covering the front surface with another sheet of plywood creates a tidier appearance and permits the introduction of a prop shelf below the playboard.

Aluminium tubing For strength coupled with lightness of weight, the square-section aluminium tubing (described on page 210) is excellent. It may be made up into rectangular unit structures, hinged, bolted or clamped together. The corner pieces which effect the joints permit single lengths of tube to be introduced or rearranged wherever required.

Two examples of the endless possibilities are illustrated (figure 34). As with wooden units, plywood shapes may be attached to the aluminium frame (using self-tapping screws) to establish shapes like arches, turrets, etc. Attach drapes with fabric tapes or, if not too heavy, with Velcro (page 228) glued securely onto the tubing.

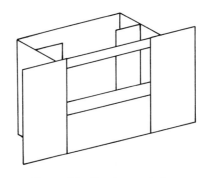

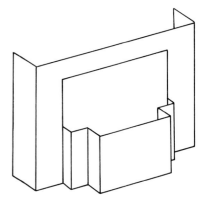

Figure 34 *Staging made from square-section aluminium tubing*

Designing stages for glove and rod puppets

Most glove puppets are presented within a stage or booth of some description sometimes with, but usually without, a proscenium arch. Rod puppets tend to be contained within a stage, though usually of larger proportions than that for gloves. More recently, however, there have been developments in terms of open stage techniques which use some staging units but which also maximise the possibilities of space. Examples are illustrated (figures 35 and 36). These techniques are particularly appropriate for rod figures in the Bunraku style (see page 126) and masked actors. See also the proscenium stage for marionettes (pages 222–223) and the wooden, table-top shadow theatre (page 240). These have the flexibility to be used for any type of puppet.

Figure 35 The Phantom Tollbooth
by Caricature Theatre, Cardiff

Figure 36 Sleeping Beauty *by the Drak Puppet Theatre, Czechoslovakia*

213

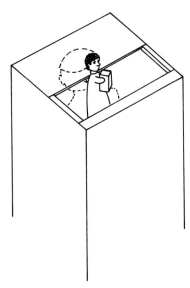

Figure 37   A walk-about stage

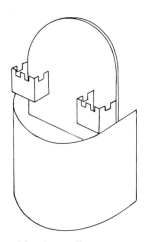

Figure 38   A castellet or castello

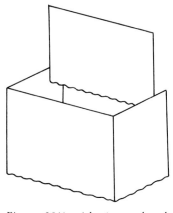

Figure 39/1   A basic open booth

214

A walk-about stage

This simple structure completely hides the puppeteer and consists of three battens attached to a plywood board (figure 37). From this framework are suspended the drapes. The whole fit-up rests on the puppeteer's head; it is held in place by a 'skull cap' rather like an academic mortar board. This may be cut from a large vinyl ball of suitable dimensions, screwed to the board and lined with sheet foam rubber. If necessary, straps to secure under the chin may be added. If the ball needs strengthening or to be made more rigid, use a suitable adhesive to glue on strips of card in three or four layers. Alternatively, screw to the board a helmet of the type used by roller-skaters.

One usually finds all manner of hooks and other devices inside to hold puppets and props, produce sound effects, etc. Pockets stitched onto the inside of the drapes are invaluable. This fit-up is especially popular with street performers who use glove puppets or simple rod figures. Some wear a harness made from strong material or canvas to hold additional puppets, etc. Usually this has a strap around the chest and two shoulder-straps.

A castellet or castello

This type of glove-puppet booth dates back at least as far as the fourteenth century. It was made to represent a castle for the enactment of chivalric episodes and, although originally a bow-fronted fit-up, may be any shape desired.

The feature of interest to us today is the use of scenery, such as turrets, to provide a second acting level and give a greater feeling of depth to the scene. A painted back cloth usually lacks the effect of depth achieved with this technique, which is capturing the attention of contemporary puppeteers in their experiments with split acting levels. The fit-up is constructed in the same fashion as other open booths.

An open booth

In its simplest form this fit-up consists of a front screen to hide the operators, and a back drop against which to operate the figures (figure 39/1). Some puppeteers dispense with a back screen but this is not really wise as it is unusual at engagements to find a suitable background against which to perform.

The minimum width suggested for this fit-up is 5 ft. This will serve solo performers well and is practicable for group work too, although larger dimensions are preferable.

The main structure is created from hinged units for which a number of possible designs are illustrated (figure 39/3). It will be seen that the main alternatives are to have small units with legs bolted on, small units on top of each other or taller units. Those with legs have the advantage of being easily adjustable; those that stand directly on the floor tend to be more stable.

The two sets of units can be hinged together in the centre for quick assembly but it is preferable to bolt them together. This allows them to be

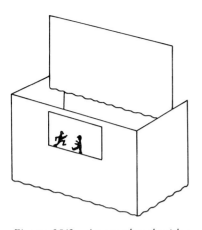

Figure 39/2 An open booth with a shadow screen

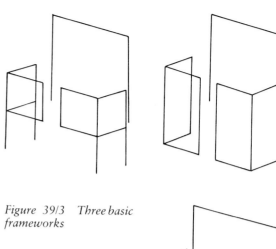

Figure 39/3 Three basic frameworks

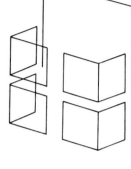

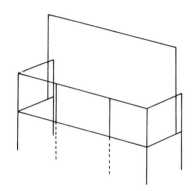

Figure 39/4 Extra legs to support a wide frame

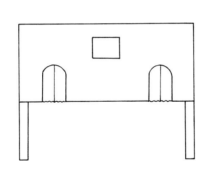

Figure 39/5 A plywood back-screen

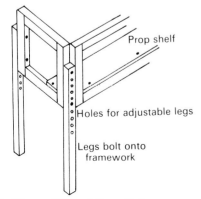

Prop shelf

Holes for adjustable legs

Legs bolt onto framework

Figure 40/1 Adjustable legs

separated and additional units included to extend the stage (figure 39/4) or to introduce a shadow screen (figure 39/2).

The back frame may be just three lengths of timber, hinged together and bolted to the sides of the main frame (figure 39/3). To this may be attached plain or scenic drapes (figure 39/1) or a back-screen cut from plywood and bolted to the timber (figure 39/5).

If a booth with legs is extended, extra legs may need to be bolted to the front centre section for extra support (figure 39/4). To make legs adjustable, simply drill a series of equally-spaced holes in the structure and the legs so that the parts may be bolted together at different heights (figure 40/1). In order to allow for changes in height, secure a separate 'skirting' curtain to the bottom of the booth with curtain wire (figure 40/2). You may find you need some of the accessories for the booth described below.

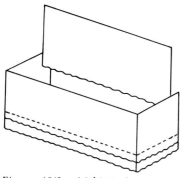

Figure 40/2   A 'skirting' curtain to allow for adjustment

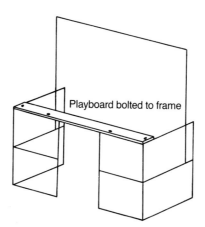

Playboard bolted to frame

Figure 41/1   A playboard bolted onto the frame

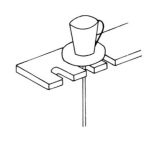

Figure 41/2   A slotted playboard for props on rods

A playboard   A plywood 'playboard' may be bolted onto the frame (figure 41/1). This is a front 'shelf' upon which props may be stood; for props on rods, it will need to be slotted (figure 41/2). The playboard can clearly also be used to determine the width of a booth if it is to be used to join two separate units; it will often need to be hinged for transporting. It is not uncommon for small playboards to be attached only where needed, to permit the puppets to come right up to the front of the booth and to allow methods of attaching scenery described later.

Prop-shelves   Shelves for props are very handy; it is a good idea to attach a strip of beading along the edge to prevent props sliding off. The shelf may be a length of plywood, like the playboard, but attached lower in the booth (figure 42/1) or smaller, triangular plywood plates which fit into the corners of the booth (figure 42/2). In either case, the corners of the shelf should be cut away to fit the framework (figure 42/3). Both methods may be used to hold the framework rigid.

An alternative type of 'shelf' is really a fabric cradle glued and tacked (or stapled) to two long battens which bolt onto the framework (figure 42/4). The advantage of this method is that props are held more securely and are not easily knocked over by the performers during the show.

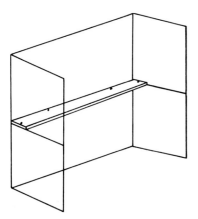

Figure 42/1   A prop-shelf

Figure 42/2   A corner prop-shelf

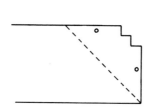

Figure 42/3   The corners of the shelf cut away to fit the framework

Figure 42/4   A fabric cradle for props

216

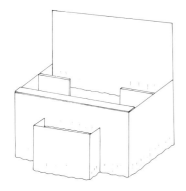

Figure 43/1 A booth with split acting levels

A hanging wire A curtain wire fixed to the inside of the main frame may be used for hanging up glove puppets when not in use (see page 105).

Note: The use of multiple acting levels has attracted increasing attention in recent years. The structure is based on the unit system, as with the booth described above. Examples of possible designs are illustrated (figure 43).

Figure 43/2 Snow White and the Seven Dwarfs *by the Naive Theatre, Czechoslovakia*

Figure 43/3 Split acting levels are used in this production, O Zwyrtale Muzykancie, *by the Lalka Puppet Theatre, Warsaw*

Figure 44/1 Petrouchka *by the*
Drak Puppet Theatre

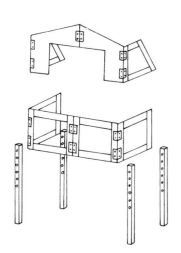

Figure 44/2 *The separate parts*

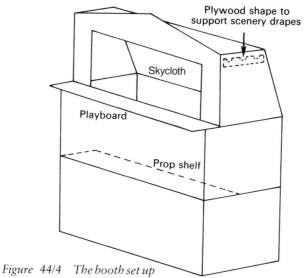

Plywood shape to
support scenery drapes

Skycloth

Playboard

Prop shelf

Figure 44/4 *The booth set up*

Figure 44/3 *Securing a hinged pros-*
cenium

Back-drop

Semi-transparent
back-drop

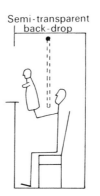
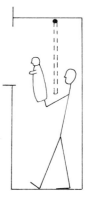

Figure 44/5 *Positions for operating the puppets*

A proscenium booth

This is a larger version of the type of booth traditionally used for Punch and Judy, a variation on which is illustrated (figure 44/1). The lower part of the booth is constructed in exactly the same way as the open booth. It differs in that a unit containing a plywood proscenium arch is added (figure 44/2).

If necessary the proscenium may be hinged in the centre. When being used it is held firm by a plywood plate on the inside; this is screwed to one half and hooks over a screw in the other half (figure 44/3).

Accessories such as playboard and prop-shelves may be added, as for the open booth. Slotted battens (see section on scenery, page 234) may be attached to the booth for supporting back-cloths (figure 44/4) and it is common for the fixed back screen (preferably slanted) to be a sky-cloth. Draw curtains may be added to cover the opening (see page 229). The opening may also be used to accommodate a shadow screen.

The height of the booth depends upon the method of manipulation to be used (figure 44/5). It is restricting to perform sitting down, and performing with your head behind a semi-transparent backdrop allows you to see the puppets clearly but places restrictions upon the background scenery. Performing standing with the playboard above your head is the most common and recommended practice.

Remember that a proscenium arch reduces the viewing angle for the audience, so keep the opening as wide as possible to allow plenty of scope for action and, if curtains are used, ensure that they draw back completely behind the sides of the arch or they will limit the viewing angle even further.

Designing stages for marionettes

For comfortable viewing, all types of marionette presentation generally need to be raised either by setting up on a platform, stage or rostra blocks or by a built-in feature of the puppet staging.

With any method of presentation, it is desirable to have a stage floor covering, such as thin carpet, hessian (burlap), or felt to provide a good surface for puppets to walk on without making too much noise.

Open stage techniques

The totally open stage style of performance is described in the section on improvised stages on page 204 (figure 12). This is most commonly used for cabaret and variety acts, though some companies are now using marionettes in this manner for other types of production. This is a particularly exciting development as it provides much greater scope for movement and action than the more traditional forms of open stage which are described below.

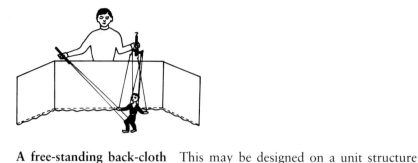

Figure 45/1   A hinged unit for a back-drop

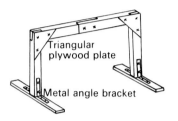

Figure 45/2   A free-standing back-drop

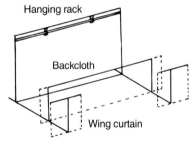

Figure 46   An open stage design with perchery and wings

A free-standing back-cloth   This may be designed on a unit structure (figure 45/1) described previously; it may also be constructed from aluminium square tubing, or may simply be a cross-bar (known as a *leaning bar*) bolted to two upright supports, which are themselves bolted to supporting 'feet' (figure 45/2).

In the latter case, triangular plywood plates (bolted on) and metal angle brackets (screwed on) are required, as illustrated, to hold the framework rigid. Drapes are attached as described on pages 228 – 229. Open-stage backdrops are usually waist-high.

A basic open stage   It is a good idea for the open stage to have not only a back-cloth but a perchery (hanging rack for the marionettes) and wings to hide both backstage activity and the puppets when they are preparing to make their entrance.

The design illustrated (figure 46) may be made from staging units with appropriate additions, from aluminium square tubing or from timber bolted together.

An elaborate open fit-up   The stage (figures 47/1 and 47/2) consists of two raised platforms (for the stage floor and operating area); a back-cloth; wings to hide backstage activity and puppets about to enter; a perchery (hanging rack) for the marionettes; and a drape suspended behind the puppeteers to concentrate attention on the stage (and give it a neater appearance).

For the platforms, use trestle tables or home-made, collapsible 'bridges' of a similar type. It may be desirable that the operating area should be

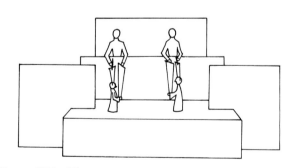

Figure 47/1   The stage

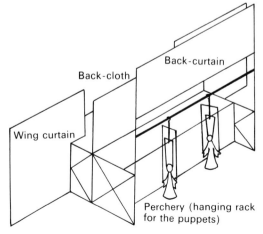

Figure 47/2   A back-stage view

higher than the stage floor, if, for example, the puppets are large, or if the puppeteers wish to be further removed from their puppets.

Bolt all upright supports for the leaning bar, perchery and back drape on to the legs of the platforms. The horizontal rods for the back drape and perchery are supported by the same uprights. For each rod use two strong dowels joined in the centre.

Cut away the back of the operating area to allow the puppets to hang freely from the perchery.

Curtains are attached to the leaning bar and to the wings (see section on back-cloths and back-screens, page 231). A shadow screen may be incorporated in the structure below the leaning bar and covered with curtains or scenery when not required.

A portable proscenium stage

Five types of proscenium stage are illustrated (figure 48). The most elaborate will make great demands in terms of construction, weight, transport and setting-up time. The simplest stage (figure 48/1) has a proscenium, stage floor and back-cloth.

Although a bridge is not essential, it is certainly desirable. A bridge behind the backdrop (figure 48/2) raises the puppeteers and is essential in situations where the puppeteers would otherwise be visible to the audience through the proscenium opening. A deeper stage floor with a bridge, or bridges, over part of it (figures 48/3 and 48/4) is desirable; it creates a greater sense of depth than the previously mentioned stages, as the puppets no longer perform close to the back-cloth. It also permits considerably more scope for action.

These stages need to be set up on a platform, or elevated by legs incorporated in their structure (figure 48/5).

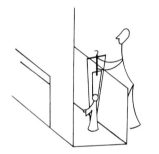

Figure 48/1 A stage with no bridge

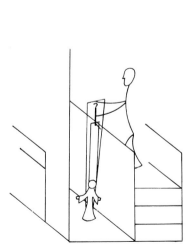

Figure 48/2 A stage with a higher back-cloth and a small bridge

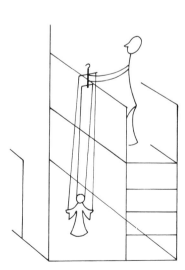

Figure 48/3 A stage with a high bridge over the stage floor

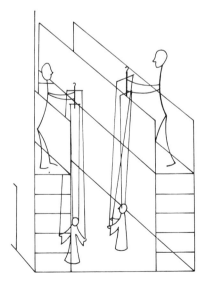

Figure 48/4 A stage with two high bridges over the stage floor: one over the proscenium opening and one over the back-cloth

221

Figure 48/5   An elevated prosce-nium stage

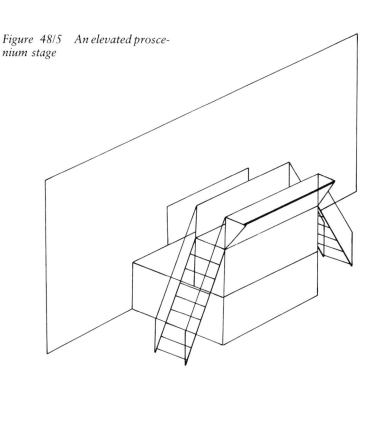

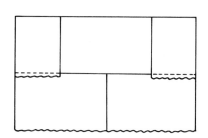

Front curtain frame

Wing support

Leaning bar

Figure 49/1   A framework for a stage without a bridge

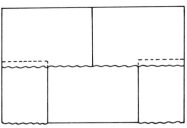

Figure 49/2   Lower curtains open for marionettes

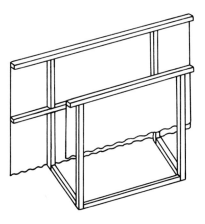

Figure 49/3   Upper curtains open for gloves, rods and shadows

Figure 49/4   A raised back-screen

222

The dimensions of stages will depend on many factors, including the size of the puppets, the needs of the performance, and the transport facilities available.

A stage without a bridge   At its simplest, this may be just a framework of timber or aluminium square tube (figure 49/1) constructed as detailed on pages 207 – 210. The front curtain frame supports two rows of curtains, the top one overlapping the lower one by a few inches.

With the lower set open, it becomes a marionette stage (figure 49/2); with the top set open, a glove or rod stage (figure 49/3). A screen fixed into the upper opening creates a shadow theatre. When used for glove and rod puppets, the leaning bar and back-screen need to be raised (figure 49/4). Wing curtains help to conceal backstage activity from the audience.

The advantage of this design is not only the flexibility for different types of puppet, but the facility to adjust the width of the acting area simply by varying the extent to which the curtains are opened. For details of curtain control, see proscenium curtains section (page 229 – 231).

Clearly, this theatre or elaborations upon it may be constructed using the staging units previously described. The aluminium tube is particularly suitable for the addition of any required features and with these even a large theatre can be reduced to a bundle or box of tubes.

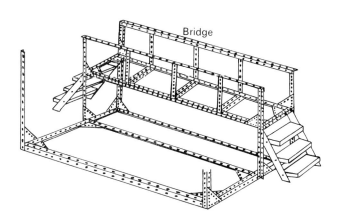

Figure 50/1   The stage floor and bridge framework built from Dexion slotted metal angle

A stage with a bridge   When a stage has a bridge it is essential that the construction of the whole framework is very strong. For this purpose 'Dexion' slotted metal angle strips are ideal.

Use Dexion also for the stage floor surround as the bridge is bolted to it. Support the bridge by four vertical lengths of Dexion. Two horizontal lengths joined at 3 ft intervals by cross pieces form the frame for the bridge floor, which is strong plywood or chipboard bolted on to the Dexion. Two more horizontal lengths form the leaning bar and back rail of the bridge (figure 50/1).

Strengthen the frame by using triangular plates, or angle struts, at the main joints. Then attach a small set of steps to each end of the bridge. (It will usually be necessary to buy these or have them made.)

It is wise to have a number of boards or metal strips bolted between the bridge floor and the upper rails to prevent anybody falling through.

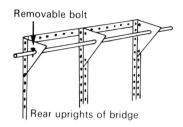

Figure 50/2 A perchery

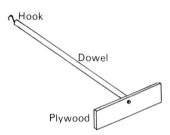

Figure 51 A clearing rod

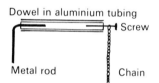

Figure 52/1 Constructing the gallows

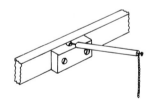

Figure 52/2 Supporting the gallows

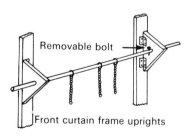

Figure 52/3 A gallows for a large stage

To make a perchery for hanging up the puppets, bolt three triangular plywood plates to the rear uprights of the bridge, one at each end and one in the centre. In each plate drill a large hole to take a strong dowel or aluminium rod, and secure the rod by a bolt at each end (figure 50/2).

If aluminium or timber staging units are to be used for an alternative construction method, the bridge and its supporting units must be strong enough to hold the considerable weight of the manipulators.

Accessories for marionette stages

A clearing rod This is a wooden 'rake' used to reach props on the stage during scene changes. It is simply a strip of plywood screwed on to one end of a dowel rod (figure 51).

A gallows for the stage Gallows are used to suspend a puppet on the stage, either if two free hands are needed to manipulate it for a special effect or if the puppet is required to be on stage but not moving.

Any form of projection with a length of chain or loop of cord will serve the purpose, but a hinged gallows is often preferred as it can be pushed out of the way when it is not needed. Two methods for constructing gallows are described; the second is better for a large stage.

1 Bend a metal rod into a right angle. Drill a hole in the end of a dowel rod, then glue one end of the metal rod and jam it tightly into the hole. To strengthen the dowel, a 'sleeve' of aluminium tubing may be glued over it. Use a screw or screw-eye to fasten a chain or cord to the other end of the dowel (figure 52/1).

Make a groove in a block of wood and screw the block to the stage wherever it is needed. The metal rod fits into, and turns in, the groove (figure 52/2). Hook the puppet's control into a link in the chain or a loop in the cord.

2 Drill a hole in each of two strong, triangular plywood plates. Hinge the plates to the staging as required. Fit the ends of a strong dowel or aluminium tube into the holes in the blocks (figure 52/3). In each end of the dowel drill a hole to accommodate a bolt (to prevent the dowel coming out of the blocks). Suspend lengths of cord or chains from the rod.

A perchery This is a rack used for hanging up the puppets during a show. A perchery attached to a stage with a bridge has been described above, but often a free-standing rack is needed.

Aluminium square tube is excellent, being light in weight, rigid and easily dismantled. Use aluminium tubing for the rails (figure 53/1). Depending on the length of the rack, intermediate supports for the rails might be needed.

A wooden rack (figure 53/2) will need cross-bracing struts bolted to the end supports.

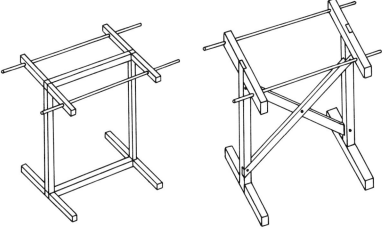

Figure 53/1 An aluminium puppet rack

Figure 53/2 A wooden rack

Figure 54 An open-stage production of The Ballad of Mr. Punch *by Alain Recoing (Théâtre aux Mains Nues), France*

Staging for mixed puppet productions

When using marionettes and other types of puppet together, an open style of performance is the simplest form of staging.

Shadow puppets may be used with three-dimensional puppets, either on the back-screen, or to the sides, above or below the main acting area. It is a very straightforward procedure to design the staging to incorporate the shadow screen, but ensure that there is room to operate the other puppets without impeding the lighting or manipulation of the shadows. Figure 55/1 illustrates a variety of possible positions for a screen. A removable screen in a proscenium arch does not allow different types of puppet to be

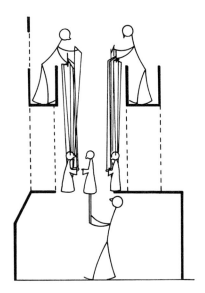

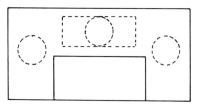

Figure 55/1 Staging for mixed puppet productions; dotted lines show possible positions for a shadow screen

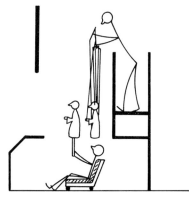

Figure 55/2 Lowering rod and glove puppet operators by seats on castors

used simultaneously; it can be introduced and removed smoothly for a particular scene but other arrangements are preferable.

The most common mixture of puppets is rods and marionettes, probably because of the similarities in their style. However, full staging for such a mix is necessarily fairly complex because rod puppets are normally held above head height and to hold marionettes at the same height will require quite a high bridge (figure 55/1). An alternative arrangement lowers the rod puppet operators by the use of foam-padded wooden seats on castors (figure 55/2) but the gains from lowering the height are at the expense of the puppeteers' freedom of movement and the loss of the depth of staging under the bridge.

It is recommended therefore that such a presentation style is used only when the needs of the performance *really* demand different types of puppet. This is usually not a viable proposition unless one has a major touring company or a fixed venue in which a permanent stage can be erected.

A permanent puppet stage

Few puppeteers are fortunate enough to have their own theatre but it has proved possible for many schools, amateurs and professionals alike to establish a permanent puppet stage in a variety of locations. Like all stage designs, this calls for compromises but a few underlying principles may be identified:

1 Make the proscenium opening quite wide: about 9 ft is ideal. The height might be up to 5 ft but sight lines will determine what is possible (figure 56/2).
2 Allow sufficient space back-stage for the performance area, the manipulators, scenery, props, and for storage. More space will be needed behind the stage than for the acting area itself.
3 Allow sufficient side space for the manoeuvring of scenery.
4 To give the greatest scope for productions, a small apron in front of the proscenium is desirable, with (curtained) arches to permit access from back-stage (figure 56/1).

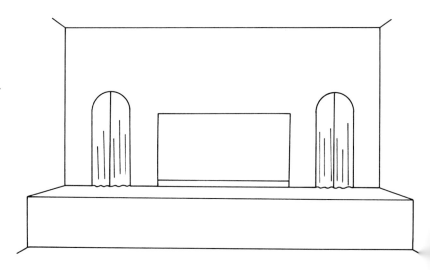

Figure 56/1 A permanent stage

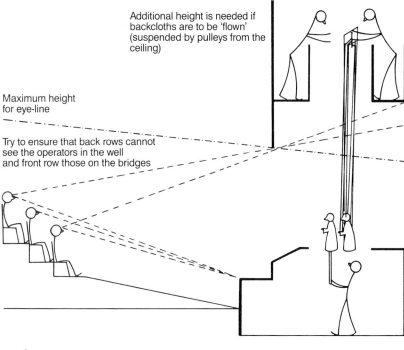

Additional height is needed if backcloths are to be 'flown' (suspended by pulleys from the ceiling)

Maximum height for eye-line

Try to ensure that back rows cannot see the operators in the well and front row those on the bridges

Figure 56/2 Sight-line considerations

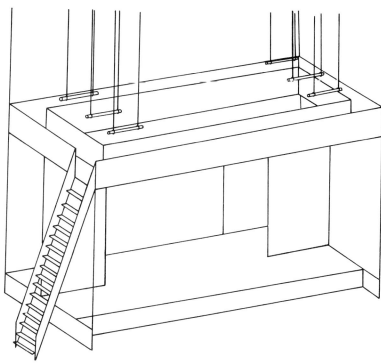

Figure 56/3 A back-stage structure

5 It is also desirable to have the facility for using all types of puppet; marionettes are operated from a bridge and gloves, rods and shadows are operated from a 'well' created by removing the stage floor (figure 56/2).

6 It is useful for the bridge to encircle the whole stage area (figure 56/3 above), allowing the use of a good depth of acting area. It must extend

227

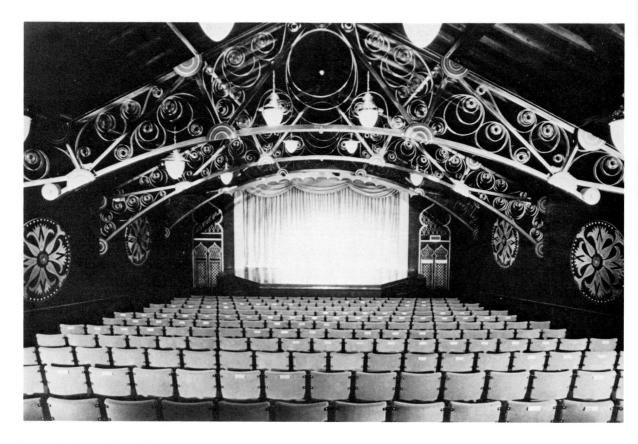

Figure 56/4 Polka Children's Theatre, London

well beyond each side of the proscenium opening to allow puppets to hang off-stage beyond the wings.

7 Tiered seating or a raked auditorium help considerably in achieving comfortable viewing.

8 Check all proposals with the Fire Safety Officer and any other relevant officials to save yourself a great deal of wasted time and expense. For public performances you will find there are even requirements for the spacing and fixing of seats, construction materials, etc.

9 Before building your own staging, try to see as many other such stages as you are able. You learn a lot by looking and asking questions.

Curtains and scenery

Drapes for the stage

Stage curtains need to be suitably lined or heavy enough to prevent light showing through, but attractive enough to enhance the staging without distracting attention from the puppets.

A richly coloured velvet is popular; crushed velvet is particularly useful for touring as creases tend not to show. However, velvet is an expensive investment for a large stage and today there are many suitable fabrics from which to choose.

With lightweight curtains, strips of Velcro tape (sewn at intervals along the curtain and glued and tacked/stapled to the framework) provide a quick and easy device for attaching them to the stage. Heavier drapes require a stronger method. *Either* use large, heavy-duty press-studs (sewn on to the curtain and tacked to the stage) *or* stitch long loops of tape to the drapes at regular intervals, take these over the framework and slip them over hooks screwed into the inside of the staging, *or* sew Rufflette tape to the curtain, gather in the drapes and then hang the Rufflette loops over hooks screwed into the framework. Sew lead curtain weights into the hems if necessary to help the way the drapes hang.

Proscenium curtains

For those stages which have a proscenium front, curtains will normally be required. Whichever of the following methods is used, attach the curtains to a batten and bolt this onto the framework in the appropriate position.

The straight curtain   Hang two curtains from a curtain wire or rail attached to a batten. They are opened and closed by two cords (nylon cord is excellent). Thread the cords through the curtain rings and over pulley wheels or hooks in the batten, as illustrated (figure 57). Tie the cords to the innermost ring (X) on each curtain. Fasten small weights on the ends of the cords to keep them taut. Pull one cord to open the curtains and the other to close them.

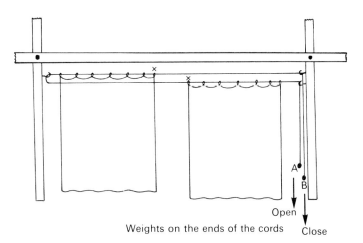

Figure 57   The straight curtain. (The curtain wire is omitted for clarity)

Weights on the ends of the cords

Open

Close

The pull-up curtain   Tack the top of the curtain to a wooden batten. Fix two screw-eyes in the top of the batten, one at each end, and tie a cord to each screw-eye. Screw three pulleys into the upper cross bar, two directly above the screw-eyes in the batten and the third wherever required to the side (figure 58). Thread the cords over the three pulleys as illustrated and knot the ends of the cords together. Pulling the cords down raises the curtain. Screw hooks into the upright support and loop the cord around the appropriate hook to keep the curtain open or closed. This type of curtain may also be used to reduce the height of the opening.

The draped curtain   This curtain is not recommended for general use as it considerably reduces the size of the proscenium opening.
    Tack the tops of the curtains to a batten so that they overlap slightly in the centre. Sew curtain rings diagonally across each drape; thread cords

229

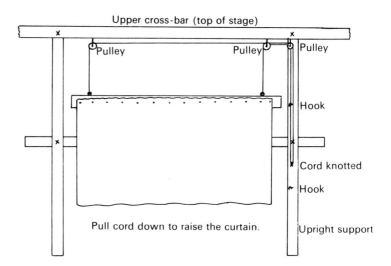

Figure 58   The pull-up curtain

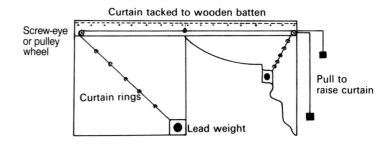

Figure 59   The draped curtain

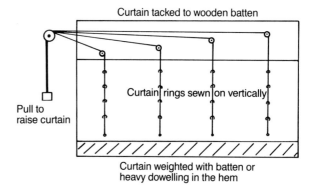

Figure 60   The drop-curtain

through the rings and tie them to the lowest ring on each drape. Thread the cords through screw-eyes or pulley wheels at each end of the batten; take one of the cords along the batten and through the other screw-eye so that both cords can be pulled together (figure 59). If necessary, weight the corners of the drapes so that they drop smoothly and quickly when the cords are released.

The drop curtain   Tack the top of the curtain to a batten. Sew about four sets of curtain rings to the curtain in vertical rows. Thread cords through the rings and tie them to the lowest ring in each row. Screw four screw-eyes or pulley wheels to the batten, thread the cords through or over these and then through/over another set at one end of the batten. Tie the cords

Figure 61/1   Pageant (or processional) opening

Figure 61/2   Archway opening

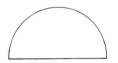

Figure 61/3   Lunette opening

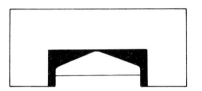

Figure 61/4   An archway drape suspended in a pageant opening

together so that when they are pulled they raise the curtain (figure 60). Weight the bottom of the curtain with a thin batten or fairly heavy dowel stitched into the hem.

Masking drapes for proscenium openings

The proscenium opening in the front curtain may be any size or shape required. The most popular shape is the 'pageant' (or 'processional') opening which is approximately twice as wide as it is high (figure 61/1). This is the best all-purpose shape.

'Lunette' (figure 61/2) and 'archway' (figure 61/3) openings are not common but, when necessary, a drape with one of these openings may be suspended on a batten to mask the pageant opening. Usually the masking drape is suspended just inside the proscenium opening (figure 61/4) but it may be fixed further back, so dividing the stage area. This latter method restricts movement of marionettes on the stage but may be desirable for a particular effect.

Back-cloths and back-screens

Whilst you will want to make the sets appealing, take care not to make them too bright or they will be distracting and will obscure the visibility of the puppets.

The effectiveness of many designs for puppet theatre lies in their simplicity. This is clearly illustrated in figure 62/1. The scenery in figure 62/2 is turned and moved to music, almost like puppets themselves, to create changes of scene, with a sky- cloth behind illuminated in a variety of colours.

A solid back-screen   Some types of staging for glove and rod puppets will have a solid back-screen with cut-out shapes for entrances and exits and possibly windows (figure 39/5). The shape and finish is often neutral so that it may represent all manner of settings, sometimes with a little extra decoration added to establish particular scenes.

The openings of 'doors' and 'windows' are usually covered by small curtains attached to the back of the board and split down the centre to permit easy access whilst hiding any back-stage activity.

Figure 62/1   Simple but effective scenery for 'Winter' in What the Four Seasons Are Talking About *by the Pinokio Theatre, Poland*

Figure 62/2 A set from the Leningrad Bolshoi Puppet Theatre production of The Fairy Story of Emilio

Figure 62/3 A batik back-cloth

232

Figure 62/4 A scene from The Fair Maguelone *by the Theatre of Puppets*

Plain drapes   Similarly, for all types of three-dimensional puppet, a plain, draped curtain serves a multitude of purposes. A fairly dark, neutral colour is usually preferred. Some performers have three or four sets of drapes in different colours which they open and close as the occasion demands.

Painted scenery   Background scenery may also be painted on plywood, hardboard or fabric (unbleached calico is recommended).

Collage scenery   A collage (material picture) can be effective, too. Use a large piece of fabric, such as an old curtain, as the base and glue or stitch the materials on to it.

Dyed fabric scenery   Fabric dyes are useful for creating a scene on white cotton sheeting. They may be painted or sponged on, either allowing them to run into each other slightly or picking out fine outlines with hot wax to keep the dyes apart. The batik process (figure 62/3) is particularly suitable for puppet theatre too:

1   Heat the wax and paint it onto all parts of the cotton that are to remain white.
2   Soak the material in a cold water dye of a chosen colour x, in accordance with the manufacturer's instructions.
3   Rinse the fabric and hang it to dry. Then apply the wax to all those parts to remain colour x, and dye the fabric colour y.
4   Repeat the process as before, continuing for all colours required. The ordering of the colours is clearly important; start with the lightest, taking into account the effect of each colour on the previous colours and vice versa.
5   Finally, boil the wax out of the material.

Relief sculptured or modelled scenery   Back-screens modelled or sculpted in relief (figure 62/4) can be very effective. One method is to establish the shape in polystyrene on a plywood base and cover it with paper and PVA glue or with stockinette. Soak the stockinette first in hot water and then in

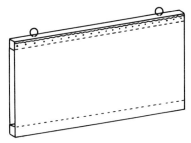

Figure 63 Background scenery hung by screw-eyes

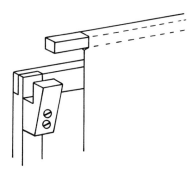

Figure 64/1 A wooden bracket to hold the back-cloth

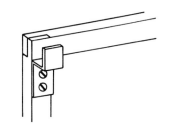

Figure 64/2 A metal bracket to hold the back-cloth

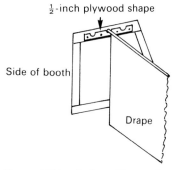

½-inch plywood shape

Side of booth

Drape

Figure 65/1 A slotted batten for suspending back-drapes

carpenter's pearl glue; squeeze out the majority of the glue and spread the fabric over the back-scene, pressing it carefully into the modelling. When dry it will be quite stiff and strong.

Alternatively, use one of the modelling materials described in Chapter 6, building onto a lightweight base of balsa wood, polystyrene, cardboard boxes, or a frame of chicken-wire, as appropriate.

Attaching background scenery

A hanging back-cloth *Either* tack the top and bottom of the back-cloth to two wooden battens *or* slip the battens into wide hems. There are a variety of ways of attaching this to the main framework:
1 Large screw-eyes in the top of the batten are used to suspend it from the framework (figure 63).
2 The top batten is extended at each end to fit into wooden brackets cut to the shape illustrated (figure 64/1); these brackets are screwed to the stage. An alternative bracket may be made from strong metal (figure 64/2).
3 A slotted batten may be attached to the sides of the stage to hold a series of scenery battens (figure 65/1). The same technique may be used for attaching solid scenery sections (figure 65/2).

Roll-up back-cloths The following technique is useful for raising and lowering back-cloths painted on calico.

Tack the bottom of the back-cloth to a thick dowel which is used as a roller. Roll up the scene around the dowel, then attach a strong cord to each end of the roller. Thread the cords over pulleys screwed into the batten. When the cords are released, the roller is lowered and the cords wind around each end of it (figure 66). Pulling the cords causes them to unwind and the roller to roll up.

Projected scenery

A translucent screen is used instead of the usual back-screen so that a scene or non-naturalistic images can be projected on to the screen from behind the booth. A rear-projection screen or a suitable alternative, such as shower-cloth, is recommended.

Arrange the stage lighting so that no strong light falls directly on to the screen. Projection techniques are described in Chapter 13. This method allows the setting to be changed as often as desired. It is not possible to use it for marionettes unless the operators work from a bridge, or they would obscure the path of the projected image.

Gauze

Theatrical gauze suspended across the stage is used for special effects. If it is illuminated from the front with the lights to the sides, not shining directly on to the gauze, any scene painted on it is visible to the audience whilst objects and scenery behind are invisible. If lighting is introduced behind the gauze instead of in front, the scene previously invisible becomes visible and the scene on the gauze will disappear. This technique is particularly effective for taking the audience within a building, or for a dream sequence.

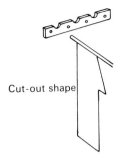

Cut-out shape

Figure 65/2   A slotted batten supporting solid scenery sections

Figure 66   (Right) A roll-up backcloth

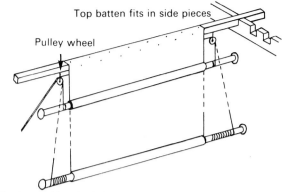

Top batten fits in side pieces

Pulley wheel

As the cord is raised, it unwinds, but winds up the scenery.
As the roll unwinds, the cord winds around the dowel

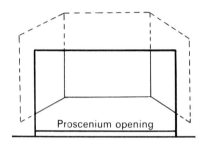

Proscenium opening

Figure 67   An inset

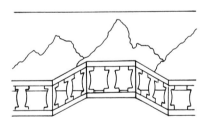

Figure 68   A screen set

Other types of scenery

An inset is used to screen off part of the stage (figure 67). This may be made in the same way as staging units or from plywood, hardboard or even strong card (for improvised stages), hinged by strips of strong linen glued along the edges. It can be folded up for packing.

Screen sets are more elaborate than insets. They are flat, cut-out shapes made into a three-dimensional background (figure 68). Finishing them in light relief adds considerably to their effectiveness. Hang a back-cloth behind the screen set. It is usually convenient for this to be a fairly generalised scene of sky, distant hills, and so on.

Plywood cut-out scenery, finished in light relief if desired, can be attached quickly and easily by cutting in the board inverted keyhole shapes which fit over the heads of large screws in the framework (figure 69). This, too requires a back-cloth or sky-cloth behind it.

Three-dimensional scenery is usually too troublesome for the travelling entertainer but it is ideal for any group with a permanent base in which to work. It may be made from plywood, polystyrene, corrugated or smooth card, or even cardboard boxes. Basic shapes can be enhanced by the use of a modelling material described in Chapter 6. Ensure that the scenery has a firm base or supporting structure so that it cannot be knocked over.

With the exception of the cut-out plywood scenery, the techniques described above are more common for marionettes, because of the complexities of supporting the scenery in a booth. For free-standing

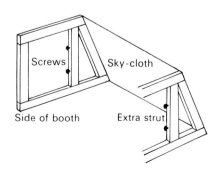

Screws   Sky-cloth

Side of booth   Extra strut

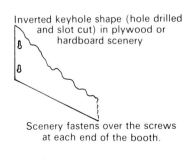

Inverted keyhole shape (hole drilled and slot cut) in plywood or hardboard scenery

Scenery fastens over the screws at each end of the booth.

Figure 69   Supporting cut-out background scenery

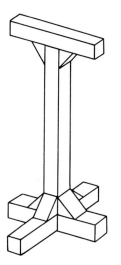

Figure 70   A purpose-built stand to hold scenery

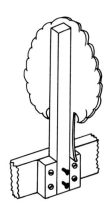

Figure 71   Scenery bolted to the stage

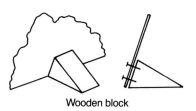

Wooden block

Figure 72   Cardboard scenery nailed or pinned to a wooden block

Wing-nut and bolt

Cut-out scenery screwed to wooden block

Playboard

Clamp

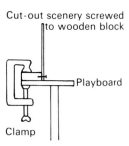

Figure 73   Scenery clamped or bolted to the playboard

scenery in a booth, telescopic lighting stands or purpose-built structures (figure 70) are used but these must be fairly heavy and very stable or held firmly by stage weights.

Cut-out scenery pieces may be screwed to a batten which bolts onto the stage. Wooden blocks may be screwed to the framework, if necessary, to help to steady the batten (figure 71).

Free-standing scenery may be attached to a board base to steady it, or screwed to a fairly heavy wedge (figure 72) and held further with a weight if necessary.

In a booth for glove or rod puppets the scenery may be glued and tacked/screwed to a block of wood which is then bolted or clamped to the frame or the playboard (figure 73).

A scenery slot   Scenery cut from plywood, or strong card, may be attached to the front or sides of any booth, and the following procedure can be followed.

Cut out the plywood shapes, leaving a strip projecting downwards to fit into a slot in the booth (figure 74). Cardboard shapes should be tacked to a strip of plywood.

Glue and screw three strips of plywood to the frame of the booth, as illustrated, to create the slot. (The top side piece of the frame must be cut away to accommodate the extra blocks of wood when the sections are folded up.) Insert the scenery tag in the slot and drill a hole through the plywood, the tag and the framework. Insert a dowel peg into the hole to secure the scenery in place. Attach the dowel to the frame with screw-eyes and thread.

The same technique is used to attach a 'scenery groundrow' to the front of a booth (figure 75). Similarly, a scenery slot may be constructed in cardboard for use in a simple booth improvised from a cardboard box.

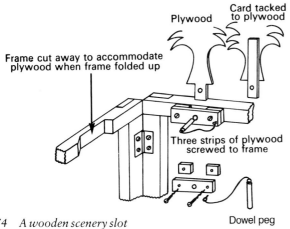

Plywood

Card tacked to plywood

Frame cut away to accommodate plywood when frame folded up

Three strips of plywood screwed to frame

Dowel peg

Figure 74   A wooden scenery slot

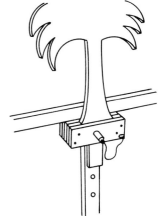

Figure 75   A scenery groundrow

A sliding slot for scenery   This technique permits small items of scenery in a booth to be introduced smoothly during a performance, without the puppeteer's hands being seen.

The 'slide' is a strip of plywood attached vertically to the main frame (figure 76/1) and the 'sliding slot' which holds the scenery consists of four small pieces of plywood glued between three plywood strips (figures 76/2 and 76/3), thus forming two slots.

The vertical slide fits into one slot and the scenery tag into the other. Insert the scenery, raise the slot to the top of the slide and drill a hole through the entire assembly to accommodate a dowel peg which is used to secure the scenery in place (figure 76/4) as described previously.

A series of holes in the slide will permit the scenery to be held at a variety of heights.

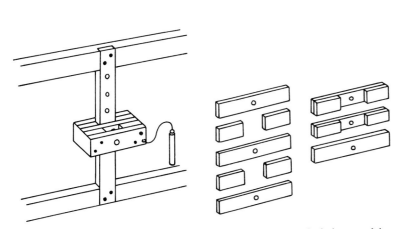

Figure 76/1   A sliding slot for scenery

Figure 76/2   Exploded view of the sliding slot

Figure 76/3   Spacers glued between the main strips

Figure 76/4   Scenery secured in the slot

Fastening props   Many of the props used in puppet theatre need temporarily to be held fairly securely in place; with marionettes, this usually means simply weighting these items sufficiently, but with rod and glove puppets there is a very real danger of them falling off the playboard.

237

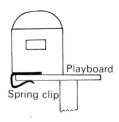

*Figure 77 The use of a spring-clip
to hold properties on the playboard*

To avoid this, some such device as a spring clip may be built into the bottom of the object (figure 77) or a projection on the bottom may be held in place by a large bulldog clip. Properties moved on rods will stand on a slotted playboard (figure 41/2, page 216). 'Velcro', the fastening tape, is useful for some purposes. Simply glue securely one piece to the bottom of the object and another to the staging. Press the pieces of tape together to secure it and pull them apart when required.

Staging for shadow puppets

For descriptions of flexible staging which can be adapted to different purposes see the proscenium booth (page 219) and the portable proscenium stage (page 221). For staging in which shadows and other puppets can be used together, see the open booth (page 214), the elaborate open fit-up (page 220) and staging for mixed puppet productions (page 225).

When not in use, shadow puppets are normally placed on tables to the sides of the operating area or on a table-top below the screen (provided the puppets are not operated vertically).

Puppets with fixed, horizontal controls are rested with the rods on the table and the figures over the edge, to avoid bending and other damage (figure 78). All other types may be placed flat on the table.

The screen   The screen may be made from any semi-opaque material. A piece of white cotton or polyester/cotton sheeting is the most common and is quite satisfactory.

Greaseproof paper may be used, but there is the danger of it tearing. Lotte Reiniger* recommends the use of a Cinemoid acetate called 'frost', used with the matt surface towards the audience. Some professional shadow-play performers use architects' tracing linen for their screens, or even a suitable shower-cloth. Occasionally a textured fabric is used to create a particular effect in keeping with the style of the performance.

Whichever material is used, the screen must be taut; if it sags or wrinkles it will spoil the performance.

For the shape of the screen, see section on scenery (page 244).

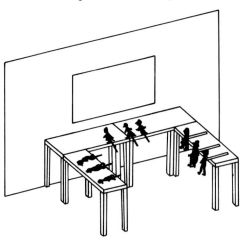

*Figure 78 Back-stage arrangement
for shadows*

Shadow theatres and shadow films (Batsford, 1970)

238

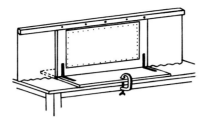

Figure 79   A picture-frame shadow screen

Improvised shadow theatres

Puppet stages improvised from a classroom shop or a clothes-horse, and which incorporate shadow screens, have been detailed on pages 203 and 206. Examples of other possibilities are described below.

1 Pin or staple the cotton screen to a picture frame. This is attached to a wooden base by means of two metal brackets (figure 79). If side curtains are required, screw a supporting wooden batten to the top of the frame.

2 If there is some fixture in the room (e.g. metal beams in a classroom) from which the screen can be suspended, fasten safety pins at the top corners and tie cords to these. Stitch, or pin, a masking curtain to the bottom of the screen to hide the operators.

   Further cords attached to the sides of the screen can be tied to tables or other heavy furniture or fixtures to keep the screen taut (figure 80).

3 The screen can be fixed between two legs of an upturned table but this is rather limiting as the other legs impede the movement of the manipulators (figure 81).

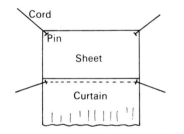

Figure 80   A screen suspended from architectural fixtures

Figure 81   A screen fixed to an up-turned table

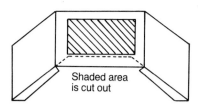

Figure 82/1 The basic cardboard shadow theatre

Figure 82/2 Decorative top-piece added

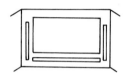

Figure 82/3 Spacing strips glued around the screen

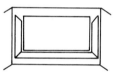

Figure 82/4 Scenery holders glued on

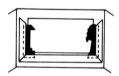

Figure 82/5 Scenery held in the scenery pocket

A cardboard table-top theatre

The basic frame is made by cutting off the top and one side of a cardboard box. Cut the hole for the screen in the centre section (figure 82/1), leaving plenty of space between the bottom of the screen and the bottom of the box. Fasten the screen over the inside of the hole using glue or masking tape, stretching the fabric taut so that it does not sag or wrinkle.

From the side removed, cut a decorative top-piece to hide the operator(s) and glue this to the frame (figure 82/2). Alternatively, if the stage is to be used for other types of puppet too, attach the top-piece by means of scenery slots (see page 207).

Items of scenery are held in a scenery pocket. This is created by gluing to the frame three thin cardboard strips as spacers (figure 82/3) and then three wide strips (figure 82/4) to form slots into which the scenery fits (figure 82/5).

This shadow theatre is best used with figures operated from behind, because of the limited space below the screen. However, a theatre may be made in the same way from a very large box which stands on the floor and which can be used for any form of operation.

A wooden table-top theatre

This theatre is made on the same principles as the improvised picture-frame theatre described above (figure 79). It is portable, easily stored, quickly assembled and dismantled, sturdy and steady without protruding struts to impede the manipulators. It also is flexible enough to use with all types of puppet.

The dimensions will depend on your transport and storage facilities and the number of operators to be accommodated but the minimum dimensions recommended for the screen itself are 42 in wide by 27 in high, to allow reasonable scope for the performance.

Use 2 in × 1 in timber (i.e. 1¾ in × ¾ in planed), ¼ in plywood and ¾ in chipboard. Figure 83/1 shows an exploded view of all the parts.

The base is made by gluing and screwing two lengths of timber to the chipboard (figure 83/2), taking care to countersink the holes for the screw-heads. Ensure that the timber is appropriately spaced to hold the frame securely (use another length of timber as a spacer during construction).

The frame consists of four lengths of timber, glued and screwed together with half-lap joints (figure 83/3). Take care to maintain the right angles at the corners. Glue and screw plywood strips to each side of the frame at the top (figure 83/4) to hold the curtain rail, having cut a slot in the rear plywood strip, as illustrated, to accommodate the hinge in the rail. A coping saw is a useful tool for this. If the frame does not fit snugly into the base, secure it with bolts and wing nuts (figure 83/4).

Place another length of timber on top of the base piece to form a lower cross-bar (figure 83/4). Drill holes through the ends of the bar and the two uprights, then secure the cross-bar to the frame with bolts and wing nuts. This lower cross-bar forms a fixture for the bottom of the shadow screen which is secured with drawing pins (thumb-tacks) to the top and sides of the frame, passes under the lower cross-bar and is pinned to the side facing the operator (figure 83/5). This helps to keep the screen taut, provides a

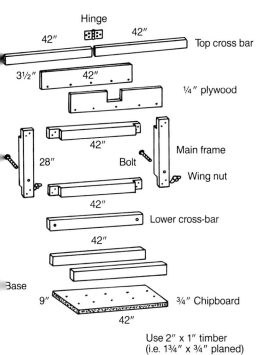

Hinge

42″ · 42″ — Top cross bar

3½″ · 42″ — ¼″ plywood

42″ — Main frame

28″ · Bolt

Wing nut

42″ — Lower cross-bar

42″

Base

9″ · 42″ — ¾″ Chipboard

Use 2″ x 1″ timber
(i.e. 1¾″ x ¾″ planed)

Figure 83/1 Exploded view of the table-top puppet theatre

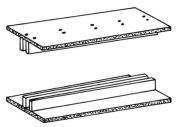

Figure 83/2 The base of the theatre

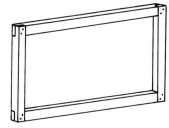

Figure 83/3 The frame for the screen

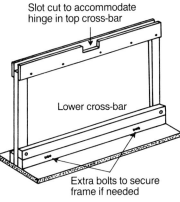

Slot cut to accommodate hinge in top cross-bar

Lower cross-bar

Extra bolts to secure frame if needed

Figure 83/4 Attaching the lower cross-bar and the plywood strips for the curtain rail

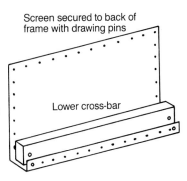

Screen secured to back of frame with drawing pins

Lower cross-bar

Figure 83/5 Securing the screen to the lower cross-bar

Figure 83/6 The lower cross-bar holds scenery and provides a ledge on which puppets can walk

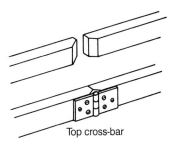

Top cross-bar

Figure 83/7 A hinged curtain rail

Figure 83/8 The theatre assembled

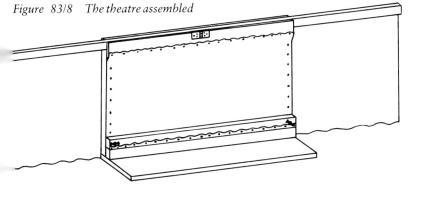

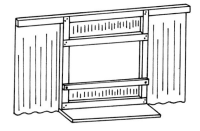

Figure 83/9 A variation on the basic design

241

ledge on which the shadow puppets may walk (figure 83/6) and the gap between the screen and the cross-bar creates a slot for holding scenery. The cross-bar can be unbolted and the screen rolled up for storage or transporting if necessary.

The top cross-bar is two lengths of timber, joined with a strong hinge (figure 83/7). Shave a little off the joining edges of the timbers as illustrated to accommodate the hinge, and keep them carefully in line and the edges tightly together when fixing the hinge. The cross-bar drops into the plywood slot on the top of the frame (figure 83/8). Curtains are suspended from it by means of a curtain wire held by screw-eyes and supported at intervals by small hooks.

Closing the curtains permits the theatre to be used as a screen for glove and rod puppets or as an open stage for marionettes. If the theatre needs to be clamped to a table-top for extra stability, ensure the table is suitably protected.

Many variations on this basic design are possible. A design for a slightly larger theatre with more space above and below the screen is illustrated as an example (figure 83/9).

A large shadow theatre

A free-standing theatre may be designed in a variety of shapes from a very basic large screen with surrounding curtains (figure 84/1) to a multi-screen theatre (figure 84/2). Always ensure there are sufficient masking screens to prevent the audience seeing back-stage activity.

Figure 84/1 A large shadow theatre

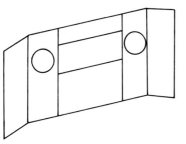

Figure 84/2 A multi-screen shadow theatre

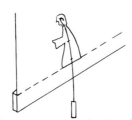

Screen on operator's side of frame

Figure 84/3 Figures operated from below: screen on operator's side of frame

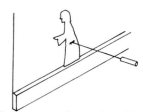

Screen on audience side of frame

Figure 84/4 Figures operated from behind: screen on audience-side of frame

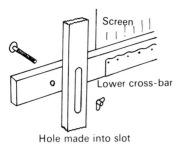

Screen

Lower cross-bar

Hole made into slot

Figure 84/5 An adjustable screen

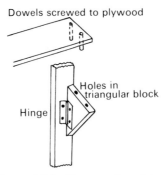

Dowels screwed to plywood

Holes in triangular block

Hinge

Figure 84/6 Construction of the ledge

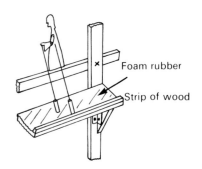

Foam rubber

Strip of wood

Figure 84/7 Holding the controls securely

Figure 85 The Story of Jacko *by Polka Children's Theatre*

The theatre may be constructed from timber or aluminium square tube, or may be based on staging units, in accordance with the techniques described for three-dimensional puppets (pages 207 – 212).

If the puppets are to be operated from below, attach the screen to the operator's side of the framework so that the puppets and scenery may be held flat against the screen (figure 84/3). If they are to be operated from behind, attach the screen to the audience side of the frame so that the lower cross-bar provides a ledge upon which the puppets can walk (figure 84/4).

Ensure that the stage drapes do not let the shadows of the performers show through or the audience will be distracted. Attach them as described on pages 228 – 229.

Adjusting the tension of the screen   This small modification is not essential but may be desirable. It involves making the lower cross-bar adjustable.

Make the hole in the vertical post into a slot to allow the bolt in the lower cross-bar to slide (figure 84/5). (Drill a series of close holes in a straight line and file out the waste.) To increase the tension of the screen, lower the cross-bar and tighten the bolts.

A ledge for characters in repose   If the puppets are operated from behind, the fit-up may have a ledge on which to rest the controls of the characters 'in repose' on the screen whilst the others are manipulated.

Make the ledge from a strip of plywood, to each end of which are screwed two short dowels (figure 84/6). The ledge rests on two triangular blocks of wood which are hinged to the vertical posts below screen level. Drill two holes in the top of each block to accommodate the dowels (figure 84/6).

Figure 86 A masking shape used with the screen

Cover the ledge with thick felt, foam rubber, or a comparable material, so that the controls do not slide about. In order to prevent the control rods slipping off the ledge, glue and nail a narrow wooden batten to the outside edge of the ledge (figure 84/7).

Scenery

Scenery for the shadow theatre need not be elaborate: beautiful scenes can be achieved by simple means. Often, as with other aspects of puppet theatre, a mere suggestion will evoke an idea. Something simple can be just as effective as, or even more effective than, elaborate scenery.

Remember that figures cannot cast a shadow if they stand in front of scenery (unless the scenery is translucent) so every piece of scenery cuts down the acting area.

The shape of the screen is the first consideration when setting the scene. With the basic shape of a large rectangle, a masking shape can be fastened against the screen to establish any other shape required (figure 86). It may be a material drape, a cardboard cut-out, a thin sheet of plywood or even a coloured sheet of translucent acetate.

The projection units described in Chapter 13 allow any shape to be established, or even changed during a performance, without the need to carry large items of scenery. These also permit textured surfaces or lighting effects to be created across the entire screen.

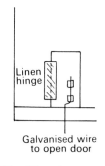

Figure 87 Hinged scenery

Constructing scenery Solid black scenery is best made from stiff card. For texture or colour, use one of the methods described for shadow puppet construction (pages 166 and 170–172).

Some parts of the scenery, such as doors, may be fixed with linen hinges (glued on) so that it is possible to open and close them. Tape a small piece of galvanised wire to the moving part so that it can be opened and closed easily (figure 87).

If the puppet is required to walk on parts of the scenery, it is useful to glue and tack wooden blocks on to the back of the cut-out scene to provide a surface (figure 88).

To create a greater feeling of depth in the scene, a horizon piece may be used (figure 89/1). Most of the action will take place below this line although smaller figures may be used above it for action in the distance. Another effective technique to achieve depth is the use of multiple layers of tissue paper. These are cut to required shapes and overlapped to produce a variety of intensities of colour or, using white, shades ranging from white to dark grey (figure 89/2).

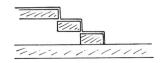

Figure 88 Blocks of wood glued on to scenery for puppets to walk on

Securing scenery to the screen Simple techniques for holding scenery in place are by means of drawing-pins, paper clips or bulldog clips (figure 90/1), suspending it on a thread (figure 90/2), or the use of double-sided adhesive tape (or a loop of masking tape) pressed onto the scenery and against the screen. There will be different requirements for figures operated horizontally and vertically.

1 Figures operated horizontally: built-in scenery slots, using the space between the screen and the framework, have been described above. If this is not satisfactory for your purposes, a more substantial scenery slot may be created by gluing or screwing a length of wood to the lower

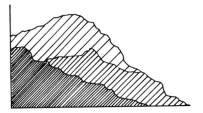

Figure 89/1 A scene from The Wooden Soldier *by the author, which makes use of an horizon piece*

Figure 89/2 Multiple layers of tissue paper help to achieve a sense of depth

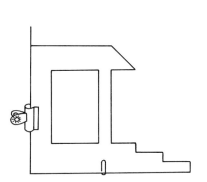

Figure 90/1 Scenery held by clips

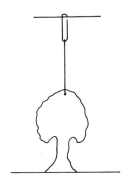

Figure 90/2 Scenery suspended by thread

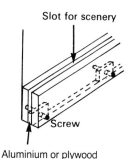

Slot for scenery

Screw

Aluminium or plywood

Figure 91/1 Operation from behind: the slot for scenery

cross-bar, with suitable plywood or aluminium spacers between them (figure 91/1). To the back of the scenery glue a stepped strip of aluminium or a block of wood and strip of plywood (figure 91/2). This fits snugly into the slot and holds the scenery firmly against the screen. A similar arrangement at the top of the screen may be necessary for large items of scenery.

2 Figures operated vertically: the arrangement described above is not satisfactory with figures operated from below as it prevents the puppets from being held against the screen. The type of scenery pocket described for a cardboard table-top theatre allows vertical operation.

Alternatively, glue button magnets into holes drilled in the lower cross-bar. Fix the screen on the operator's side of the framework with the screen stretched across the magnets. Screw a series of hooks into the top cross-bar. Sew small curtain rings to the top of the scenery; these hang from the hooks. Glue strips of metal (e.g. tin) to the bottom of the scenery; these are held by the magnets (figure 92).

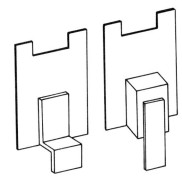

Figure 91/2 Stepped strip of aluminium glued to scenery or to block of wood on back of scenery

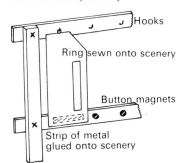

Hooks

Ring sewn onto scenery

Button magnets

Strip of metal glued onto scenery

Figure 92 Securing scenery for operation from below

13 Lighting and sound

Lighting equipment

Most puppeteers use some form of artificial lighting to create atmosphere, enhance modelling and focus the audience's attention. Recent developments, the availability of small, economical home lighting units and the increased awareness of safety make home-made lighting unnecessary and unacceptable. One purpose-built lighting unit is described here, but this should be undertaken by a suitably qualified person.

The lighting equipment most useful for puppeteers is described below, but do compare prices, check the availability of accessories and ensure that the units you select meet your particular needs. There is a lighting system to suit every budget. In order to help the reader determine which is appropriate for him, guideline prices (inclusive of tax) are quoted. These will inevitably date but provide a means of comparison.

Note 1: Each of the professional lights described here has a tilting fork which allows the lantern to be adjusted to many positions and there is a variety of mounting devices which allow it to be attached to a ceiling, wall, metal pipe, telescopic stand or part of the stage.

Note 2: There are larger, more powerful and more expensive versions of most of the lights described, but these are usually not suitable for the needs and resources of puppet companies. Further information may be obtained from the companies (see Appendices).

Spotlights

Economy-priced units: (Price £6 to £20 including fitment)
Ordinary light bulbs are not generally suitable as the light emitted is not usually adequate, nor directional, and they often create considerable glare. Reflector spotlights are preferable. These may be held in a photographic reflector (figure 1), display lighting fitments (figure 2), or in home lighting units (figure 3).

The type of bulb shown in figure 3 is a reflector spotlight, commonly found in 60 watt or 100 watt ratings. It is not a photographic lamp, is available in a range of colours and lasts for a considerable time, providing good, clear lighting. Figure 2 shows a sealed-beam reflector spotlight (100 watt or 150 watt) which is powerful with very efficient built-in reflectors. It is sturdy and needs no separate reflector.

A variety of colours is available for each of these bulbs and some can be found in quite small sizes. The wide range of fitments now available allows you to select whichever will suit your staging needs.

Profile spotlight: 250/500/650 watt (Prices £65 to £180)
The profile spotlight is excellent for all types of open stage performance,

Figure 1   A Photax Interfit reflector with a non-focusing lamp-holder and clip-on frame

Figure 2   An Attralux spotlight (sealed beam reflector) with the fitment adapted to fit onto an aluminium tube

Figure 3   A clip-on spotlight fitment

Figure 4   The CCT Minuette TT profile spotlight

Figure 5   The Rank Strand Harmony 15/28 variable spread profile spotlight

for a front-of-house spotlight (i.e. one placed in the auditorium) with proscenium theatres, and for shadow play. It may also be used for side lighting within very large marionette theatres, provided that the lamp is not too powerful.

By the very nature of the lens configuration for a profile spotlight, these will be longer units than, for example, comparable fresnels or prism convex lanterns, and the flexibility of these latter types may make them much more satisfactory than profile spotlights for use *inside* a puppet stage.

Among the accessories that can be used with the spotlight are colour filters, a colour wheel and an iris diaphragm mask which gives a variable circular beam. Built-in shutters permit the beam to be shaped.

The profile spotlight illustrated (figure 4) is one of the cheapest models in the range and is particularly useful in that one can sharpen or soften the edges of the beam, and an interchangeable lens system allows the angle of the beam to be varied between 26° and 46°. The throw of this sort of light would be around 9 metres (c. 30 feet).

The next step up in more sophisticated lights (figure 5) starts at about three times the price but might be a good investment for a major front-of-house spotlight.

Follow spots: 150 watt upwards (Prices £265 to £1,000)
These lamps, for projecting a spot to follow a character on stage, are normally not necessary for puppet theatre work. They also tend to be very heavy, far too powerful and very expensive. However, the model illustrated (figure 6) is a small version which may be useful and is more modestly priced. Like most follow-spots, it has built-in iris, colour magazine and dimming facility.

Pebble convex and prism convex lamps: 250 watt–650 watt (Price £60 to £70)
These lamps (figures 7 and 8) provide a useful compromise between the profile spotlight and the fresnels described below. They avoid the filament projection that one gets when working at close range with a profile and the flare around the edge that one gets with a fresnel.

The angle of the beam is usually variable from about 10° to 60°, making this a very useful compact lamp for puppet theatre work.

Figure 6   The CCT Minuette follow spot

Figure 7   The CCT Minuette M650 pebble convex lantern

247

Figure 8   The Rank Strand Minim PC 500/250w prism convex lantern

Figure 9   The Rank Strand Minim F fresnel 500/250w lantern

Fresnels: 250 – 650 watts (Price £60 to £70)

Fresnel spotlights (figures 9 and 10) have a soft-edge circular beam, the spread of which may be varied (by means of a sliding knob) from a near-parallel beam to a medium angle flood. Thus, they are versatile lights which can be used with colour filters and are recommended for side lighting within a fit-up as the light is easier than that of a profile spotlight to blend on the stage.

Rotatable barn-door attachments (figure 10) may be added to shape the beam but do check that the lantern you choose can be used with barn-doors and colour filters *simultaneously*; those that cannot are not suitable for puppet theatre.

Floodlights

Economy-priced reflector floodlights: 150 watt (Price £6 to £20 including fitment)

Reflector floodlights (figure 11) are the flood equivalent of reflector spotlights. They are not generally used for open-stage performances as they give too great a spread of light but they may be used for floodlighting within a fit-up and for shadow play.

They use the same sorts of home or display lighting fitments as described for reflector spotlights.

Floodlight: 200 – 500 watt (Price c. £55)

This professional floodlight (figure 12) has a wide-angle, evenly distributed beam and can be used with or without colour filters. The light is useful within larger proscenium stages: two or three floodlights provide an ideal wash of light over the acting area to consolidate the spotlighting. In this respect they are preferable to batten lights as each lamp can be directed individually, but they do tend to need to be placed 4 – 5 feet away from the area they illuminate.

The disadvantage with floodlights is that they tend to illuminate too large an area for puppet theatre use. The model illustrated can be used with a barn-door attachment to provide some control over the spread of light, but not all makes have this facility.

Figure 10   A CCT Minuette M650 fresnel with barn door attachment

Figure 11   A reflector floodlight

Figure 12   The Rank Strand Coda 500/1 floodlight (200-500w)

248

A hook clamp (with a safety chain) is generally the most useful method for mounting floodlights; the hook clamps on to a metal pipe. However, most of the mounting fixtures for spotlights can be used with this lantern too.

Compartment floodlighting: (Price 3-light batten, c. £140; 4-light batten, c. £180)
These are battens of floodlights for overhead lighting (figure 13); they are usually obtainable in 3 compartment and 4 compartment lengths. Each compartment has a 200-500 watt bulb and a separate colour filter. Each batten has two hangers for attaching to a metal pipe or other suitable fixture.

These battens may be used over the proscenium arch in a large marionette theatre or for overhead lighting (where possible) with open-stage glove or rod puppet performances. However, the battens tend to be rather large and heavy for puppet theatres and individual floodlights are generally more satisfactory.

Striplights

Non-fluorescent striplights: 60 – 70 watt (Price inc. fitment c. £5.00)
These are tubular lights, about 12 in long (figure 14) and intended for household use, generally within units. They are useful to the puppeteer as footlights and for special effects, such as the illumination of a sky cloth.

Figure 13   The Rank Strand Coda 500/4 compartment floodlight (200-500w)

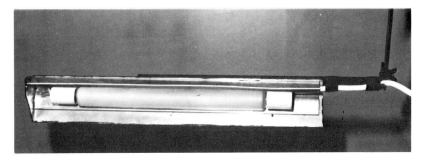

Figure 14   A striplight held in a fitment made to fit onto the side of the stage

Striplights have special fitments which may be screwed into any type of home-made light box, a well in the stage floor or on to any part of the stage. Often it will be found desirable to have runners on the box for colour filters.

Fluorescent tubes are not suitable for this type of use.

Fluorescent striplights: 36 watt (Price incl. fitment from c. £6)

Fluorescent tubes, while not suitable for normal stage lighting, provide a very good diffused light which is ideal for many types of shadow play as the control rods do not show on the screen. They are available in various lengths.

With the fitment securely attached to a base board to hold it steady, it is particularly useful to stand it on a table top for children's shadow play as the tube does not get hot.

Projectors

A projector can provide excellent lighting for shadow play and for the rear projection of scenery and other images for all types of puppet. It does impose constraints on the performers' movements, the method of operation and stage design as sufficient distance between the projector and the screen is required and this area obviously must be kept clear. The projector must also be positioned facing straight on to the screen or the image will be distorted. Projectors are not suitable for general stage lighting as the light is too harsh.

To avoid the image of a scene or slide change, use two projectors linked to a dimmer desk with a cross-fade facility. It is then possible to dissolve from one scene to the next and move each projector onto the next slide or scene whilst it is not projecting. This also permits the superimposition of images.

Overhead projectors: (Price from c. £110 to £460)

These units have become increasingly slimline and portable recently. They give a crisp light and allow silhouettes of scenery, or images on transparencies, to be projected onto a screen.

The transparencies are coloured with suitable felt pens, glass painting colours or shapes cut from transparent, self-adhesive film (e.g. Letrafilm). For silhouette effects, textured materials and cardboard cut-outs may be used or you can paint on the acetate with quick-drying black enamel. Coloured acetate sheets can be used to cover the entire area and non-naturalistic images can be achieved by standing perspex or glass objects (e.g. drinking glasses or ashtrays) on the projector or by moving them out of focus. With ingenuity a variety of effects can be achieved.

To keep transparencies flat on the projector, mount them in cardboard frames. Some overhead projectors have an attached acetate roll which can be wound on so that the image or scene moves across the screen. It is possible to create the sensation of a figure walking some distance whilst actually remaining centre-stage but it is very difficult to do this convincingly and is probably best avoided.

Slide projectors: (Price from c. £70 to £450; lenses from £20 to £200) Carousel slide projectors hold a large number of slides and require the minimum of attention during a performance. The disadvantages of slide projectors are the noise from their built-in cooling fans and the substantial distance needed to cast a large image. A wide-angle lens is essential to reduce this distance.

You can project photographic slides of either real scenes (but this tends to be out of keeping with puppets) or, preferably, of your own designs. Scenery and other images can be projected in this manner in silhouette or in full colour.

A purpose-built projection unit This unit is very flexible and has the advantage of providing a considerable spread of light (e.g. up to 10 or 12 feet wide) at a comparatively short distance from the screen. The cost is only a fraction of that of the other projection units described.

The unit (figure 15/1) consists of a bulb in a light box which is mounted on one end of a wooden bar. On the other end of the bar is fastened a scenery frame, a rectangular wooden frame with grooves to take cut-out cardboard silhouette scenes or large home-made transparencies of scenery. The light projects the images on to a shadow screen, or a back screen for other puppets. Large colour filters may be inserted into the frame too. The central wooden bar fastens on to a telescopic stand.

The box This is made of aluminium. It has one open end and ventilation slots across the back and along the sides (figure 15/2). Paint the inside matt black, using heat- resistant paint, to prevent reflection. (If a really sharp image is to be obtained, the light must not be diffused in any way.)

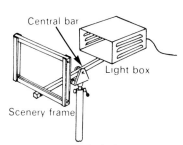

Figure 15/1 The lighting unit mounted on a stand

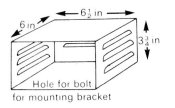

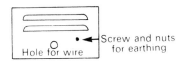

Figure 15/2 The light box

The light A small quartz iodine bulb (24 volt/150 watt) is most suitable. This is inserted into a bulb holder which is screwed to a piece of plywood (to insulate the bulb holder from the light box). The plywood is screwed in position near the back of the box by a screw through the base of the box (figure 15/3).

Wiring the light The light is connected to the mains via a small transformer which converts the current to 24 volts. A fairly heavy three-core wire is used to connect the bulb to the transformer. Drill a hole (c. ½ in diameter) through the back of the light box to accommodate the wire. Insert a rubber 'grommet' into the hole to grip the wire and insulate it. (Grommets are obtainable from motor accessory shops for car wiring.)

Connect the 'live' and 'neutral' leads to the bulb holder and the 'earth' lead to the inside of the light box by a small screw, held by two nuts. The other ends of the lead are connected to the appropriate terminals of the transformer. The transformer is plugged into the mains, again by means of a three-core lead.

It is a good idea to incorporate a plug and socket between the transformer and the light box to allow them to be separated for packing. (It is wise to use a different type of plug from the one connecting the transformer to the mains so that the light box cannot be plugged straight into the mains by mistake.)

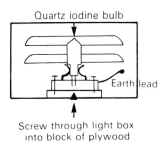

Figure 15/3 Mounting the bulb

The scenery frame This consists of two lengths of wood with two grooves in each (it can be bought already grooved) and four connecting strips which are glued to the grooved pieces and further secured with

251

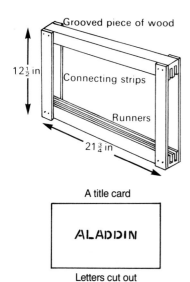

Grooved piece of wood

Connecting strips

Runners

$12\frac{1}{2}$ in

$21\frac{3}{4}$ in

A title card

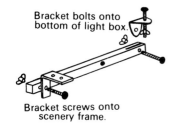

ALADDIN

Letters cut out

Sellotape, Scotch Tape, Takibak or *Contact* to hold in place loose centres of letters

Figure 15/4   The scenery frame

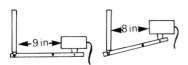

Bracket bolts onto bottom of light box.

Bracket screws onto scenery frame.

Figure 15/5   The central bar

Figure 15/6   The distance between the light box and the frame alters as the central bar is angled to permit the light to shine through the frame

veneer pins (figure 15/4). The grooved strips form the horizontal runners which hold the scenes to be projected. It is important to have two grooves for a number of reasons.

1 One scene can be inserted as another is removed.
2 A title (painted on acetate or cut as a stencil from card) can be projected above a scene.
3 A masking card, giving a particular shape to the screen, can be retained in one runner whilst scenery within the shape can be changed in the other runner.
4 Colour filters can be used in one runner and scenery in the other.

The central bar   Use a 15 in ($\frac{3}{4} \times \frac{3}{4}$ in) length of wood for this supporting bar. The light box is attached to one end of the bar. Cut a slot in the bar to accommodate a metal L-shaped bracket; fasten the bracket to the bottom of the light box and to the central bar by means of bolts with wing nuts, so permitting adjustment (figure 15/5).

A smaller bracket is used to attach the scenery frame to the other end of the bar. Screw the bracket to the bottom of the frame and bolt it to the central bar (figure 15/6). This is also adjustable.

A form of 'U' bracket permits the unit to be mounted on a stand or other fitment. Make the sides of the 'U' from two pieces of strong plywood. Glue and screw them to each side of a piece of wood the same thickness as the central bar. Drill a hole in each piece of plywood to accommodate a bolt upon which the central bar pivots (figure 15/7). Drill the hole through the central bar at the point of balance when the light box and scenery frame are attached. Washers used between the central bar and the plywood help to tighten the joint. Use of a wing nut on the bolt allows adjustment of the bar.

Drill another hole downwards through the bottom of the 'U' bracket; this accommodates a bolt which is used to secure the whole unit to a suitable fitment. A spigot adaptor (see opposite page) may be screwed on to the bolt so that the unit can be mounted on a telescopic stand.

Note: The dimensions given have been used successfully but are only a guide. (No light should spill over the outside of the frame: arrange the dimensions so that the edges of the beam fall on to the frame itself.) For screens of different size, simply alter the distance between the light and the screen.

The scenery   Scenery for projection can be made as described above for overhead projectors. When cutting out silhouettes from cardboard, leave the edge of the sheet as a frame as shown in figure 15/8.

Other items of scenery can be taped to the front of the frame if required – e.g. dry grasses have been used to good effect.

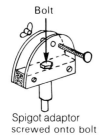

Bolt

Spigot adaptor screwed onto bolt

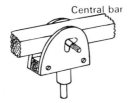

Central bar

Figure 15/7   The 'U' bracket

Figure 15/8   A cardboard silhouette for scenery

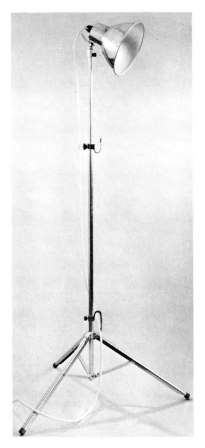

Figure 16   A Photax Interfit lighting stand with a reflector mounted on top.

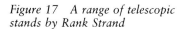

Figure 17   A range of telescopic stands by Rank Strand

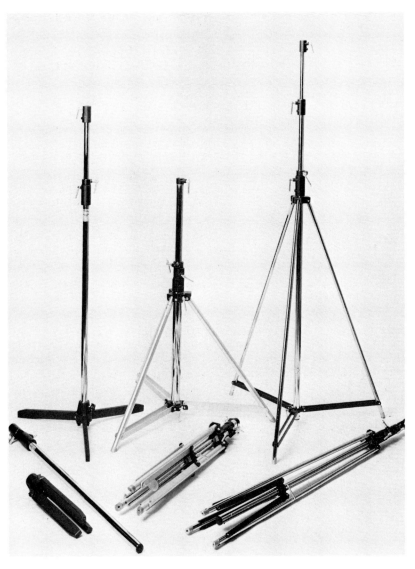

Telescopic stands for lights

When lights have to be stood outside a booth they are – unless it is a permanent theatre – mounted on adjustable telescopic stands. When professional stands are used, a spigot adaptor screws over the lamp's suspension bolt; the adaptor fits into the top of the stand.

Aluminium stands: (price from c. £30)
Photographic shops generally supply these lightweight telescopic stands (figure 16) complete with a reflector mounted on top. The base of the stand folds up for transportation.

Stands without the reflector may be used with *very* lightweight units but most professional lights would be far too heavy for the stand and there is always the danger of the stand being knocked over, so position it with care. For these reasons the more expensive professional stands described below are much better value.

253

Professional lighting stands: (Price £55 to £85)
The range of stands illustrated (figure 17) are sturdy, strong and capable of holding the professional lights described. They are also useful for supporting items of scenery provided they are suitably placed so as not to trip the operators.

The lighter and cheaper of the stands adjusts between 4 ft and 7 ft 6 in; the two braced stands, which are both the dearer price, are progressively heavier and adjust from 3 ft to 5 ft and from 5 ft to 11 ft respectively.

Lighting control

For nearly all puppet presentations the individual lights are carefully directed before the performance and remain in the same position throughout. Occasionally, in a very large open-stage show, it may be desirable to use a 'follow spot' – that is, a spotlight which is moved to follow a character around the stage – but not often. Therefore, in terms of lighting control, the puppeteer is concerned simply with 'raising' and 'dimming' different lights.

A useful dimming manoeuvre, satisfactory for use with a small amateur fit-up, is simply to slide a piece of card over the light. (It will fit into the runners for colour filters.)

Ideally, each light should have its own dimmer control but, for economy, lights may be paired if the desired effect can be achieved and *provided the maximum load specified for each channel is not exceeded.*

If you are using a microphone and dimmers, do check that the dimmers do not cause interference with the sound system; a slight hum might be inevitable.

Economy lighting controls: (Price from c. £7)
Small, lightweight dimmers with up to four control knobs (you can occasionally find them with more), which are intended for use in the home, are sufficient for small stages. Most units handle a maximum of 250 or 400 watts per control channel. The most useful type of unit has a series of individual control knobs, with one master-dimmer which overrides them all.

Medium-range control units   (Price £125 – £500)
The major problems with professional lighting control units are the size, the weight and the price, but there are few manufacturers of more modest units intended for schools, amateur dramatics, puppet theatres, etc. These units have integral controls and dimmer packs and are reasonably versatile.

The model illustrated (figure 18) is the cheapest and most basic found; its two slider dimmers control four outlets, each with a capacity of 650 watts. Increases in capacity and versatility are matched by substantial increases in price.

Professional lighting controls   (Prices: Control desks from £75 – £620; Dimmer packs c. £525 each)
These units (figure 19) are designed to enable the very heavy dimmer packs to be accommodated out of the way whilst the lightweight control desk, linked to the packs by long cables, can be situated wherever it is needed. The smallest desk has six channels and one master fader, but the larger

Figure 18   The Rank Strand Act 2 dimmer unit, here shown wall-mounted

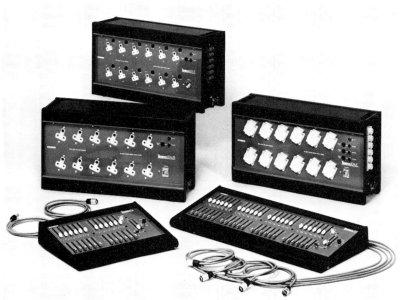

Figure 19   Examples from the Rank Strand Tempus range of dimmer packs and control desks

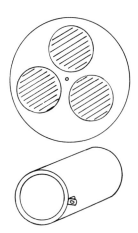

Figure 20/1 *A colour wheel to bolt onto a light fitment*

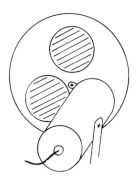

Figure 20/2 *The wheel attached to the fitment*

desks have a variety of facilities, including two pre-sets (i.e. you can set the desk ready for the next lighting change) and automatic cross-fading from one lighting arrangement to the next.

The desks increase in size in multiples of six channels up to a total of thirty-six, but each increase in channels requires an extra dimmer pack too, so the expense and the weight increase very quickly. These systems are excellent, however, for getting the best from a lighting scheme.

Colour lighting

Like all forms of lighting, coloured lighting should be used with caution. If carefully used it can do much to produce or enhance atmosphere but equally it can have a very destructive effect if used carelessly.

Any light may be coloured by covering its source with a colour filter. Cinemoid or Chromoid (coloured transparent acetate) is the best material for the filters; it may be purchased in sheets or pre-cut sizes and then mounted in metal frames which can be bought in sizes suitable for different lights.

In a fairly large-scale production where a substantial number of lights are in use, changing colour is a comparatively simple matter: one set of lights is dimmed and another is raised. In a smaller show, with perhaps only a few lights, filters may have to be changed during the performance. To remove hot filters and replace them by hand is a difficult and clumsy business which is not recommended and, indeed, often not possible because of their situation. The only effective solution is the use of a colour wheel which may be purchased with or without remote control; this permits the light to blend smoothly from one colour to the next.

A colour wheel may be home-made from strong card (or even aluminium) but you must check that the material can withstand the heat of the lamps with which it is to be used. The wheel consists of two pieces of strong card with three, four or five corresponding circular holes cut in them. Between these pieces of card are placed pieces of coloured acetate, each covering a hole. The diameter of the holes is slightly larger than that of the light they are to cover (figure 20/1). The acetate and the two enclosing pieces of card are stapled in position. The wheel is fastened to a bracket (by a nut and bolt through its centre) and the bracket is bolted to the side of the light box (figure 20/2).

The attributes of colour Of the primary colours, red, green and blue, red is the strongest and blue the weakest, which should be borne in mind when planning lighting effects.

The primary colours may be combined to give the secondary colours thus:

red and green	give	yellow
red and blue	give	magenta
blue and green	give	cyan (blue-green)

Of the primary colours, red and green are said to be 'complementary'; that is, they kill one another if superimposed and enhance one another if placed side by side. This attribute is shared by all the colours of the spectrum to a lesser degree. Red and green are the 'true complementaries' but all the 'warm' colours have their complementary amongst the 'cool colours. (Thus with four lights it is possible to produce complementary secondary colours.)

Colour lighting effects Cinemoid and Chromoid colour filters can be bought in a wide range of colours (a sample book can be purchased from Rank Strand Electric). The following are recommended to produce, or enhance, certain 'standard' effects:

Candlelight	No 3	Straw
For a 'murky' scene	No 55	Chocolate Tint
To cool the light	No 17	Steel Blue
To warm the light	No 52	Pale Gold
To 'boudoir' the light	No 54	Pale Rose
To sharpen the light	No 50	Pale Yellow
	or No 1	Yellow
Sunlight	No 50	Pale Yellow or Yellow may be used but it is often better left as plain white
Blue sky	No 18	Light Blue
	or No 32	Medium Blue with strong 'sunlight' on the acting area and on some scenery to show it is a warm day
Cold sky	No 18	Light Blue
	or No 40	Pale Blue with Steel Blue on the rest of the scene
Moonlight	No 17	Steel Blue
	or No 40	Pale Blue
Sunset or Firelight	No 34	Golden Amber
	or No 35	Deep Golden Amber

Never use Primary Red (No 6) or Ruby Red (No 14) for firelight.

Chromoid is the high-temperature filter essential for use with certain lamps. The colours quoted above are the Cinemoid range but most have a close Chromoid equivalent (add the prefix '1' to the reference numbers).

Principles of lighting the puppet theatre

It must be recognised that some types of puppetry activity (e.g. many educational applications) will have no need of artificial lighting, but most other performances will be enhanced considerably by it.

There are no hard and fast rules for lighting any more than for other aspects of puppet theatre, but certain guidelines may be offered. Fundamental to the use of artificial light is that it should enhance the puppets and the performance and not obscure visibility. The very size of most puppets introduces problems of visibility; this is compounded by their proximity to the back-drop in many stages so it is sometimes difficult to see them distinct from the scenery.

As a basic principle, therefore, it is suggested that whenever possible, the puppets should be lit separately from the sets. One of the major problems this poses is where to put the lights in a small stage, so consideration must be given to this when designing the stage. When separate lighting is not possible because of staging limitations or economics, then try to choose colour filters which will enhance the puppets and subdue the sets. Additionally, avoid very dimly lit scenes; puppets will often require more light than their live counterparts for a comparable scene.

Accessible colour filters can be exchanged during scene changes but they will be very hot and there is little time, so avoid the practice whenever possible. If you do have difficulties with space you may find it preferable to use a smaller number of lights with remote-controlled colour wheels but this reduces the flexibility achieved with more lights to blend together to create the desired effect.

Many performers go to great lengths to prevent heavy shadows being cast by puppets or scenery. Whilst one might properly seek to eliminate unwanted shadows (by reducing or redirecting light, or compensating with another light) do look also for the dramatic potential of certain shadows and utilise them where appropriate. There is, however, one type of shadow that performers should do their best to avoid – those of themselves operating back-stage, which can be cast in huge dimensions on nearby walls and ceilings. These are very distracting and can destroy the illusion that is being created. For back-stage lighting use blue, low-power bulbs, heavily shaded so that light does not spill onto the stage area, nor create such unwanted shadows.

Completely open stage performances, which do not use traditional fit-ups make possible all manner of lighting arrangements, particularly as they do not have the limitations of space of actual puppet stages. However, you must remember that the larger the performance area, the more lanterns you will need to light it effectively.

Apart from lights for special effects and backcloth/cyclorama illumination, lighting may be categorised into: side lights, front-of-house spotlights, overhead lights and footlights.

Sidelights These provide much of the illumination for most puppet presentations. They may consist simply of two spotlights cross-lighting the stage, but for more elaborate productions it will generally be necessary to have a mixture of lights. Prism convex and pebble convex spotlights and fresnels are particularly useful because of their versatility and compactness. Some requirements will call for occasional use of floodlights and possibly profile spotlights.

These lights within the fit-up may be placed to each side of the proscenium opening and behind wing-flats. Sidelights may also be placed well clear of the stage in the auditorium, more commonly with open staging techniques but also with proscenium stages if the light is carefully directed through the opening.

The number of lights needed will depend on the size of the stage but, as a guide, a fit-up with an acting area about ten feet wide might have a minimum of three or four lights to each side. When lighting a small open stage, two spotlights are the minimum necessary to highlight modelling, eliminate heavy shadows and prevent the 'flatness' created when only one light is used; just four spotlights increase the scope considerably.

Front-of-house spotlights A major spotlight placed in the auditorium aids illumination and helps to balance the lighting. One 500 or 650 watt profile spotlight is usually satisfactory as its beam can be shaped precisely and it is important that light does not spill on to the stage curtains. There may also be front-of-house spotlights placed to the sides of the auditorium, for which each of the spotlights described above may be of use.

Overhead lighting This is generally by floodlights (individual lights or a batten) placed over a proscenium arch or suspended above, and just in front of, an open booth. Such lighting enhances modelling and scenery and blends with the sidelighting for the overall effect. Care must be taken however to avoid lighting the tops of the puppets' heads, casting heavy shadows on their faces. For this reason, overhead lighting is often omitted, especially in small proscenium booths.

Footlights Footlights help to achieve clear illumination, but usually their main purpose is to balance overhead lighting. Thus, in the puppet theatre with little overhead lighting, footlights are not often necessary.

In the human theatre floodlights would be used but in a puppet theatre these would often obscure the figures, be too powerful and too close to the puppets. When a little lighting of this sort is needed, some performers would use ordinary striplights in a suitable lighting box designed to carry coloured filters. It is not generally good practice to mount striplights as a groundrow inside an open booth; the puppets will be acting for much of the time close to the lights, the flare of which on the puppets' costumes will call undue attention to itself and destroy any effect that might otherwise be achieved.

Back-cloth illumination The illumination of the back-cloth is normally achieved in puppet theatre by floodlights mounted in the wings or by a groundrow – often striplights rather than floods, depending on the size of the staging and the space available. Overhead illumination will be possible in some fit-ups.

Fresnels might also be found useful. Generally speaking, one would try to avoid those lights which have a hard-edged beam.

See Projectors (page 250) for details of rear-projection effects.

Lighting for glove and rod puppets

In principle, these puppets need side and back lighting from the wings to illuminate puppets and sets. An overhead floodlight batten is useful but footlights are not recommended. Front-of-house profile spotlights are also helpful, but need to be used with care or they may emphasise the small size of the puppets. Illumination of a cyclorama or sky-cloth helps to create depth. The following notes detail how this is often translated into practice.

Open booths A good way of lighting a small booth is to use reflector spotlights or sealed beam reflector spotlights mounted on plywood extension arms attached to the two front corners of the stage. Often there is little space in the booth but small, clip-on, home spotlights may be introduced to highlight the backcloth or sets.

For larger booths, fresnels and other spotlights mounted on telescopic stands to either side of the stage, just in front of it, are efficient. It is usually possible also to introduce lighting from the wings and under the backcloth, but it should be arranged so that shadows of the puppeteers are not cast on the sets. A front-of-house profile spotlight mounted on a stand is desirable. If conditions permit, coloured overhead floodlighting may be used but the travelling show will seldom find a suitable means of securing it.

Proscenium booths   It is difficult to illuminate a small proscenium booth with lighting in the auditorium and lighting within the booth itself may be too close to the puppets. The most satisfactory solution is to mount small spotlights to the top corners of the booth, outside the proscenium arch. Backcloth illumination is achieved with striplights.

With a large proscenium booth, some lighting may be placed outside the booth – a front-of-house profile spotlight and other sidelights – provided that they are carefully directed through the proscenium arch but, wherever possible, mount the main lighting inside the booth in keeping with the principles outlined above. Overhead floodlights may be suspended above the proscenium arch or from a batten supported in front of the back-cloth.

Some stages are designed with a projection outside the booth, above the proscenium arch; this houses fresnels or spotlights and allows light to be shone into the booth and very precisely directed.

Lighting for marionettes

In stages with no bridge, the puppets can be operated at no more than arms' length from the back-cloth, so clearly it is very difficult to light puppets and sets separately. When there is a bridge, it is possible to place lighting under the bridge floor and in a well below stage level to light the backscreen and increase the sense of depth on the stage. When back-cloths cannot be illuminated separately, it helps if they are not too light in colour, so as to reduce the effect of unwanted shadows cast by the puppets.

Most people accept that the puppets' strings will show; some performers seek to disguise them by the use of low level spotlights directed at the puppet, but this can produce heavy shadows on sets and limits the entire lighting scheme.

Open stages   For small, open stage performances, two reflector spotlights or sealed beam reflector spotlights, one on either side of the stage and cross-lighting the acting area, are the minimum requirement. At least *two* lights to each side (preferably prism or pebble convex spots, or fresnels) are recommended, however. The nature of open staging usually makes overhead floodlighting impracticable.

For larger, open stage work, more such sidelighting may be needed, possibly supplemented by floodlights, though fresnels will often serve the purpose and provide a useful compromise. A front-of-house profile spotlight is desirable.

Proscenium stages   Marionette proscenium stages are usually illumin-ated, in keeping with the principles already stated, by sidelights, overhead lights (if conditions permit), at least one front-of-house profile spotlight and, occasionally, footlights. A groundrow, however, is more frequently used for illuminating the backcloth than as footlights at the front of the stage.

Front-of-house lights to the side of the auditorium illuminate the apron of the stage, which would otherwise be in shadow. Whilst an overhead batten may be attached to the inside of the proscenium arch or under the floor of a bridge, it cannot be fixed in any intermediate position as it would impede the movement of the puppets up and down stage.

Lighting for shadow puppets

In principle it is possible to use any source of light for shadow play. Normally there should be only one source of light: two lights may produce a blurred shadow. Some professional performers use a selection of lights and projectors for specific purposes and might even need a purpose-built rack to contain the array of light equipment.

Daylight Position the screen between a window and the audience. Ordinary daylight gives sufficient light for shadow-play and the diffused light enables the performers to stand behind the screen without casting shadows on it. Only puppets held against the screen will create shadows.

Whilst bright sunlight gives a stronger shadow, it creates problems in that the shadows of window frames and performers may show. This source of light also moves so, whilst you may position yourself to avoid such shadows, you may find the window frame appearing on the screen during a performance!

A torch (flashlight) or bicycle lamp This will provide sufficient illumination for a small table-top screen. Stand it on the table, behind the screen, taking care not to cast the shadows of your hands on the screen.

'Live' light A candle or oil lamp is ideal for shadows. This type of light is in keeping with the nature of the shadow puppet and, more important, the flickering light gives added movement to the figures, which is not possible with any other kind of lighting. Needless to say, safety considerations make it unacceptable for some purposes and some venues.

Such lights usually stand on a table behind the screen, but traditional forms of shadow-play (like that of Java) would use an oil lamp hanging just above and in front of the puppeteer's head.

Electric light An overhead room light may be used if the screen is set up just in front of where it hangs, with the light above and between the operator and the screen. This is not as satisfcatory as the following methods.

An angle-poise lamp (reading lamp) with a heavy base or an old table lamp without its shade will provide an adequate light. It must be positioned so that the performers can operate without casting their shadows on the screen and without knocking it over. In practice, this means it is usually placed just to one side of the screen.

A professional floodlight or spotlight mounted on a telescopic stand provides a good, crisp, clear light that illuminates the screen evenly. Take care with how it is positioned or the source of light will be very obvious and distracting as the audience looks at the screen. With these more powerful lights, as the puppet is moved away from the screen, the size of the shadow will increase, whereas, with techniques described previously, it will tend to fade.

A purpose-built lighting unit described on page 251 is excellent for large-scale work, but the performers do have to operate from below screen level or their shadows will show. The facility for projecting scenery means that a small folder of cut-out scenes is all that is required to work with a very large screen. This unit is the most satisfactory for permitting the size of the puppets' shadows to be increased substantially (by moving the figures towards the light source) without too much loss of definition.

Overhead projectors give a crisp light and allow scenes to be projected on to the screen. It is possible to lay small shadow figures horizontally on an overhead projector and project the shadows and scenery together, but the operation is fiddly and this seldom results in good movement. It is recommended therefore that the puppets are operated against the screen in the usual manner. Note the possibilities for creating a variety of images, described on page 250.

Slide projectors also allow the projection of scenery and have to be used with the operation of the puppets from below screen level. They provide a sharp, satisfactory light but impose more constraints than the two other projector units described.

Organising the lighting

A routine is suggested for tackling the lighting for a particular production. In a small stage with a few lights, this may mean simply adjusting existing lights and trying different colour filters and dimmer positions. With more ambitious productions a systematic approach becomes more necessary.

First, determine what you would like to achieve; compromises may be necessary but you must be clear about your aims. Wherever possible, design scenery with a view to your lighting needs, particularly asking yourself: 'Where am I going to be able to put the lights?' Note which lights have a fixed position; this provides a starting point for your lighting plan, around which you can arrange the movable lights.

Next, determine a colour filter for each light; you might have to modify this later, but it is a basis on which to work. Now prepare a full plan showing which lamps are linked to the same circuit and numbering each lamp with its switchboard channel; show its position, arrow the direction in which it points and note where it is focused (figure 21). As the performance takes shape, keep this plan up to date.

Clarify lighting needs during rehearsals when you see the puppets under the lights. A list of cues ('the cue sheet') may now be prepared; number each cue on the script and on the cue sheet (figure 22), note the page, the cue number, the timing of the change (i.e. whether to take 30 seconds, snap-on or off, etc.) and a description of the effect. Modify the plan again as necessary and prepare a provisional 'switchboard plot' (figure 23), showing the cue number, the timing and the action to be taken (i.e. the number of the light and its switchboard position – full on, half, three-quarters, and so on).

Figure 21 A lighting plan

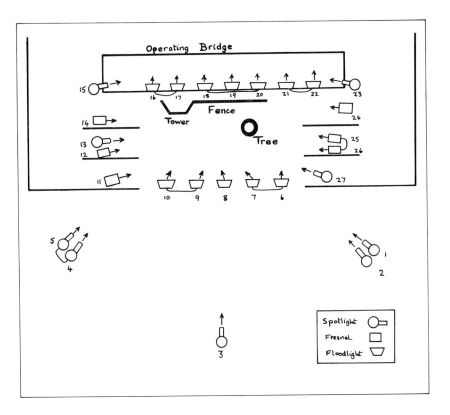

Lighting Cues : Act Three

Script Page	Cue	Timing	Effect
39	Opening	Preset	Glowing gates of Hell
39	1	30 secs.	Gates opening slowly, illuminating centre stage
40	2	SNAP	Devil appears — highlight figure
43	3	20 secs.	Thunder and lightning
46	4	15 secs.	Scene transforms to seashore

Figure 22 A lighting cue sheet

Switchboard Plot : Act Two

Cue	Timing	Action		
Opening lines	Pre-set	$\frac{1\ 2\ 4\ 5}{1/2}$	$\frac{14\ 15\ 16\ 17}{F}$	
1	SNAP	$\frac{6\ 8\ 10}{1/2}$	$\frac{13\ 18}{3/4}$	$\frac{15\ 16}{F}$
2	30 secs.	$\frac{12}{F}$	$\frac{15\ 16}{1/2}$	
3	15 secs.	$\frac{1\ 5}{1/2}$	$\frac{3\ 15\ 16}{3/4}$	$\frac{12}{F}$
4	SNAP	$\frac{3\ 15\ 16}{FULL\ MINUS}$	$\frac{14\ 17}{3/4}$	$\frac{12\ 19}{1/2}$

Figure 23 A switchboard plot

The rigging may now proceed. Fix the lights in position, insert the appropriate colour filters and adjust the focus as required. Again, modify the arrangement as necessary and note the finalised details on the switchboard plot.

Some adjustments might be determined as the show is performed, but the main continuing task is the regular checking of the equipment. Are all the bulbs in good order? Are the reflectors and lenses clean? Are all moving parts moving freely? Are the wiring and plugs in good order and all connections secure? Do any fuses need replacing? Do you have sufficient spare fuses and bulbs handy?

Finally, remember that the control of the lighting needs to be undertaken with as much care as the control of the puppets. Very basic things, like the way the house-lights go down (slowly and quietly) are often badly handled (the audience is suddenly plunged into darkness). It calls attention to itself, destroys the atmosphere and, with children, creates wild shrieking and the like.

Sound

Recent developments in the quality and compactness of sound systems coupled with reasonable prices, have revolutionised puppet theatre sound. The complete system can, nevertheless, add up to quite an expensive outlay, but reasonable equipment is essential.

Remember that sound equipment may appear remarkably loud under home conditions but in a large hall it may be barely audible, so amplification equipment might be necessary. Whatever system is adopted, it is recommended that separate loudspeakers are used, as built-in speakers usually cannot cope with high volume without much distortion. Larger extension speakers permit greater volume with better tone and less distortion. It is worth noting though that there are now some small loudspeakers with high volume capabilities.

Loudspeakers should be carefully positioned on each side of the stage in front of the curtains or the sound will be muffled. Some performers add a third speaker either just above or below the stage. Sometimes forward-facing speakers in front of thick curtains cannot easily be heard by the performers backstage; there is then a temptation to turn up the sound but, if it is a comfortable level for the performers, the front rows of the audience will suffer terribly. This is a very good reason for having an extra loudspeaker backstage for the benefit of the puppeteers. It also underlines the importance of checking the sound out-front at each venue and adjusting it accordingly.

Other aspects of sound, recording show tapes, etc. are discussed in Chapters 14 and 15.

Any of the following portable sound systems may be suitable, depending on your particular requirements but do take care. It is not uncommon to purchase an amplifier and then to search in vain for a microphone that will both meet your needs and be compatible with the system. First, ensure the system permits the use of the tape facility and microphone *together*, and that their relative volumes can be balanced. A system in which you switch to *either* tape *or* microphone is clearly unsuitable. If a number of microphones are to be used, a mixer unit will be needed to blend and balance the various sources.

Secondly, choose the type of microphone carefully; it can cost anything from £20 to £800. Usually it will need to be a clip-on (lapel/tie) model or a neck microphone with a suitable halter to restrict it from moving whilst you are operating the puppets. It must be capable of picking up your speech clearly without you having to direct your mouth down towards it and it must be capable of being used with a reasonable length of lead to the amplifier. If the lead is too short, you will be restricted but, with some microphones, increasing the length can result in loud interference.

Radio microphones are a means of liberating yourself from the restrictions of leads. These have either an integral transmitter or a short lead to a pocket-sized transmitter carried on the hip. The remote receiver is then plugged in to an amplifier input. A complete set comprising clip-on microphone, transmitter and receiver can cost around £460 but, like many technological developments, in real terms they are getting cheaper all the time. An additional combined microphone and transmitter may cost c. £180.

Also ensure that your dimming system for the lights does not produce an audible hum in the sound system and do remember, when you use a live microphone, all back-stage asides are amplified too.

A radio-cassette player (from c. £80 to £200) These units have developed so much in recent years that many provide excellent tape deck reproduction, even without extension speakers. The volume may well be sufficient for small shows which do not need microphones.

A cassette tape deck with amplifier and loudspeakers (Tape deck from £80; amplifier from £40; loudspeakers from £85 per pair) A good quality tape deck is important, used in conjunction with a compatible amplifier. Hi-fi amplifiers are not sufficiently sturdy for the rigours of a travelling show — and may not be powerful enough anyway. A good public address unit is preferable, but beware of cheaper models which give poor sound reproduction. The ability to mix taped music and live voice (via microphones) is highly desirable, though a mixing unit will be needed for a number of microphones, to blend and balance the various sound sources.

An integral sound system (from c. £130) Certain manufacturers, particularly those catering for the education market, now produce single units comprising cassette tape deck, microphone input, extension speaker socket, amplifier and speaker, all in one cabinet. They are very compact, sturdy, reliable, powerful and excellent for transporting purposes. Similar home entertainment 'sing-along' units which have appeared recently may be worth exploring for some purposes (e.g. Philips D6550 'Karaoke' amplifier).

A reel-to-reel tape deck with amplifier and loudspeakers (Tape deck from £500 to £3000; amplifier and loudspeakers from £200 to £2000) Reel-to-reel tape decks are preferred by some companies, in pursuit of high-quality sound. These are obviously larger and more cumbersome than cassette players but may be worth the trouble and investment. The use of these would obviously be pointless without high quality amplification equipment. Those with speeds of 7½ and 15 i.p.s. are preferable; the latter is better for quality in music reproduction and for editing purposes.

14 The performance

Fundamentals

Anybody who is planning to produce a puppet performance ought first to consider a number of very basic issues which have a direct bearing on all decisions about that production.

Why a performance with puppets?   Is it a hobby, a way of earning a little extra money, an intended career, a demonstration performance to accompany a workshop or lecture, a class project, or a way of conveying a message (e.g. health or hygiene)? Perhaps it appears a suitable medium for a piece you wish to perform. The reasons for coming to puppet theatre are usually many and complex but it is worthwhile identifying one's own reasons because it will influence what you might tackle. For example, an undergraduate drama production might explore themes for which the professional might find difficulty drawing an audience.

For whom is the production intended?   It is essential to have a clear sense of audience in order to select and to structure the performance appropriately. It is also important to be realistic about performing for children or for adults: once you are identified with children's shows it is difficult to sell your shows to adults. Yet it is really only in the children's market that most professionals can make a living. Very few are successful at combining the two.

Where are you to perform?   This is, of course, linked to your target audience. Schools performances tend to be the most popular with professionals, probably because of the regular income from an established circuit and a guaranteed full house – usually reasonably controlled – every time. Those performing for adults aim at venues such as arts centres and arts associations as most professional theatres are either too large or unwilling to engage puppet companies. Community centres and associations are often willing bookers but some performers feel this is more like ordeal by fire. Libraries, museums and other local groups or institutions are increasingly booking the smaller shows as part of their widening sphere of activities. There is often scope here too for the amateurs or semi-professionals, who also get a fair number of bookings for private parties, fêtes, and so on.

Christmas and New Year is always a very busy time, but all those large firms wanting entertainment for their children's parties offer one of the two hardest ways of making a living; one is often squashed between the jelly course and the film or disco! The other way is street theatre – but as Paul Hansard warns,* it is fine if you are happy to earn monopoly money, but no good for earning a living.

*Paul Hansard *A Puppeteer's Guide to Self-Advertisement* (Puppet Centre Trust pamphlet)

Figure 1 A puppet show within a puppet show: Petrouchka *by the Hungarian State Puppet Theatre*

Consider also the space available for construction and rehearsal; these can be as important as the venues in determining your staging, the scale, and other considerations.

The time-scale for the production The time-scale helps to determine what is feasible and how ambitious you might be. It also gives deadlines to work to, which so many puppeteers seem to need. Remember that it *always* takes longer than you think, especially the construction, so the danger is that the performance will be under-rehearsed – and it will show.

Puppetry in schools suffers in the same respect. Children often spend hours making puppets, rarely to use them. There is a need to move the construction along fairly speedily to allow scope for developing the performance and, the larger the group, the more time is generally needed to prepare the performance. A half-day puppetry workshop with children working on their stories in groups might include a ten minute demonstration, about fifty minutes for construction, fifty minutes for developing the performances and thirty minutes for presenting them.

With this time-scale, it usually pays to tell the children that they have forty minutes for construction, then give them a little extra time to finish off – and allow for clearing up too. Of course, a little trading-off of time is possible; simple shadow puppets, for example, might take less time to construct and allow longer for working on the performance. More ambitious school projects require a comparable time-scale; be realistic about what you undertake and allow about one third – and certainly no more than a half – of the available production time for construction.

For adults, puppet theatre is really a much bigger undertaking than people appreciate and most puppeteers budget their time badly. Gretl Aicher (Salzburg Marionettes) says it takes ten years to build a show; John Wright (Little Angel Theatre) says it takes four years. With a major production most big companies need a year to eighteen months, calculating it on the basis of two people full-time for that period. A smaller company with a more modest production might take just as long because it cannot afford to have somebody working on nothing but one production for all that time. There is also the 'gestation period', for many productions have been simmering away for some time – even years – before the work proper begins.

Time is needed for simply finding and purchasing the materials you need and perhaps the equivalent of ten full working days for the construction of each puppet. Do not forget to allow for construction of staging and scenery too. All this assumes that the work on the text is well in hand and that you already have the lighting equipment. Time must also be found for the publicity, administration and performing the current show!

One can see why so many shows are under-rehearsed. It is essential to allow the equivalent of five days' rehearsal (6 – 7 hours per day) for every fifteen minutes of playing time. It is not a good idea to try to extend the working day as long rehearsals produce diminishing returns.

What will it cost?   Or, to be more realistic, what can you afford?

Those engaged in amateur puppetry or education do not have major cost problems with puppets as the activities can be as cheap or as expensive, as simple or as complex as you choose. The real problems of expense arise when trying to earn a living from puppet theatre because this immediately involves administration, publicity and travel costs and the scale of the enterprise is usually much greater too.

People's time is the major part of the production costs. If you have to engage somebody to undertake construction, for example, and if a puppet takes two weeks to make, then whatever you have to pay for two weeks' work, plus materials, is the cost of a single puppet. In the face of such costs, some performers are tempted to save money in various ways, particularly on the sound. But the performance experience is a combination of vision *and* sound so beware of such temptations.

Finance comes to the fore also when considering the realities of maintaining a company for, once you start to act like a regular touring company, you have got to keep churning out the work. Barry Smith points out that, if you are in live theatre, you need minimal sets, minimal costumes, a good text, a group of good actors and, in six weeks, you can turn out a production, so you can create two or three productions a year without much problem. But the time-scale for creating a production with puppets is quite different, so it is almost impossible to undertake long tours, keep good, mature artists in the company, keep the performances fresh *and* work on new productions. You would need a designer, writer, musician and a couple of puppet makers all permanently on the staff – and the cost would be enormous.

The companies that are most effective seem to be those that have the stamp of one or two people on them, like Barry Smith and Alan Judd (Theatre of Puppets), Ray and Joan DaSilva (Norwich Puppet Theatre) or John and Lyndie Wright (Little Angel Theatre), so many companies now work in a fairly ad-hoc way and negotiate on performers being available as and when they are needed.

Many small companies survive by being subsidised by their members providing free labour, free storage and the facilities they have in their own homes. If all of these were properly costed and charged to the companies, they might not exist.

Companies that tour schools can probably keep going from the schools' work once they get established. Most other companies can keep themselves afloat whilst touring and might have a little left to plough back into the company for the next production or to cover some of the previous production costs.

Puppeteers who are fortunate enough to secure regular work in television series often use the income to subsidise the production costs of their own shows.

Grants are sometimes available but the sources currently have less finance for an increased number of applicants. Usually, these are project grants for a particular production rather than a regular revenue grant to help with administration.

What talent is available?   And what talent is needed? Who is going to direct the production, write the script, tend to design and construction, prepare the music, manipulate and speak for the puppets?

Many needs will be met from the talents within the group. Others might require additional performers to be involved, whilst some people might be taken on for short periods to fill particular gaps during preparation.

Puppeteers draw upon various sources for their voice actors and musicians; they make use of the local community, secondary school orchestras, youth orchestras, university departments, etc. They make it widely known that they are looking for people; they contact local theatres with notices of auditions. Those who apply might be auditioned live or invited to send specimen tapes, as appropriate. People *want* to do these things. There is nothing wrong with using volunteers, but get the best volunteers you can.

What materials and equipment do you already have?   And what more are needed?

What transport is available?   This also influences the staging and how many people can be included in a travelling show. Note what happens if the height of the puppets is increased by half: the dimensions of the props are also increased by half so that a prop that is $2 \times 2 \times 2$ ft (8 cubic feet) becomes $3 \times 3 \times 3$ ft (27 cubic feet). In other words, you have increased the volume of what you must store and transport by nearly three and a half times.

How can you publicise the show effectively?   Clearly you have to have the bookings arranged by the time the show is ready, but it is both time-consuming and expensive. Some performers maintain that you need to budget at least as much money for promotion as you do for production costs – plus a lot of time.

Even when you have an established reputation, you are only as good as your last show, so you need to maintain standards and spend a lot of time writing literally hundreds of letters. Publicity is all about contacts – getting in touch with the right people for the sort of show you are promoting, so research this thoroughly and know to whom to write. They may be headteachers of schools, local education authority advisors, regional arts councils, directors of forthcoming festivals, etc.

It is essential to have an attractive and appealing brochure – something to catch the eye and make the recipient want to read further. Something must distinguish it from all the other literature they receive daily, so get a good designer if you do not have the skills yourself. But do get quotations first for both design and printing or the bills will be a considerable shock. Local colleges' design departments sometimes welcome requests for help as a source of student projects; then your costs will be reduced to materials and printing.

Your brochure should describe the show and reflect its style as accurately as possible; make clear your technical requirements, the price and any other details (travel expenses, accommodation, if applicable). Ray DaSilva advises: 'If you are a new company trying to establish yourself, it is advisable to find one overall concept for a particular show and to reproduce that everywhere to unify it – special letter-headings, leaflets, posters, programmes, advertisements in the local paper, all reflect one theme.'

Some performers use local radio and television too, but that is expensive unless one gets a feature in a local programme. Remember that no *one* thing works: it is a combination of things. The best form of advertising is word of mouth, but you cannot ignore the other forms.

Some potential bookers, such as arts officers or education advisors, might ask for a 'showcase' performance. This is a free show at a local venue where those potential bookers can decide whether they wish to engage you. It can be very helpful in breaking into a new circuit and establishing enough bookings to make a tour viable: travelling great distances for single shows is seldom profitable and would probably not even cover costs.

It is good practice always to have written agreements and to take an invoice to the venue in case it is required: do all you can to facilitate the payment of your fees. Private bookers and theatres usually pay quickly (often on the spot) but institutions such as eduction authorities take some time, so budget carefully and be prepared to wait for payment.

If the show is successful, clearly this is a prime target for future publicity but remember that, if you are re-engaged, you will need a new show and, as

Paul Hansard warns: 'Do not go more than once a year, for you will ruin your scarcity value.'

What is involved in touring a show? Touring involves very mundane considerations like being away from home, finding time to do your washing and the whole business of living without a base or a real social life. For school tours, for example, you perform twice a day, five days a week; you are finished by four o'clock but, as Ray DaSilva points out, it may be four o'clock in the middle of nowhere.

There is also a lot of hard work, humping heavy loads, and you can begin to feel like furniture removers with the getting in and getting out of venues, especially in converted town halls where the performance space is usually on the first floor. You really do need a strong constitution and the ability to go plodding on.

You also have to cope with acoustic problems, particularly echoing, and sight-lines can be difficult as you cannot design a show which is going to suit perfectly all situations. Barry Smith meets this problem by designing productions (which are often open-stage style) that will be seen to best advantage in a moderately-raked auditorium of a studio theatre with an audience of up to three hundred.

It is important to remember, too, that the members of a touring company have to live together; they are going to see each other from breakfast time for the rest of the day. When choosing a company, directors will therefore take some account of cultural interest, dietary requirements and various habits, such as smoking. Inevitably there will be upsets from time to time; the larger the group the greater the risk you can take and two extremes may balance each other within a company, but it is a much bigger risk in a small team.

On the positive side, the rewards for a touring company are considerable, particularly the immediate contact with the audience after the performance, which the puppeteers often do not have in a theatre. Touring also means, of course, that you can reach audiences whom you would never see in a permanent theatre.

'Variety' shows

Until recently, shows consisting of variety or circus acts were, with few exceptions, the domain of the marionette. However, some of today's more imaginative puppeteers have shown that all types of puppet can provide first-class entertainment of this sort, although it is still the marionette that dominates the scene.

Puppet 'variety' is popular amongst puppeteers, especially solo performers who cannot present a play by themselves. It is also much in demand for children's parties, live variety shows and cabaret. The staging may be as elaborate, or as simple, as desired and most of the acts can be used for both adults and children with only a slight adaptation of the 'patter'. The choice of material will depend partly on the puppeteer's skill in construction, partly on his skill in manipulation, but also on his own taste and the requirements of his audience.

A programme might well consist of a sketch or two and a number of acts involving tricks and 'transformations'. The sketches need not be

Figure 2 The Ballad of Mister Punch *by Théâtre aux Mains Nues (Alain Recoing), France*

elaborate; it is the idea and its execution that matters. Albrecht Roser presents an act in which a clown plays with a balloon and the balloon ends up chasing the clown. The idea is simple but the precision timing and exquisite manipulation make it extraordinarily effective.

The following are some of the trick acts that might be used to make up the performance:

> weight lifter; juggler; extending or collapsible puppet; acrobat; tumbler puppet; dual-controlled dancers; contortionist; stilt walker; lion and lion tamer; clown with collapsible chair; performing dog (or other animal); Scaramouche (puppet with many heads, one inside the other); puppet puppeteer; come-apart puppet (e.g. dissecting skeleton)

Many of these turns are traditional and have been performed for hundreds of years, notably by the Italian Fantoccini puppets. Each has to

273

be fitted into an act and this requires some ingenuity and imagination. The dissecting skeleton cannot just walk on, come apart and walk off. If the puppet is to ride a monocycle, what is he to do whilst he is on it? It is no use offering the audience a copy of what it has seen before, so you must try to find your *own* slant.

Animals are very popular with both adult and young audiences and can be used for many of the above acts (e.g. an acrobatic monkey or a bear on a monocycle). It is also possible to design one puppet so that it can perform many acts: a tight-rope walker can be a contortionist; a juggler can be an extending puppet.

Some puppets may simply perform to music; some may talk directly to the audience or to other puppets. All these techniques may be employed within the same show, depending on the acts. Where the show involves audience participation it is as well to have a few 'filler' acts prepared as it is impossible to gauge how protracted this will be.

Much of what is said about the preparation of a play is relevant to variety. The attainment of timing and precision, however, is of supreme importance. Variety of all things must never be allowed to drag.

Plays

The scope open to puppet theatre is extensive and there is wide agreement that puppets should do that which they do well and not attempt that which the live actor can do better. There must be a reason for doing it with puppets: the puppets must bring something to the piece rather than be used for a trivial version.

It is worth noting how much of puppet theatre originates with the narrative form. This underlines the view that good live plays are often not good puppet plays, and also the difficulty of finding playwrights who can write specifically for puppets. But also note that good stories do not always make good plays either; a possible story must always be considered with a view to its dramatic content. What sort of imagery does it contain? How much of the story can be translated directly into action? Puppets that just stand still and talk are not interesting to watch.

Any material that you may think of using should be considered from the point of view of copyright (see Appendices). There is much that is not in copyright but it pays to make certain.

The lack of suitable published material and the widespread confidence in the craft coupled with inexperience of performance, leads to a tendency to create puppets without any thought as to what they might perform. They are literally 'characters in search of an author'; this is a difficult way of approaching the performance, it can be most frustrating and the quality of the resulting show usually reflects this. The advice is – especially for the beginner – start with your theme, your text or story outline, and know where you are going.

Of course, the puppeteer might intend to write an original play. This will involve the development of a plot, settings and characters, from which a scenario and script can be created. The most difficult aspect of this is undoubtedly the plot itself and, no matter what advice is given by different 'authorities', there is no simple formula; plays for puppets are not

Figures 3 and 4 (overleaf)   Scenes from the Drak production of The Sleeping Beauty: *the scene is set back-stage of a human theatre performance*

universally reducible to certain elements. However, the suggestions for the scenario and script (pages 276 – 279) do contain some guidelines which should be helpful.

Principles for adapting a story

As the performer has been inspired by the story, one assumes that he will wish to retain the style and essence of the source and keep as much of the original dialogue as is appropriate. Some stories will demand a good deal of inventiveness from the writer but with others the dialogue just seems to flow. Never lose sight, however, of the need for *action*.

The actual processes of developing a scenario and script are discussed below, but the process of adaptation requires certain preliminary steps. First consider whether there are events which do little to move the plot forward or develop the characters; these might be deleted first. Are any characters superfluous? Are there any events or situations which are difficult to depict with puppets? Can these be deleted or, if they are essential, how could they be achieved or even suggested?

Scenes in books can change from page to page, or perhaps several times in a single page. Clearly too many scene changes will not work with puppets, so could the action be confined to three or four scenes? Additionally, are there in the text any brief but important scenes which need *elaboration*? This will be a demanding task needing a good deal of care.

At what point in the story should the play open? It need not start where the book does; very much depends on what achieves the best dramatic impact without confusing or boring the audience. A good deal has to be achieved in this scene, in terms of story and character development, atmosphere, etc.

But be clear that the process of cutting down does not imply that one must reduce everything to a single, simple storyline; this would only trivialise the story. There must be development of character and plot; there may be a sub-plot. In a sense, writing for puppet theatre is rather like writing a good book for children; all that has to be achieved in an adult book also has to be achieved effectively in a children's book, but with far fewer words. So it is with puppet theatre: it is drama condensed.

Having made these basic decisions one is ready to progress to the business of developing the scenario and the script.

The scenario and script

The approaches of Ray DaSilva and Barry Smith (Chapter 15) emphasise the differences that exist in script writing and, clearly, there are no hard and fast rules. However, a few pointers may be given to help the puppeteer who has not yet developed his own approach.

When you have chosen your material and prepared a brief outline of the story, this can be developed into the scenario, an account of 'who does what and where'. It is useful to include preliminary stage directions too. The number of characters and changes of scene that is going to be possible is limited, so it may be necessary to do away with, or combine, some of the characters and places of action. Ensure that all important action takes place on stage. It is not usually appropriate for a character to enter and say what he has just done if it is an essential aspect of the plot.

From the outset it is most important to keep in mind the shape of the play. Each development vital to the plot should be noted and the whole series of actions arranged in the most telling order. At the same time it should be decided which are the characters essential to the development of the plot so that the stage can be kept clear of those that are not important and the number of manipulators required in any scene kept to a minimum. Remember that the manipulators need much more space than the puppets and beware of crowd scenes.

It is important also to be very strongly self-disciplined about the length of the show. Most puppet shows are too long and would be much more effective if they were tightened up dramatically and reduced in length. So many performers make this comment about shows they see but rarely reflect it in their own productions. It has been suggested that the length of a puppet production, compared with the human theatre, is directly proportioned to the height of the puppets compared with the live actor. There are many examples which show this to be something of an exaggeration but the essential notion is quite a sound one to keep in mind.

The limitations of particular types of puppet, the size and shape of the staging will impose all manner of restrictions as well as offering many possibilities. It might determine whether, for example, you can write in action that requires great height or width.

Take care not to plan scenes that will necessitate long scene-changes; the audience will become bored and you will not be able to sustain the mood or the flow of the production. Have as few breaks as possible (most peformers do not have an interval) and either change settings in full view, choreographed as part of the performance, or try to limit scene changes to two minutes – and *under no circumstances* longer than three.

With this in mind, decide where the climax comes and make sure that no

Figure 4 The Sleeping Beauty *See previous caption*, p. 275

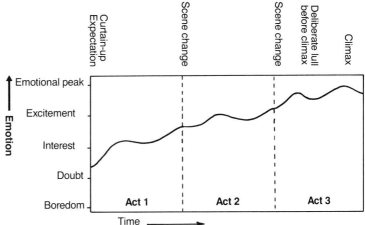

Figure 5 Building interest and emotion

intermediate action in any way detracts from it; remember that if the audience is to participate fully in the climax they must understand fully how it came about. To have to take recourse in explanations at the end of a play is highly undesirable. Jan Bussell* suggests a very useful graph for building interest and emotion across the performance, emphasising the need to end each act on a peak which will carry the audience into the next act with a sense of anticipation, suspense, excitement, etc. A similar chart is illustrated (figure 5); it is not appropriate to try to sustain a high level of emotion throughout, creating a horizontal line high across the chart. Variety of pace and emotion are essential; the audience cannot sustain a high level throughout and it does not make good theatre.

Consider the way in which Hitchcock created suspense – not by surprise after surprise, but by *building*, changing pace, juxtaposing. Comedy may be pointed up by a subdued moment and tragedy can be heightened by light relief. But treat the writing with great care or it can become ludicrous

*Jan Bussell, *The Puppet Theatre* (Faber, 1946)

277

and destroy the continuity of the play. The audience must be kept interested in what is coming next.

This has important implications for how and where the play begins for it must be a moment which holds the audience, captures their interest and quickly sets the tone of the play. It is very good practice for the first character to enter and *do* something as soon as the curtain goes up. It is not usually a good idea to start explaining the plot the moment the play starts. For the first few minutes many people do not really listen to puppets: they are too busy watching it – taking in the type of puppet, method of operation and the conventions of the performance.

Here the question of explanatory dialogue soon arises. Shakespeare might have used the Prologue most effectively to set the scene but this does not often work well with puppets. We need to *see* the important action and a play that opens with two puppets giving a lengthy exposition is both clumsy and boring; it does not make good puppet theatre.

The step from the scenario to the final script can be taken in a variety of ways. If the piece originated with a script, clearly the scenario and final text will have developed together: in identifying the major elements of the scenario, you would also be identifying the significant aspects of the script. What is now needed are the links to enable the play to flow with continuity.

If the play originated with a text, storyline or other theme, then it might be a case of a suitably experienced writer converting the scenario into a script or a process of improvisation which is recorded, transcribed and then adapted and refined as necessary. If the improvisation process is adopted, puppets should be used for this, even if the puppets for the play in question are not yet made. It is not wise to use human acting as a basis for puppet acting: speech tends to become more important than action.

It is important to take account of the intellectual level of your target audience. Whilst puppet theatre should challenge the audience intellectually, they clearly must be able to grasp the point. In a show for young children seen recently, the story depended on the two characters not being able to see each other but, though the children laughed at the funny puppets doing funny things, it became clear that they did not really understand. They were not able to decentre and see the situation from somebody else's point of view; because *they* could see both puppets, they could not grasp that the characters could not see each other.

Similarly, you have to find the appropriate level for the dialogue: again, do challenge the audience and do not patronise them. Most people have experienced puppet shows where dreadful shrill voices repeat equally dreadful and soppy dialogue, like: 'What shall I do now? Oh, I know, I'll go and see if Mrs Rabbit's in. Oh, here I am at Mrs Rabbit's house and here she comes. Hello, Mrs Rabbit.' So much puppet dialogue, argues Barry Smith, is a sort of television talk. It is filling in the time, with no shape or direction or good purpose to it – partly, of course, because puppet theatre is short of good writers.

Whoever is assigned the script-writing must have a sound knowledge of what puppets do well, what they do badly, and must have a grasp of puppetry fundamentals – such as the need to avoid long speeches. They need to have *seen* a range of puppet theatre and worked with puppets themselves. There is no substitute for first-hand experience and the writer will find it immensely helpful to have been involved in directing a puppet production too.

The decision about whether to use taped dialogue needs careful consideration. Generally, the advice is *don't* – unless it is really necessary and you are going to achieve a high quality tape. A poor tape will ruin the show, a good tape still needs first-class manipulation technique. Technical hitches while the tape runs on is a sure way of a serious piece degenerating into a farce. You also have to consider the capacity of the live voice to hold the attention of the audience and the need to allow for audience response and participation.

In relation to audience participation, there are many ways in which to involve your audience, the most important of which is the way in which you hint or suggest, inviting the audience to supply with the imagination those other dimensions that puppets cannot achieve. The way in which the audience brings something to the performance is a powerful aspect of puppet theatre. Some shows do not get off the ground because there is absolutely nothing needed from the audience. Any puppet show must at least acknowledge that there are other people in the hall. Frequently the notion of audience involvement is interpreted in terms of verbal participation, and for certain types of performance there is, indeed, nothing wrong with encouraging a little response of this sort – provided you can control it and it contributes to the performance. But often it is not controlled; on the contrary, in some shows for children they are encouraged to generate louder and louder noise, almost to the point of hysteria. The result is a loss of concentration on the story or the dramatic entity.

By contrast, the puppeteer should be able to play on his audience, to bring them right back to think deeply, to feel. He must be able to move them in the ways in which they are moved in a theatre; do keep this in mind when preparing the play.

Finally, how do we know the play has finished? Sometimes this is not at all clear: the curtain drops, the audience hesitates, somebody starts to applaud and the house lights come up, but nothing inherent in the performance signals effectively that the play has finished. This is not to suggest that some naive little line should be inserted to say, virtually, 'that is the end', but the style of ending, the use of music, lighting, etc., together with the way in which the story concludes and the posed stage picture *can* communicate effectively that the piece has ended.

However, once the drama has been resolved do not draw out the finale or the impact of the moment will be lost. Bring down the curtain fairly soon.

Music for the show

The function of music in the theatre is to enhance mood and atmosphere and to link scenes and bridge intervals so that these qualities are sustained. Music should never force itself upon an audience's notice.

If you have any doubts about the contribution of music to a performance, try a simple exercise even without puppets: do the same

Figure 6 Culhwch and Olwen *by*
Caricature Theatre

speech (from Hamlet, perhaps) with a background of music from *West Side Story* and then with music from the *Tom and Jerry* cartoons. Also compare television dramas with and without music. There are good dramatic reasons for having no music at times but there are equally good reasons for including it in other pieces. Basically the question is: what does it do for this particular piece?

Do ensure that the music selected is appropriate and that the reproduction quality is good. Live music is usually too difficult to arrange but, when it *is* possible, it brings a whole new dimension to a production.

It is usual to precede curtain-up with a short appropriate piece but music at the end of a peformance is usually thought to detract from the effect of the final curtain. Sometimes, however, the dash and vigour of a variety finale can be given a final polish by a suitable piece being played after the curtain falls.

It pays always to listen to music with a critical ear, noting down what certain passages suggest to you (and where they come on the record) and how certain pieces might be used. Such a reference book can save considerable time when music is needed.

Finally, always check performing rights and royalties (see Appendices).

Voice work

Too often people think that they need to put on funny voices for puppets but it is not so. Instead you need to breathe properly and to project the voice well and clearly. Barry Smith, an expert voice teacher, emphasises that you must be very crisp and clean on your speech tunes and rhythms. You must have very clear changes of intervals in the voice (in the musical sense) to match the changes of thought. A radio actor, he argues, can slide through tunes but not a puppet voice. It has to be on *this* level, then on *that* level; then the next thought comes, then another thought – and those intervals have got to be very clearly defined, much more so than with most straight acting or radio work.

You also need a character voice and in this respect you can learn a lot by studying the voice work in Disney films as it is very much the same technique. However, there is much to be gained by taking lessons from a good voice teacher.

Manipulation and movement

To make each puppet exciting to watch and convincing in his role, it is important to try to introduce as much variation of gesture as possible, within the limits of characterisation. Remember that puppet theatre is much more akin to mime and dance than it is to human theatre and that a puppet's movement, if it is well done, is very crisp, clean-cut and drawn in the air very precisely, like that of a dancer.

When exploring the range of movement and gesture, it is a very good plan to try to perform the play entirely in mime. The limitations of speechlessness often force a deeper exploration into possible ways of conveying meaning through action. A far wider range of action and gesture is discovered. Whilst experimenting with movement, study gestures and try to relate them to emotions.

Fundamental to good manipulation is total concentration on the part of the puppeteer; the moment he stops concentrating on the puppet, it loses a lot of its power, so keep your eyes on your puppet and act *through* it. A common weakness with beginners is to hold the puppets rather lifelessly while they are themselves acting away, not projecting this through the puppet. An interesting illustration of this concentration and identification is to try to operate convincingly, say a rod puppet, whilst reading from a text; it will not be very successful for sure. Now, hold the text in the puppet's hand and try it again; as a puppet focuses on the text, so can you, because you have the *same* focus, and a different quality of movement will be achieved. This emphasises also the importance of knowing the play thoroughly. You cannot use a script when performing.

One thing at a time is another rule: do not wiggle the puppets about nor slur all the movements together. John Wright (Little Angel Theatre) says: 'Every line should have an action and every action should have a meaning. Never put in unnecessary movement.' Deliberate, clear-cut, clean movements are needed and, generally speaking, the principle is *new moves on new thoughts*. Particularly watch the puppets' eyelines so that they are inter-relating: think about where the puppet is focusing. Pace is also important but take your time and let us see the puppet think.

The first thing that many people think of in terms of puppet movement is the head and hands but it is the *whole* puppet that communicates character, emotion, etc. so do not neglect the other aspects. At the same time, economy of movement and economy of gesture is required; it also helps to have plenty of intrinsic movement in the puppet and its costume, so that you supply just what is required and let the puppet's natural movements do as much as possible.

How do we know which puppet is speaking? If the audience is to believe that the puppet is speaking, words and actions must synchronise and it must be possible to tell which puppet is speaking by other means than by recognising the voice. The art in this lies in subduing the actions of the figures that are silent (without allowing them to appear lifeless) so that all attention is focused on the speaking character. The silent figures can help in this with appropriately subdued gestures, such as nods of assent, directed towards the speaker. The convention that the puppet who is speaking moves is often carried too far and the puppet nods or jiggles to every syllable of speech; just use the puppet's movements to emphasise important words or phrases as people do. If the puppet has a moving mouth, do not just open and close it continuously while that puppet is speaking: match the mouth movement to the spoken word, opening the mouth on 'open' words and noting the amount of space needed between the lips for different words. Lip synchronisation is a very difficult skill to master while concentrating also on the overall puppet movement. To study expert technique, watch Ronnie LeDrew's manipulation of Zippy in Thames Television's *Rainbow* programme, Basil Brush or the Muppets.

Sightlines are important in terms of ensuring the audience can see and that the puppets do not disappear from view (they must not sag below the stage level and must be raised as they move upstage – i.e. away from the audience). With glove and rod puppets, it is necessary to establish the height of each puppet above the playboard and in relation to each other, and to keep the puppets walking on the same level. This is complicated by the different heights of the operators.

Pay attention to the way the puppet takes and leaves the stage. Often this is out of character with the movement of the figure on the stage. In any type of performance the puppet must make an effective entrance. Faulty entrances and exits most frequently occur with marionettes, which are allowed to swing or drop down on to the stage. This immediately destroys the illusion. To be sure of a good entrance, the puppet should be in action before it comes into view. Rod and glove puppets are often allowed to pop up out of the floor, which is equally undesirable; make the most of doorways, arches and wings, bringing the puppet up to the appropriate height *out of sight* and then walking it into view. In a booth with none of these devices, it is a good idea to imagine a set of stairs and have the puppet walk up these into view. The same comments apply of course to exits.

There are limitations in using a mirror for practice. While it has a place for checking details, one learns to *feel* when the puppet is not moving appropriately: over-dependence on a mirror hinders the acquisition of this skill and prevents proper concentration on the puppet. Take advice from a director, let the performers take turns sitting in the auditorium and, where possible, make good use of a video-recorder.

Try to avoid having to operate sitting down because it limits you so much. Give sufficient attention to the movement of the puppets whose characters are more difficult to portray (witches and villains are often much easier than princesses and heroes). And make full use of the conventions of puppet theatre; puppets do not have to do everything themselves: in Chapter 15 Barry Smith describes the techniques of using the puppeteers, in view of the audience, to do things on behalf of the puppet, 'as if he were doing it'.

Figure 7 Playboard Puppet Theatre: A waddle and a quack

Very difficult actions can draw undue attention to themselves by being bungled *and* by being performed with ease to the amazement of the audience. Both draw attention to the puppet as a puppet and break the atmosphere of the play. Variety acts may thrive on provoking the audience's wonder and admiration, but not plays: 'attention should not be distracted by a clever piece of production. Production is only good and clever when it gains its effects unnoticed.'*

It is widely recognised also that puppeteers need some kind of movement training to help them to empathise with the movements of other people, because you can transmit to the puppet only that with which you are in empathy. This does not mean that you necessarily have to be able to *do* it yourself; you may not be able to move like an elephant but you can empathise – or 'know yourself as elephant'.

This section has been concerned with the manipulation and movement of individual puppets, which need to be seen and choreographed in relation to the overall stage picture and the movements of other characters. This process is part of the business of rehearsal and is discussed below.

Rehearsal

Adequate rehearsal is essential for perfecting performing technique, developing confidence, smoothing out technical and production problems, discussing methods of presentation and considering all the aspects of design, lighting, sound, scenery and costume.

*Jan Bussell *The Puppet Theatre* (Faber, 1946)

283

Rehearsal should never be rushed and a couple of hours at a time will usually be as much as the performers can take without a break. It is helpful to draw up a schedule for rehearsals and try to keep to it, and it is essential for the manipulators to be thoroughly familiar with the play before rehearsals begin.

A word should be said here about the director: there is a lot of sense in inviting somebody from outside the group to come in to direct or, at the very least, to offer constructive criticism. So many puppeteers tell you what they are going to do next and it sounds fabulous; they show you the designs and they are marvellous; they make the puppets and they are brilliant; they present the show and it is *boring*. If one person has conceived, designed, constructed, directed and performed the piece, you are not going to get a fresh, objective view. Perhaps the puppeteer *is* aware of certain weaknesses but, as he puts the show together, he learns to live with them so that they are no longer glaring. It needs that fresh person to come in to remind him of these shortcomings because, by the time he realises that the show has misfired, he may be so far into it economically that it is difficult to retrieve, especially for an elaborate, professional performance where the economics are of considerable importance.

When the director first works through the play with the manipulators in order to arrive at a general scheme for movement about the stage, he is not concerned with the gestures of the individual characters but with the overall patterns of movement; with arranging groups and positioning individual puppets to the best visual and dramatic effect. This process is known as 'blocking'. Every move or series of moves that is determined is noted in the master script and simple diagrams illustrating these are drawn opposite the appropriate speeches.

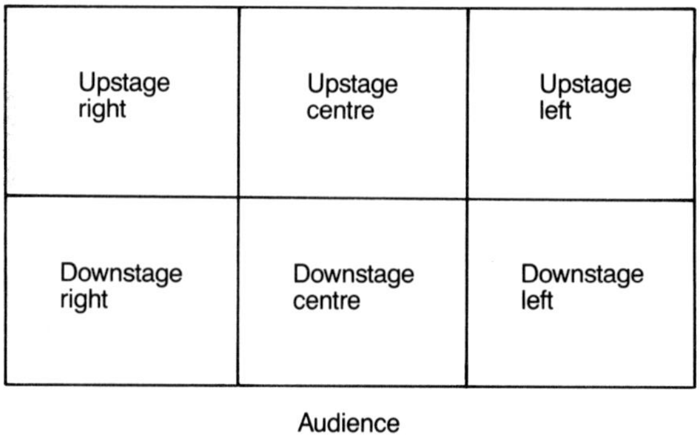

Upstage right	Upstage centre	Upstage left
Downstage right	Downstage centre	Downstage left

Audience

Figure 8   The main stage positions

Figure 8 shows the six major stage positions: down-centre is the strongest, followed by up-centre, then down right and left; up-right and left are the weakest positions and not usually suitable for major action. The major character will often utilise the area down-centre, or down right or left, but do aim for variety in the use of space.

The next step is to decide on the basic actions of the individual characters, introducing their most important gestures and determining the cues for them. To this foundation, details of action can be added and the complete pattern of the puppet's movement built up, so that it flows smoothly from one position to the next, but always with due regard for the overall stage picture.

The figures, of course, do not need always to walk directly from one spot to another. Their paths might sometimes involve a circular pattern, a loop, etc; make the most of the space and let the puppets *use* it. But be careful not to have characters crossing one another all the time as this can cause problems for the manipulators; they have either to pass each other or to exchange puppets at every cross-over.

The puppeteers' own movements should be worked out at this point and off-stage positions fixed for the puppets so that they can be found without hesitation. The back-stage choreography is of immense importance.

While puppets need to relate to one another, do not let them permanently present a profile to the audience; turn them slightly. Do not let the characters 'upstage' each other – that is, do not position a figure so that another has to turn his back to the audience to deliver a line. And, as you develop the movement, watch your lighting areas so that one puppet does not steal another's light.

Essentially rehearsal is a process of taking a broad view of the play, getting the underlying structure right, then looking at smaller and smaller units to refine the detail, and finally putting the package together again. It is important that the play should be sufficiently rehearsed as a whole.

Part of this process will involve the delegation of a wide variety of tasks to be covered during the performance for, in most puppet companies, there can be no distinction between who does the performing, the stage management, etc. Generally, everybody does everything, though major characters might be operated by particular members of the company and a very complicated lighting scheme with frequent changes might demand its own operator. The organisation of these tasks is all part of the choreography referred to above. Resulting from this, the performers will have their own individual schedules of tasks:

Scene 3: Standby on bridge.
          Take puppet from DC. Hang on rack and check.
          Work owl in tree after clouds disappear.
          Open gate to sound cue.
          12 14 16 Down to $^3/_4$ (lighting change) when wolf appears.
Interval: Remove tree and fence.
          Place rocks in circle, centre stage.

With all this activity going on, a very dim blue light backstage can be very useful.

Prior to the dress rehearsals there is a need to include technical rehearsals which do not involve running through the whole dialogue, but which practise curtain cues, lighting cues, music cues and sound cues. Very basic details are checked, such as the space for entrances and exits. Setting out the puppets, props and scenery should all be practised until they become instinctive. It is important to rehearse also the setting up and 'striking' (taking down) of the stage so that the whole operation becomes smooth and efficient.

It has been noted that one should organise intervals so as to avoid long pauses which destroy the continuity and lose the concentration of the audience. The puppeteers may be furiously busy backstage, but the audience sitting in the auditorium is not. Scene changes should be timed and rehearsed until they are as smooth as the rest of the performance and

Figure 9 The Sea Witch from The Little Mermaid *by the Little Angel Theatre*

no unintended sounds should be heard by the audience. Soft-soled shoes are essential.

Another routine matter should be the checking of all equipment: examining all puppets, controls, strings, scenery and props before and after each rehearsal or show. Checking the packing of puppets, properties and other equipment when going to and when leaving a show is very much facilitated if a list is kept.

An emergency kit containing a small selection of tools, fuses, glue, tape, etc. should always be kept handy (and tidy) for running repairs.

The performance

All the elements of construction and preparation are united in the performance; it is the moment when all aspects of the puppeteer's art are on show and it is essential that his work is shown off to the best advantage. From the moment the performer arrives for an engagement he is on show and he must be professional throughout.

Paul Hansard, a highly polished performer whose presentation is always impeccable, suggests that it is a good idea to send an advance reminder-card to confirm the details of the times you are arriving and due to perform. Make sure your equipment is in first class order *and* appearance, and that your transport is in good running order. It is *essential* to arrive on time, to set up efficiently and to be ready to perform on time.

No venue will be ideal but do not complain about its shortcomings; make the best of the situation you find. Be prepared for every type of electrical socket and carry yards and yards of cable; the sockets always seem to be in the worst possible places. Be totally self-sufficient and *never* ask to borrow anything.

During the show there must be complete silence back-stage. Even whispers can carry and spoil the illusion that is being created. It is always a debatable question among puppeteers whether the performers should allow themselves to be seen after the show – assuming that they have not been working in the open. Some come forward to take a bow, some come forward with one of the puppets, others prefer to remain unseen: the question remains as to whether the magic and illusion of the puppet would be destroyed by the appearance of the performers.

After the first few performances of a new production, the puppeteer should pause to take a fresh look at the whole show, to reassess it in the light of how the audiences received it and reacted to it. If there are any improvements that can be made, he should make them, not be satisfied with anything less than his best. Every effort should always be made to improve the standard of any production. The show reflects and represents months of work but it is by the finished production that the puppeteer's work is judged.

15   The professionals on the performance

This chapter presents the approaches of Barry Smith and Ray DaSilva, directors of well-established companies of international repute. They tend to draw upon different types of material and to some extent different kinds of audience. They have quite distinct styles and approaches to the performance but it will be seen that they do have much in common.

Their accounts, based on interviews, provide valuable insights into puppet theatre and clearly underline that there is no 'right' way of doing things (though there might be some 'wrong' ways). The reader is invited to draw upon these approaches as appropriate, but do not simply copy organisational details: look to the underlying principles, for each director's approach to the text, to music, etc. must be seen in the context of his performance concepts.

The approach of Barry Smith

Barry Smith is the director of Theatre of Puppets (co-director Alan Judd).

Barry first became attracted to puppets in 1943 when he witnessed a demonstration by Paul Brann, the director of the Marionette Theatre of Munich Artists. He was further inspired in these early years by the work of Olive Blackham, director of the Roel Puppets.

In 1954 he trained in theatre at the Central School of Speech and Drama, London, and discovered other major influences in the ballet master Sigurd Leder, and the Alexander Principle of Movement. For eleven years after drama school he worked as a freelance voice and speech tutor, mainly at the Royal Academy of Dramatic Art but also with other companies, including the Royal Shakespeare Company and the National Theatre. He was voice coach to Sir Laurence Olivier for his part as *Othello* at the Old Vic Theatre.

He founded Theatre of Puppets in 1969 'to carry puppet theatre beyond the narrow field of children's entertainment alone but, nevertheless, encouraging young people to share with an adult audience the delights and discoveries of theatre with puppets.'*

His productions have included *The Chrystal Palace*, based on Planché's fairy extravaganza (1844) and *The Vampire*, a gothic melodrama (1820). *Playspace* was a collection of light-hearted and surrealistic turns, the experiments with which over several years had an important influence on British puppet theatre. In 1972, *Starchild* (Grimm's *The Giant with the Three Golden Hairs*) was a landmark in puppet theatre and his (1975) version of Marlowe's *Dr Faustus* is regarded by many as his most

*Animations, Puppet Centre Trust, April/May 1980

288

Figure 1 Planché's The Chrystal Palace

(Figures 1 to 8 all by Barry Smith's Theatre of Puppets)

successful production. By now the company consisted of three instead of the original five. Samuel Beckett's *Act without Words*, as performed by Theatre of Puppets, is one of the most compelling testimonies to the power of the puppet, and the recently produced *Isabella or the Pot of Basil* (Keats) is a magical piece of theatre.

What constitutes good puppet theatre? There is a quality – possibly not unique to puppet theatre but certainly unique to theatre – that puppets can have peculiarly strongly. It is the very reverse of charm. There are moments of unnerving strangeness: it is something to do with the juxtaposition of unexpected things, something to do with the suspension of disbelief and puppets can be peculiarly moving and disturbing in a quite irrational way. When that happens, that is what puppet theatre can be about.

The nearest analogy I can find is that of the conjuror. Intellectually, you know that what is being done is a trick; it cannot possibly really happen, but on every other level, you are seeing something impossible happen. It is the tension between what you know intellectually and what, emotionally and imaginatively, you are convinced is happening, which is really the attraction of conjurors, which makes you gasp. I think that puppets can have a similar effect when suspension of disbelief really occurs with them; intellectually you know that it is a doll being manipulated but on the imaginative level you are absolutely convinced it is real. This can give delight, it can make people rock with laughter.

One of the best examples of this I saw in the Salzburg Marionettes' production of *The Barber of Seville*. At the end of a song, which was beautifully done, he sat down and just crossed his ankles: the timing was perfect, the movement was perfect, and the audience went through the roof with joy at that simple gesture because somehow it was so real it

289

transcended the reality of the actor – even though we all knew it was artificial. It was this tension between the two things that gave the audience the sheer delight, sheer joy.

The difference between this and trying to look real is that it is catching the essence of something, not just a carbon copy of being lifelike.

What is appropriate and what is not in terms of literature for puppets? I am always astonished at what you can get away with in puppet theatre.

Alan Judd adds: it is a bit like the old rule of making films: it is practically impossible to make a film of a long novel – the best bit of literature to pick from is a short story because then the film can do its own kind of playing and expansion in its own terms. If you have an enormous novel, all you can do is cut it down. In the same way, take something that is a masterpiece; try to do it with puppets and you will only belittle it. You cannot make it any better.

Barry continues: you want to adapt first-rate second-rate material like Keats' *Isabella*; Oscar Wilde is another one, and the fairy stories. You can pull them about, whereas Keats' *La Belle Dame sans Merci* is an absolutely perfect work of art: you must not touch it. You cannot add anything to it or bring out any aspect of that work in any other medium.

Also, I think you have got to think about puppets being rather like children; they have got to work always in the here-and-now and absolutely in concrete terms. They cannot philosophise, cannot really look back over the past; they have got to be in the moment or moving forwards. This is a fundamental principle.

In our *Faustus* I was amazed at how much of the final speech we could keep intact, that wonderful speech with the clock striking the hours:

> *Faustus*   Ah, Faustus,
> Now hast thou but one bare hour to live,
> And then thou must be damned perpetually!
> Stand still, you ever-moving spheres of Heaven,
> That time may cease, and midnight never come;
> Fair Nature's eyes, rise, rise again and make
> Perpetual day; or let this hour be but
> A year, a month, a week, a natural day,
> That Faustus may repent and save his soul!
> *O lente, lente, currite noctis equi!*
> The stars move still, time runs, the clock will strike,
> The Devil will come, and Faustus must be damned.
> O, I'll leap up to my God! Who pulls me down?
> See, see where Christ's blood streams in the firmament!
> One drop would save my soul – half a drop: ah, my Christ!

Faustus was talking about concrete images, in the moment. The parts we cut were the philosophising around the images, around his state of mind. But, if he is stating his state of mind *in that moment* and expressing it *through images*, then that funny little eighteen inch puppet can sustain it perfectly well. The audience must do the philosophising, not the puppet.

There are two pieces at the *bottom* of my list for turning into puppet theatre: *Alice in Wonderland* and *A Midsummer Night's Dream*. For all its

Figure 2 Dr. Faustus: *Mephistophi-lis rising out of Hellmouth*

imagery, the humour and power of *Alice* is conceptual, through the power of words. It is a very English kind of humour, rather like that of Ken Dodd, but it is *verbal* – verbal imagery – and for all the white rabbits, caterpillars and all the other things in *Alice*, it is conceptual verbal humour and you cannot really translate that into three dimensions. This is why *any* visual adaptation of *Alice* sooner or later will fall down; finally you have got to come to those words because the image is static. The image really is not doing anything and it is summed up perfectly by the Cheshire Cat who disappears until there is nothing but the smile. It is verbal: it is in your head.

A Midsummer Night's Dream is a *wonderful* play. The fairies and fairyland are built up through a tapestry of verbal images, *word* images – this is the magic of it – and it is not the stuff of puppet theatre at all. Consider the mechanicals: you run into the problem of these workmen playing the parts of actors as best they can. The joy and the emotional response from the audience are because they are trying so hard and they mean it from their hearts, although it is uproariously funny. But if you

291

make them into puppets, once they come on in the *Pyramus and Thisbe* play, dressed up, they are *different* puppets. They *are* the character, not somebody *playing* the character, so the whole point of the piece is gone. They are amateur workmen playing a part on that great night and something strange touches them all – they transcend themselves in the art of coarse acting. Moreover, the whole background of *A Midsummer Night's Dream* is made up of verbal tapestry; there are all kinds of writing styles in it which go to delineate the various worlds – the human world, the fairy world, the world of the mechanicals – and all this is lost in puppet theatre. Puppet theatre cannot add anything to this.

How do you first approach a possible text?   Not taking the text just on its face value, but saying 'what is this really about?' I owe largely to my training at Central School of Speech and Drama, where they just went on and on about it: 'Now come on, what's this really about? Now, Barry, why did you do it that way? Why did you say that line that way? Why? Why? Why?' You felt almost as though you were being analysed out of existence or that all your wonderful talent was disappearing up the spout, but they were dead right and Alan Judd has carried on the same sort of discipline. I come out with a new idea for a production and he will say 'Yes, but what's it all about? Why are you doing it? That's a bit of "wouldn't it be fun if"...'

But always, when you get a fairy story or a Grimm's folk tale, surely you must say: 'What's this all about?' You have got to get through the surface of the stories until something starts twitching like the diviner's rod, and you say 'Hey, there's something down there; let's find what it is.' You have a kind of little buzz about something that happens in the story and you say 'That's fascinating; why has it got me?' So you stop and look under the surface to find what is really there.

One of the things that distresses me is when I see companies take classic folk or fairy tales and demean them, treat them trivially, exploit them in a jokey, superficial way.

What then says to you: 'This is a piece we should do?'   There is sometimes a feeling that we have just got to get a new production together. This does play a part: it gives a sense of urgency. I have been fortunate in being able to do the productions I have really wanted to do and the desire to do something comes from a kind of gut feeling that this is going to make good theatre.

Certain constraints operate in making such decisions – the artists available, the budget, the number of people we can afford in the company, the audience, what is going to sell – maybe I don't always make inspired decisions about that! But, finally, I do it because I really want to do it; it is a piece which is making fresh demands on me, something which perhaps I have not done before.

Having decided on your production, what is your next step?   You must get your text or your scenario (outline of the action) sorted out; that is most important. And the actual physical shape of the production – the kind of puppets you are going to use, etc. These things happen simultaneously. Take, for example, *Isabella*: I thought of it more or less in terms of particular kinds of puppets; I had images floating about in my mind for some years and then, having seen Bruce Schwartz perform, I thought: 'That's it, that kind of puppet and that kind of presentation is

Figure 3 Keats' Isabella or the Pot of Basil: *Isabella with the head of Lorenzo, her lover*

right for *Isabella*. I can see my way to doing it now.' Very often I have an idea or a piece in mind, but cannot see my way through. I do not need to have all the details, I just need that final clue to say: 'Of course, that's the way.' Once I have got that far, I'm home and dry really, most of the other problems can be solved.

What does working on the text involve?   To put it crudely, picking out the bits that will work with puppets – and you have got to see it visually in your head. I'm editing all the time, and perhaps writing text where really necessary to make the links.

Isabella was mainly a case of editing, juxtaposing – doing a scissors and paste job. Also thinking about it in terms of stage action, in terms of music, what is happening on stage, projections and so on. All that is going on, so one is seeing the total thing, not just the words.

Faustus was also an editing job – editing the text in a way that would work with what I had in mind. I think one was asking what it meant to the

Figure 4 Starchild

audience of the day; how much or what aspects of that experience could be valid now? I came to the conclusion that it was a piece of popular theatre, cashing in on a best-selling book that happened to have a genius as one of the writers.

Starchild was written for us but it was a round-the-table thing time and time again; we would discuss the action and the sub-text very strongly – what the puppets could do and could not do. Then the writer would go back and do some more writing, but it was in many ways a committee job from which the writer would go away and shape the text.

Writers not very experienced with puppets find it very difficult to write for them, to compress action into a few sentences. They go through a lot of dialogue – wrapping – in order to get to the point. I think the text becomes more worthwhile and powerful if you set up a kind of juxtaposition between the words and the image that the puppet is making – and between those words and that image the audience makes a connection, as a kind of sparking gap which is where the audience is doing the work. This is the great secret, making the audience work and to stop trying to do it all for them. Your word, your music, your image – let the audience start making connections, imagining what is going on.

For example, take the verse about autumn in *Isabella*

> ...So sweet Isabel
> by gradual decay from beauty fell

You can have quite a still image of the figure there and those words going on. Something happens between the two: the audience are working. This is what a lot of people working with puppets forget; their function is to make the audience do the work. You set it up but let them discover what is going on inside the puppet's head or its heart, what the ideas are in the sub-text, and so on.

Design and construction   The design and the making of the puppets, I can do. It starts after the text or the scenario is written and the mode of staging is decided. Everything then hangs fire on the puppets; we do not work with lay figures but the actual ones to be used. They may not be completely finished but I try to get them in a workable state.

How do we decide whether to use a masked actor or a puppet for a particular character? It is scale really *and* what seems appropriate. What, in my experience, does not work is using a life-sized puppet. You get neither the advantages of an actor nor the flexibility in time and space of the smaller puppet; I suffered from this and it was a very conscious effort to pull back the size.

When we came to *Faustus*, we had a smaller company and everything was scaled down. I felt at first as if I were failing or losing face in some way and then realised, of course, it was nothing of the kind. I discovered the strength of being smaller and deliberately made the puppets small – traditional glove puppets. And the smallness of the *Faustus* figures meant we had wonderful flexibility on the stage. When you are using small puppets, you can get away with outrageous things.

The designer comes in quite early in the production. The relationship of the design of the puppets and the whole concept of the sets, etc. involves a lot of negotiation and discussion with the designer but we never have any real problems with it. The designer may produce initial designs which you might reject in the early days but he is prepared for this.

Alan Judd interposes: people talk an awful lot about design and concept and content, etc. but essentially what you do is put the thing on so that things do not clash. If something sticks out, you change it.

Barry continues: the designer's brief is usually the actual dimensions and shape of the space we are going to work in. I am not a set designer at all and I am very limited in how I can actually set up a space in which to work. With *Faustus*, though the designer was given the space we were working in, she made her designs in such a way as to make that space quite perfect and magical. She would take my ideas for the space we were using and make it so right in a way I never could.

Where does the music or the composer fit in?   It depends on the purpose of the music. If it is incidental music, either you choose music which is absolutely fitting, as in *The Fair Maguelone*, or you choose something deliberately anachronistic but somehow the juxtaposition sparks something off. The music for *Faustus* was folk-rock – Emerson, Lake and

Figure 5   Mephistophilis and Faustus

295

Palmer – and it worked because we were presenting *Faustus* as a piece of popular folk theatre; that's what it was to the audience of its day. Can you convey that spirit to a modern audience to get a similar reaction? I think the music helped with this.

We had music specially composed for two productions. The *Starchild* music a charming folk-rock band composed, I think very successfully. We used the songs to provide the sub-text, so the words of the songs are about what is going on underneath the surface. I do not know how much people really listen to the words of a song; this is one reason why I like to bring an audience 'down', to achieve that quality of attention. It is the most rewarding response you can get from an audience, particularly of children. Curiously enough, *Maguelone* worked wonderfully in this way with children; you could hear a pin drop for half an hour.

The overall pace of *Maguelone* is fairly steady; it is not a quick razzamatazz piece at all but there is always something happening, a continuous flow of movement going on. It is not 'super-charged' at all in the way that most people think children's entertainment has to be. It is really quite esoteric and tricky in places. All of the music was chosen before we got to the rehearsal and was changed as necessary along the way. We usually choose the music first, then time it in rehearsal, make adjustments and then make up the final performance tape by about the last week of rehearsal.

When we prepared *Isabella*, the composer would produce about thirty yards of music for each sequence! We would rehearse each sequence, find out how long it was going to last, then give the composer the time; he would tailor those musical ideas to the time needed.

Finding the musicians is a matter of luck – if you are moving in certain circles, you meet certain kinds of people. You keep your eyes and ears open for opportunities and contacts.

Rehearsals Prior to rehearsal you will have had read-throughs of the script, discussed the text and the characters, but then the first thing to do in rehearsal is to get the whole thing 'blocked' so that people know where they are going: the sheer mechanics of moving around the stage and making a note of stage management is needed quite early on. This is part of the movement of the whole performance for the puppeteer, working the lighting board with the same care and attention as working the puppets.

You break down into smaller and smaller units with more and more detail and then you keep going back to the total thing. Blocking can take the first week of three weeks' rehearsal and you start breaking down in the second week; by the third week you are starting to build up again and getting it right. By the last three or four days' rehearsal you will be running the complete show, stopping where necessary to look at detail, but in relation to the total package.

You must not get the puppeteer confused about sorting out the puppet acting – directing the individual acting performance – with the total tempo and structure of the scene. Though they are obviously tied up to a certain extent, if you are getting the tempo rhythms right in a scene and you see bits of individual acting going wrong, leave it; make a mental note and come back later. Do not break in the middle of it to work on a lot of detail.

One tends to spend most time on 'cutting it down' to the least that has to be done to get the effect. Most puppeteers *do* too much; if we don't know what to do, most of us do everything. Most companies not only do too much acting and too much talking, but they do it for too long as well. It is something to do with the feeling that, if you are not doing something or talking, you might disappear.

Until people have got confidence knowing actually where they are, their entrances and exits, and larger issues with props and stage management, it is no use trying to coax them into a performance; they are too worried about the mechanics. Once you have got the major positions, you can work within that framework. Then it is a matter of working it out and building up a muscular memory, so that your fingers are always ahead.

The problem with puppets is that you can have a wonderful movement for them but how do you get out of that into the next? Every movement you do has got to be a preparation for the next; it is very difficult indeed to get the effects you want *and* to get them flowing.

In puppet theatre you have got to work very hard at *continuity*. You must involve your audience in a process from the moment they walk into the auditorium. I am always rather excited when we set up Pierrot in repose on his box, spotlit in dim light. The audience come in, see it and start talking about it; expectations are aroused from the moment they come in. That process must not falter; if the audience is caught up in the process, it does not matter if the process is a slow one, provided the movement is there.

My pieces tend to move rather slowly anyway, but I am interested in deliberately cooling an audience down, trying to take the whole thing onto a subtle level. I like pace; I like noise; I like to have the audience joining in when I am doing *Punch* or *St George* or any of those things, but one has to distinguish between *pace* and *speed*. Lupino Lane gave the advice to a beginner in slapstick comedy: 'Take your time, take your time.' The more I do, the more I see the value of this. Watch Laurel and Hardy or Morecambe and Wise: they seem to have all the time in the world and this comes through immense technical confidence. You have to *think quickly but take your time*. Your mind has got to be way ahead, but take your time with what you are doing.

It is always a problem to determine how much you expect the puppeteers to bring to the performance as compared with what you impose. Puppet theatre tends to be much more pre-set by its nature, because so much has to be prepared beforehand, so puppeteers tend to have a stricter, more limiting framework than an actor or a singer or perhaps even a dancer.

I try to have a firm framework within which we all have to work and there is a concept of the production there before you go in, which by its nature cannot be changed very much. But within that, I like to create as much space as possible for the puppeteers to create and invent for themselves. This happened with Gillie Robic playing Isabella; within the framework I tried to give her as much of a free hand as possible to create the character and to make the scene work. Eventually, to a large degree everything stands or falls by the skill of the puppeteer. So the puppeteers have a chance to really perform and show their skills.

Almost everything else is secondary; your text or your scenario are of the utmost importance, but then it is the performers. The designer for me comes much lower down the hierarchy, although of course design is still important and you must have a good designer.

As you get confidence in yourself and your own abilities, then you begin to get confidence in what other people can do and leave them alone to get on with it. It is very difficult sometimes still: I get bees in my bonnet about certain things, but I have got easier slowly. I used to hiss at people in the wings and give them notes while they were on stage; I used to do this quite a lot. It must have been very difficult for people to work with me in the early days as I was directing the show as it was going on, probably through lack of confidence.

Working in view of the audience   Pierrot was made as an experimental figure after seeing Bunraku. We played around with him in the company; one or two acts evolved for him and we started to use him. One or two ideas we tried didn't work out and those we dropped.

Then I had the idea of using a mask to create the character. Eventually we evolved five acts and I had the idea of putting them all together into a complete act. We considered spreading it through the whole programme, between other pieces as we were unsure how it would work as a whole piece. It was only after I had done the act for a few months that I really began to think what it was all about. It is about the persona, the mask we all wear and what is underneath.

One of the attractions of Pierrot and why he can be done in so many kinds of venues is that he inhabits the same space as the audience. Faustus, by comparison, is in a framework of some kind: he inhabits that confined space. I am not sure what sort of difference that makes, but it does make a difference to the effect he has on the audience. Audiences now are so used to seeing something inside that frame of the television screen, that when they go to a theatre I think it is perhaps more interesting for them to discover theatre going on in the same space as they are in. Though good theatre is good theatre anyway.

The technique of bringing the puppeteer out in front of the audience, getting him to appear on stage with his puppet, is very fashionable; it is a cliché now. It all goes wrong when it becomes coquettish, in a sense flirting with the audience. It is a difficult technique to learn: sometimes puppeteers are acting their socks off; sometimes they look as though they are up in front of the magistrate and about to be sentenced. They might instead acknowledge the audience, let the audience see their eyes, actually present themselves but not flirt with the audience nor try to pretend they are not there. When the action proper starts, they focus on the puppets and direct their energies into the puppet.

The puppeteer is a *supporter* who is active in quite a different way from the puppet he is supporting. This featured prominently also in *Starchild* and *Act without Words*. There were no established principles to follow: we just worked intuitively on what seemed right. In *Starchild* the boy (a Bunraku-style rod puppet) has to handle a variety of props such as a bag and a number of talismen. The puppeteers, who were working in full view of the audience, were used in a supportive role to do these things on his behalf in an almost ritualistic manner. The bag was placed around his necl

Figure 6   Pierrot in three masks

and the talismen were handed across and put in the bag *for* the boy, as it were. It was *as if* he were doing it. We took hours on that.

Performing for children   I have never minded doing work for children. Some people do say: 'Barry Smith hates children.' It's not true, not true at all. I love working for children but we have been forced to polarise – the only way I can do *Isabella* or *Faustus* is to pull right out of the children's market. If one is identified with children's shows, they simply won't take you seriously as a performer for adults. One of the minor reasons why we did *Isabella* was to make an absolutely clean break. It is not suitable for children at all: probably the only piece we have which is not accessible to youngsters. It is dealing with areas of experience and language that have not come into their lives yet. If one could work with young people and adult audiences simultaneously, nobody would be more pleased than me.

We have been thinking it would be interesting now to do some young people's work with some real guts in it: most work presented for children is both sentimental and exploitative. I think attitudes to children are very

Figure 7 Samuel Beckett's Act Without Words

Figure 8 Duchess Grognon, Envy and Fairy Chrystallina from The Chrystal Palace

strange indeed. We deny them any kind of reality and we deny the reality of our own childhoods. We will not face up to that reality recollected with clarity and honesty.

One of the most abominable things about children's entertainment is the assumption that they all love being treated as a great gang together. So many children *hate* school parties, loathe being with a mob of other children, and yet we persist in thinking that this is what children like. Very few children really do like being surrounded by a mob of other screaming children. But if you are a 'kid', you are part of an exploitable market.

Why do we persist in beaming on children the kind of fictional golden ideal? Of course a child can experience moments of sheer bliss but that's not all: it can be very painful to be a child. What is being done for children, in puppet theatre in particular, seems to bear little resemblance to the inner life of a child.

The approach of Ray DaSilva

Ray DaSilva is director of the Norwich Puppet Theatre, and the DaSilva Puppet Company.

For many years his name has been synonymous with quality puppet theatre. It is one of the most successful British companies ever and has advanced the cause of puppet theatre on many fronts – not least the training it has provided to so many of our puppeteers. Ray is widely admired as a director; he is perceptive, his standards are high and he has no pretensions about his work.

When Ray and Joan DaSilva married, they were presenting Ray's magic act in variety, but he also had a Punch and Judy show, as a result of his early attraction to puppets and model threatres. In 1956, they took these acts to Canada where they added a puppet cabaret act to the repertoire, returning to Britain in 1962 to tour working men's clubs, a 'baptism of fire'.

Then based at Godmanchester, Huntingdon, they started to build a repertoire of touring shows with a company that has since varied in size between seven and seventeen puppeteers, producing a wide variety of performances ranging from a highly spectacular *Snow White* (1967), capable of performing to audiences of up to two thousand, to Prokofiev's *Peter and the Wolf* or *Paper Tiger*, which is based on a Japanese legend.

One of the aims of the DaSilva Puppet Company was to establish a performing base where its own work and that of other puppet companies could be presented under the best conditions and 1978 saw the beginnings of the move to Norwich where the semi-derelict St James' Church, a splendid medieval building, was to be renovated as the Norwich Puppet Theatre. The theatre opened in December 1980 with *Humbug, Humbug*, an interpretation of Dickens' *A Christmas Carol*, whilst the touring company performed nationwide with *Pinocchio*. It has drawn also upon the DaSilva Puppets' existing repertoire and its most recent new production was a remarkably ambitious version of *Alice*.

Since 1981, the doors of the theatre have been open to visiting companies, in keeping with the theatre's stated policy, and the Norwich Puppet Theatre, whilst struggling – like all puppet companies – to cope with the current economic pressures, is continuing its building development and establishing itself as a major centre for puppet theatre.

The role of the director   My role changes daily from the chap who sells ice creams, to the chap who cleans out the drains, to the chap who helps in design. In our present situation, I have to be a Jack-of-all-trades, but I feel I ought to be master of one. My job in the first place is as a co-ordinator and a pointer-of-the-way. This does not necessarily mean I dictate everything – though to be honest I dictate quite a lot really. I try to take the people we have and steer their ideas into the production we are doing.

I sometimes present alternatives and there is a certain amount of freedom, as there is in the performance. For example, we have performed *Peter and the Wolf* for years but each time it is done, although there is an overall pattern (they have to get from A to B within so many bars of music), how they do it depends to a very large extent on what they give me during rehearsals. I build on that; if they do not give, I have to dictate. For this reason, in this company there does not seem to be an overall house design style, though people who know puppet theatre might be able to say: 'that is one of Ray's shows'. The show we do reflects the talents of the people that we have at the time.

I do delegate tasks to members of the company and, whilst I may have an overall veto, I do not use it very often. People talk about the scale of puppet theatre permitting a unity in the performance but the price paid is that one person thinks he can do it all. I think I can do them all – badly! I recognised this twenty years ago. I think our approach now works very well. I *am* capable of modelling a head and doing the other tasks; I like to think the

Figure 9   Pinocchio

Figure 10   Prokofiev's Peter and the Wolf

Figures 9 to 15 all by The DaSilva Puppets, Norwich Puppet Theatre)

people to whom I give the different jobs do it better. But I know exactly what I am asking them to do, and if anything is wrong I have a good idea of what is the matter with it, so this probably does bring some unity to the production, although full credit must go to the people who do the actual nitty-gritty.

Deciding what to perform   There are three *main* criteria, though there might be others as well. There are lots of things that puppet theatre can interpret in a way that live theatre cannot – to bring another approach to a piece – and that is the first criterion: something that puppetry can do in a special way. The second criterion is that I have to like it and want to do it. The third criterion is that I have to be able to sell it. We have to consider our sponsorship too but I do not let this dictate the show. The show comes first.

Occasionally, we put on something that may not be so saleable but that is worthwhile doing – perhaps something experimental and exciting which I think Norwich Puppet Theatre ought to be doing. We *have* done all sorts of weird and funny things too; this is something puppeteers have to do.

I would never attempt to do, for example, *A Midsummer Night's Dream* or *Peter Pan*, mainly because of the criteria listed above, but also take *Peter Pan*: you might say that all those things flying about is a natural for marionettes but it is not, because you lose the point of it all – the thrill of those *humans* flying.

I think the prime thing all the time is the *visual* element. Some people concentrate more than I do on the message; I would not want to undervalue that but we have to play for a very broad audience, so we try to think in terms of what will appeal visually.

Figure 11   Paper Tiger

Developing the scenario   First we think in terms of a title. This comes very early because the title is the selling point; the play may then be adapted to suit the title. To start with, I do not write words: I draw pictures – compose a storyboard – and then fill in the gaps.

I have never started with a text to translate into a puppet play. Usually the words came last in my productions. I have looked at plays but they are so impossible! I have never yet found a text written for live theatre that I feel I can translate immediately into puppet terms, nor a puppet play that somebody else has written that I can put on without too much work on it.

With *Paper Tiger* we had no title to start with. It was inspired from one member of the company practising his origami: some of his models had an inherent puppetesque quality. I thought we could build a show on those simple design concepts. We thought of all sorts of ideas like *Paper Chain*, *Paper Chase*, etc. and eventually came up with the theme of *Paper Tiger*, which means that a creature appears to be much more powerful than he is – a front that people put on. That gave us the message for the show. Then we thought of the thousands of shapes that can be formed from a folded piece of paper and we got onto the idea of transformations. We read a lot of Japanese stories and collected a lot of background information, looking for transformations. We wanted a character transformed so we identified the different sides of the character by different coloured papers rather than shape. We had the notion of an antagonist and protagonist who, in order to combat one another, each change into different creatures. We also listened to a lot of Japanese music and built the play from there.

After the scenario what is the next step?   We listen to music. Very often the music suggests action too and we try to use quite a bit of music within the show. For *Paper Tiger* we used some records; we also persuaded the Japanese School in London to record some songs for us and somebody else

303

to compose music for us. So the visuals and the music come in very early. It is rather like a ballet in a sense.

The eventual script we have tried to evolve in various ways, with varying success. In one production we had ideas, storyboard, music, scenic ideas, puppet designs and gave the lot to an excellent writer who understood puppet theatre and within the context she did a very good job. That was excellent. Prior to that, we had gone to a writer who put in all manner of things we found impossible to do; the thoughts expressed and the language were quite inappropriate for puppets to handle.

The design and development of the production   The designer comes in very early on. I draw up some rough ideas, the setting, etc. Then on one production the designer and I went off to look at the actual area in which the play was set (the Black Forest), did a lot of drawings, took photographs, listened to music, watched local dancing, etc. He then did lots of sketches, as a result of which the story changed again. It is very much an organic thing, moving along on a front together. There is not one thing in front of another at that stage until we feel that we have explored long enough and it is time to get something down.

At that point, we write a very basic script in very crude style. But it is not at all rigid, just a working script. We now also sort out the logistics: for example, what market do you have in mind? What can that market afford? How many puppeteers can we afford? So finance comes in at this early stage. If you can afford only two people, can two people handle all that is required? And the staging designs and technical aspects come in: we need a parade of soldiers – do we paint them all on one cut-out board, or have a sort of conveyor belt, or a revolve, or what? These will affect the design and perhaps the storyline. We don't sort out *all* the problems then, of course; some we have not even thought of yet.

At this point, we do some serious design: the puppets come first. We might have an overall design concept – such as designing all the scenery as though it were a jigsaw puzzle – but these rough designs are put on one side and we concentrate upon the puppets as they are the main thing.

We work out their size (which will depend on the logistics as well), relative sizes and sketch them to scale. We add the colour and come up with pretty firm ideas about what the puppets should look like; then we actually start making them.

If it is a new production, very often we make practice puppets – either existing ones adapted or even instant puppets. Then we have a run through with these practice figures, which uncovers all sorts of problems. It gives you a good idea of what the puppets may be required to do so that you can build this into their construction. Until now, the design of the puppet had been the *visual*; the try-out helps to define the technicalities. We might also find we need a duplicate, or even triplicate, of the puppet if it is to perform highly specialised actions.

We spend about twenty-five percent of our production time on the design and logistics, all before the script is prepared. The script would not be coming into play until about halfway through the production period.

The 'work-out' sometimes helps to determine the script too. Although we have the rough script, I try to get actors at this stage to explore the puppets. I would like to have puppeteers who have a knowledge of acting but in this country there are not that many acting puppeteers. Our actors improvise a script based on the roughs that we produce, and we usually record this but we do not use it. We transcribe it and refine it continually until we get the words down to a bare minimum.

I do not suggest this is *the* way to do it; it is not a model for anybody else, just a method that suits us.

Now we are about halfway through the production period and we must get the tapes made as we tend to use pre-recorded tapes, the preparation of which for a schools' show could take as much as three months for one person. This is when we engage the actors; the composer has prepared his music by now which might be adjusted right up to the actual recording session, and the musicians also have to be engaged. We have made all the arrangements with the recording studio and then we record a series of different tracks which we blend into one, as detailed below.

At the same time, we must be organising the photographs so that we can start selling the show. Usually, the only pictures we can produce for this are of the puppets, which is fine for most things. If we have somebody with graphic design in the team, we start involving them in the design of leaflets, brochures, programmes, posters and we start thinking about merchandise. If there is to be anything we are going to produce to go along with the show, it might take three or four months to prepare and get printed or made.

The lighting   We get involved with lighting right from the design stage, because we have to think about costume, painting the sets, etc. and how this will look under stage lights. I do not pretend that at that early stage we light all our designs with different colours to see how it will look; experience counts for a lot in knowing what colours respond to what. But we do think about lighting in terms of both colour and the actual physical places in which to put lights.

It is important, if you possibly can, to light the puppets with different lamps from those used to light the scenery, but I am very aware of the problems of doing that. I enjoy John Wright's (Little Angel Theatre) lighting better than anybody's, certainly better than mine. Again, it is a question of style and the lighting should support that. I think I tend to use less realistic lighting – perhaps more pantomime lighting. John Wright's is very gentle and I admire that very much; it creates beautiful pictures and that is his style.

It is important to get a unity between all these different aspects and not to let the whole thing fall down in any one area, which it can so easily, including in our productions: we reserve the right to make mistakes!

The use of taped dialogue   The taping of a show is acceptable for certain purposes if it is done well, but my general advice to most people is to avoid taping the show. This is especially true in the eductional situation where children are using pappets.

The tape suits our needs here and the style of our show, but I would not try to tape something like Punch and Judy – that would be ridiculous, though I have heard of it happening. Some types of performance are much more appropriate with live voices and where the performers can respond more directly to the audience. One recognises though that, for economic reasons, puppeteers have often to perform a number of times a day, and there are the physical problems of operating puppets and speaking live from within a stage, behind curtains. There are already so many constraints on finding puppeteers who can do what you want them to do, it makes it even more difficult if you also have to ensure that they can speak for a beautiful princess *and* a dragon.

However, if something goes wrong on stage, you have little room to improvise with a tape, unless it is a show with an intermittent tape just for background or special effects.

Creating the master-tape   Producing the actual tape is quite a complex business; our method is not particularly original. The actors will have read the play together and rehearsed it before we get to the recording studio as studio time is *very* expensive (the actual recording of *Jack and the Beanstalk* took about two days and *Alice* about four days). I think the voice actors should know exactly what the puppets look like; they enjoy having an improvised session with them and it is most valuable – it makes all the difference to the performance they give. The voice work needs to be more clearcut, more staccato for puppets than a recording for radio. We record our voice track – and we record *everything* – we keep all the takes, the mistakes, repeats, etc. and we then edit it *very* carefully. It could take two or three weeks just to edit the voice track for a fifteen minute show.

Once you are into a show, if you need to make changes in the tape in the light of audience response, it is more difficult than, for example, giving your actors notes. This is why we keep all our original material, so that I can re-mix a section if I need to, but it is a chore as you will appreciate when I explain the rest of the process.

Once we have recorded the voice track we might listen to a phrase and split it right in the middle because we prefer the ending when it was said another time. We edit to make the best of the material we have.

Then we record the music on another track. The original voice and music tracks for *Alice* each consisted of four fifteen-inch spools of tape. We now start thinking about sound effects, and there are two types: background effects, which are going on all the time and creating atmosphere, and spot sound effects. I do the former first; I think of the atmosphere of the scene in two senses – the environment and the mood or feeling and I decide what acoustic I am going to have going on all the time in the background. When I am preparing the background, I might decide to have, say, a clock ticking away all the time, which the audience will be very aware of as the scene starts, but then I will take it right down so that you can hardly hear it, but it is just there. It is like painting a picture: if you put on too many layers, it gets muddy. There might be gaps in the scene where there is suspense or where somebody is walking about or thinking, where I might bring up that little bit of background. I record sufficient of that background to keep it running all the time I am doing the mixing so that I can just bring it up and down when I want to. I also use tape loops, echoes and pre- echoes and all the other techniques and usual gadgetry of sound.

The other soundtrack is the spot effects, the funnies, the things that have to be synchronised with the puppets: doors opening and shutting, etc. Sometimes, several of these might be mixed together; background sounds also get mixed together as scenes change, and so on. When you get visual

Figure 12   Alice

scene changing, you also get sound changing at the same time. We then mix all these things together on to one master-tape, which is great fun! It also requires great concentration.

Clearly then, the decision to re-edit a tape brings a chain of implications, but we do have reference points to which we can go back within the master-tape. It might be a silent pause, a note of music or a point where there is only one track being fed on at that moment, so if we want to alter three or four words, we might have to go back and alter only about half a minute.

Principles of working with a tape   A lot of people would imagine that you are a slave to the tape, but you need not be. They think the tape is grinding on relentlessly and you have to keep up with it but this is far from the case. Once the company gets to know the tape thoroughly – every nuance of it – the tape works for them and you exploit that tape in different ways. The soundtrack is always the same, but the audience is different and every performance is different.

To give an example, in *Jack and the Beanstalk*, when Jack climbs down the beanstalk, he pauses and looks up; you can hear the Giant coming, the thunder, etc. Sometimes a child in the audience quite spontaneously shouts: 'Fetch the axe!' Jack says: 'Ah, the axe' and off he goes to get it. He brings it back and looks at it; someone shouts: 'Chop it down!' He will

Figure 13   The Giant from Jack and the Beanstalk

Figure 14   The auditorium of Norwich Puppet Theatre

look at them and perhaps they shout it again; then off he goes. If the child had not shouted 'Fetch the axe!' Jack would come down, look up thoughtfully and then say 'Ah, the axe!' as if he had just thought of it and off he goes.

So in the actual writing of the play you can plan for, and build in, the possibility of this audience response. But I do not mean in any way that you leave gaps; it is the worst possible thing to leave gaps for laughter or other audience reactions. You cover that gap: if there is a likelihood of audience reaction at that point, you put something in that does not matter if it is covered by laughter. Even dialogue can be used, like the puppet saying to himself: 'What am I going to do now?', or music, but *no gaps*.

The other important thing is that the performers work ahead of the tape; every action is preceded by thought. If I have to synchronise a puppet picking up something with the sound of it on tape, I get the puppet to *look* at it first and to *think* about what it is going to do. Even the way it thinks varies: it might look at the audience as if to say 'Shall I? Shan't I?', or scratch its head, or look at another character or peer at the object intently. *Then* it does it and the speech comes afterwards. You think, you move, and then you say: 'Here is a coin', or whatever. You do not say: 'Here is a coin', think and then pick it up. This is why the performers have to be ahead of the tape. They have to know what their next line is going to be, way ahead, so that they can set it up, so that the puppet can take a breath – and the puppets do have to take breaths and prepare themselves. A lot of puppeteers forget that.

Rehearsals We now have a master soundtrack; we play it to the puppeteers and they *always* say 'Impossible!' without fail. 'Rubbish.' 'Change the tape!' but it is a *very* rare occasion when we have to concede to that. When you start the rehearsal, you are learning something for the first time and it is inevitable you cannot do it the first time. But when they have done it a few times and developed the expertise of getting a piece of scenery onto the stage, or whatever, it all comes together and we can progress with the rehearsal process.

The logistics come very early in the production, as I said earlier, and in my pictures, my storyboard, we have the main blocking; we use models too and move them about to see how they look. We talk it over and jump in at the deep end and do it, we all know what the aim is but we have a little freedom to experiment and I sit out front to see what it looks like. So we build the main pictures and then fill in the detail and the flow between them.

What you then have to do as the Director, the things you have to correct, depends on the skills of the people with whom you are working. Usually we have a mix of experienced puppeteers and trainees. The trainees, you have to tell about thinking and getting ahead of that tape and not to worry; there is a lot of reassurance required. A lot of people feel they cannot do what you want within the given period of time and that the technical difficulties are insurmountable but after you get over certain hurdles it is straightforward.

I enjoy directing. It is probably the most rewarding aspect of my work – taking somebody's contribution and helping to develop it without taking it away from them.

I have copious notes and plans, and I very often use video. If you say to somebody: 'This is how I would like you to do it', they may say 'But that is how I *am* doing it.' You say: 'Well, no, not quite...'. If you take a video of the show the puppeteers can see it for themselves; we would do this in the later stages but not in the early stages or they will be completely demoralised. Our large-scale shows we rehearse for four or five weeks; our schools' shows we can do in a minimum of two and maximum of three weeks; about two-thirds of the way through, we can introduce a video.

One thing we never do under any circumstances is to show the puppeteers a video of a previous production of that show. This is very important because I like the show to be just as much theirs as it is mine. I also like them to go away from the dress rehearsal and the first show feeling that it falls short of perfection; if they feel that they have arrived, then it does not build. They can then go forward and the show will continue to grow.

When it comes to things like dropping a puppet or catching a string in the scenery, you try to anticipate this in rehearsal and you organise it so that your tree is 'puppet-proof' as far as you are able, or you allow for it and learn to cover such contingencies. You try not to panic too!

It is absolutely essential to have somebody out front for rehearsals. It is useless trying to perform in front of a mirror; a mirror is occasionally handy just to check out a small detail but you cannot be a slave to the mirror and you have to have somebody you can trust out front.

It is very important that you allow your puppeteers rest, though we do a nine-to-five day with the usual breaks and a five-day week. I usually have to work weekends as well trying to sort out all kinds of problems that have been uncovered. We have quite a lot of leeway in the rehearsals and, if I find that something is flagging, then we do something else for a while.

Once the show is in performance, there is usually not very much to do to it. You *are* doing fine tuning all the time (and giving praise where it is due). It is a matter of maintaining the standard, watching the development of a show and not ignoring it, but going out to see it, maintaining a continual contact with the performing team. Otherwise, they imagine you are sitting back in the office smoking cigars whilst they are out earning the money to keep you – which is not the way it is at all.

The permanent puppet theatre   The whole idea of us having a permanent theatre in the first place was so that we could control the environment in which we present our shows. I think puppeteers usually like to control everything! I felt a need to control the environment as I felt our shows were often being presented in unsuitable settings.

As to the actual running of the theatre, our policy here is very broad and some may argue that is not a good idea, but it is marvellous that we are gradually building up an educated clientele. We have a large number, and very broad base, of visiting puppeteers and we acknowledge that many of those companies do work which is better than ours. Once puppeteers can get over the hurdle of acknowledging that, the scene will develop more.

Puppeteers who are busy working, of course, do not always see very much of the work of other puppeteers and fifteen to twenty years ago they tended to be very narrow-minded about their work: that was puppetry and what other people did was was not puppetry. There is probably still an element of this, but the situation is much improved.

Figure 15 . A scene from Alice

The financing of the theatre is subsidised very heavily from the touring operation. What we do in the theatre is very much a luxury. Visiting companies cost us a lot of money. We do get a grant from the Eastern Arts Association to *help* to pay towards the cost of visiting companies; we have to subsidise the rest. But we need those visiting groups very much.

APPENDICES

Note: Whenever the French spelling of *marionnette* is used, it refers to puppets in general, not specifically string puppets.

1 Puppetry organisations and centres of activity

UNIMA (Union Internationale de la Marionnette)

The international puppetry organisation founded in 1929 and reconstituted in 1957. It has members in more than fifty countries and 'unites the puppeteers of the world'. UNIMA activities include a major festival and congress every four years, contacts and information for members travelling abroad, information of international puppetry affairs and events, and regular bulletins. Viewed in a national context, the various UNIMA Centres or sections may not appear to be very active, for it is in the international context of festivals, seminars, other events and contacts that the significance and influence of UNIMA is felt. There is a tremendous spirit of friendship, co-operation, of wanting to know and wanting to share. Enquiries to:

Australia:	Norman Hetherington (President), 17 Sirius Cove Road, Mosman, New South Wales 2088
Belgium:	Hubert Romain (Secretary), Maison de la Culture, Avenue Golenvaux, 5000 Namur
Canada:	Mrs Pat Overgaard, 887 Keith Road, West Vancouver, B.C.
France:	Julie Dourdy (Hon. Secretary), 86 rue Notre Dame des Champs, 75015 Paris
Great Britain:	Percy Press II (Hon. Secretary), 16 Templeton Road, London N15
Spain	Ana Maria Tempestini (Hon. Secretary), Edif. Horizonte Bl. IV-6°A, Tomares-Seville
Switzerland:	Margrit Gysin (Secretary), Gartenstrasse 2, 4410 Liestel
United States of America:	Allelu Kurten, (General Secretary), Browning Road, Hyde Park, NY 12538
West Germany:	Postfach 200551, 4690 Herne 2
Other countries:	The Secretary-General will supply details of officers in specific countries (please send international reply coupons): Jacques Félix, B.P. 249, 08102 Charleville-Mézières, France

Britain

The Puppet Centre Battersea Arts Centre, Lavender Hill, London SW11. *Telephone:* 01-228-5335. Open: 2.00 – 6.00 p.m. Monday to Friday; other times by appointment.

The Puppet Centre Trust, formed in 1974, is a national and international reference centre which serves the interests of all those engaged or interested in the art of the puppet, in performance, education or therapy. Its facilities include an excellent library and reference resource, a workshop, a modest collection of craftsman-made puppets for demonstration and practice, a specialist bookshop and a mobile exhibition.

Following a federation with the Educational Puppetry Association, an Education and Therapy Unit was established and the Trust now has an Education Officer, funded by the Inner London Education Authority.

Puppet Centre publications include a two-monthly periodical, *Animations*, a *Directory of Professional Puppeteers* and lists of performers in various categories. It has a flourishing programme of adult classes and courses, master classes, workshops for all ages and abilities, including for school children and handicapped people, and two annual bursaries for the further training of professional puppeteers.

The Puppet Centre has recently acquired the Hogarth Collection of puppets which was one of the best private (international and historical) collections in the world. It is not normally on display in the Puppet Centre but is available for exhibition hire nationwide.

The British Puppet and Model Theatre Guild Founded in 1925 as the British Model Theatre Guild, this organisation subsequently became the British Puppet and Model Theatre Guild. It is the oldest existing puppetry organisation in the world.

Enquiries to: Mr G. Shapley (Hon. Secretary), 18 Maple Road, Yeading, Nr Hayes, Middlesex.

The Punch and Judy Fellowship An association of Punch and Judy 'Professors' who meet at the 'Punch and Judy' public house in Covent Garden. Contact: Percy Press II, 16 Templeton Road, London N15.

The Brewery Puppet Centre, Brewery Arts Centre, Kendal, Cumbria, *Telephone:* 0539 25133
A developing, very active centre with workshops and performances.

Cannon Hill Puppet Theatre, Midlands Arts Centre for Young People, Cannon Hill Park, Birmingham 12, *Telephone;* 021 440 4221
Regular daily performances in a 200-seat theatre; lecture- demonstrations, courses for teachers, workshops for children, professional training. A major British company, directed by John Blundall.

Darlington Puppet Centre Darlington Arts Centre, Vane Terrace, Darlington DL3 7AX, *Telephone:* 0325 483271
A recently established puppet centre, the development of which includes workshops for children, a library and performances at the centre, in the town and in local schools.

Harlequin Puppet Theatre   Cayley Promenade, Rhos- on-Sea, Colwyn Bay, Wales, *Telephone:* (Christopher Somerville) 0492 82062
Open in summer season, includes a summer school and private tuition available throughout the year. Directed by Eric Bramall and Christopher Somerville.

Hayward Marionettes,   Abbots Bromley, Staffordshire.
Enquiries: D. Hayward, Edinburgh House, Bagot Street, Abbots Bromley, Nr Rugeley, Staffordshire
A 50-seat theatre taking block bookings only and performing solely on Thursday evenings; also a growing museum collection.

Little Angel Marionette Theatre,   14 Dagmar Passage, Cross Street, London N1 *Telephone:* 01 226 1787   Director: John Wright M.B.E.
A leading British company with a 100-seat theatre: performances at weekends for young children (Saturday mornings) and older children and adults (Saturday and Sunday afternoons); frequently has weekday performances during school half-terms and holidays and at certain times of the year. All types of puppetry presented, and seasons with guest companies, British and foreign.

The Little Puppet Theatre   Vicarage Road, St Agnes, Cornwall *Telephone:* 087 255 2154
120-seat theatre with summer season: facilities include workshop sessions and lecture-demonstrations and the development of a small studio is planned. The theatre is developing as a centre for other arts too.

Norwich Puppet Theatre   St James', Whitefriars, Norwich *Telephone:* 0603 615564   Director: Ray DaSilva
A development incorporating a theatre, workshops, a travelling workshop, courses for teachers, etc. The home of the DaSilva Puppets, a major British company.

Polka Children's Theatre   240 The Broadway, Wimbledon, London SW19 *Telephone:* 01 542 4258 *Box Office:* 01 543 0363   Director: Richard Gill
A 300-seat theatre, attractively displayed exhibition, workshop for courses, adventure room, full facilities for the handicapped.

The Puppet Barge (**Movingstage Marionette Company**)   Winter and Spring: Camden Lock (Regent's Canal), London. June to September: Tours the waterways of Southern England. Contact: Gren and Juliet Middleton, 78 Middleton Road, London E8

Australia

The Puppetry Guild of Australia   An organisation with separately administered sections in different areas. Each organises its own activities, including festivals, performances, lectures, demonstrations, films and meetings, and facilitates contact and advice. For information on the Guild and details of current officers in regional sections, contact: Norman Hetherington, President, 17 Sirius Cove Road, Mosman, New South Wales 2088

Carelew Arts Centre, 11 Jeffcett Street, North Adelaide, South Australia 5006. Tutor in puppetry: Joseph Neevcy

Clovelly Puppet Theatre Director: Edith Murray, 'Moonahwarra', Larson Road, Springwood, New South Wales 2777
A centre now run by the Creative Leisure Movement: the theatre offers performances and workshops. It has been the introduction to puppet theatre for a number of established puppeteers.

Marionette Theatre of Australia Sailors' Home Building, Sydney, New South Wales
Formed in 1965 as part of the Australian Elizabethan Theatre Trust, it became an independent organisation in 1979.

The Nutshell Puppet Theatre Director: Mrs Nancy Johnson, 54 Ord Street, West Perth, Western Australia 6007
Established in 1971, the theatre includes a 50-seat theatre, library, workshop, etc.

The United States

Puppeteers of America Founded in 1937, this is a large organisation with a membership in many countries. It aims at the improvement of the art of puppetry in all its forms through educational programmes, annual conferences, workshops, exhibitions and festivals. Its publication, *The Puppetry Journal*, is published quarterly, it has a Puppetry Store and a considerable number of affiliated regional guilds. Membership enquiries to: Gayle G. Schluter, 5 Cricklewood Path, Pasadena, California 91107.

The Center for Puppetry Arts (Executive Director: Vincent Anthony) 1404 Spring Street, Atlanta, Georgia
Facilities include a 300-seat theatre, workshop and conference areas, a display of some important exhibits, education room and reference library.

The Educational Puppetry Resource Center, 294 29th Street, San Francisco, California 94131
Offers consultancy programmes, puppetry library, occasional workshops, displays, audio-visual kits and a Resource Guide. Publishes *Puppetry in Education News*.

The National Puppet Center, 815 1/2 King Street, Alexandria, Virginia 22314 (Washington DC, Metropolitan area)
Is developing facilities for the performance and study of puppetry in a converted old vaudeville/movie house.

The National Puppetry Institute, (Director: Frank Ballard) Box U-127 P, The University of Connecticut, Storrs, Connecticut 06268
An independent body housed within the university; a centre for research and development in puppetry, is building up facilities for professional and para-professional puppeteers, for the investigation of the social role of puppetry as an entertainment, as an educational aid and for therapy.

For details of Regional Guilds and other centres of activity in the USA, contact the Puppeteers of America.

Other countries

Deutches Institut für Puppenspiel   Kohlenstrasse 70, 4630 Bochum 1, West Germany
A very active institute which has a range of training courses in aspects of puppet theatre. One can select and enrol for whichever of the courses one needs. Its journals (qv) are highly regarded and of practical and academic significance. Bochum is also the venue for an annual puppet festival and competition for amateur companies.

Institut International de la Marionnette   7 Place Winston Churchill, 08000 Charleville-Mézières, France
A major centre for professional-level courses, research, seminars, workshops and short courses concerned with therapy. There is a three-month specialist course each year on a particular aspect of puppet theatre. The Institute maintains a close association with UNIMA, providing the office facilities for the UNIMA Secretary-General.

2   Museum collections

Performing Arts Collections a catalogue published by Editions du Centre National de la Recherche Scientifique, Paris, contains information about all theatre collections throughout the world and includes puppets. It is especially useful as it lists not only the museums, libraries, etc. which contain collections, but also details of the type and amount of material in each.

The UNIMA Anniversary book, *International Puppet Theatre* (published by Henschelverlag Kunst und Gesellschaft, 1980) includes twenty-six pages of up-to-date details of major museums and collections worldwide. Some of the most interesting collections are listed below.

Britain

London
Bethnal Green Museum of Childhood, Cambridge Heath Road, London E2 Extensive collection including puppets of all types, dolls and toys

Horniman Museum and Library, London Road, Forest Hill, London SE23 Small collection of English, Belgian, African and Asian puppets and theatrical masks from all over the world

The Museum of London, 150 London Wall, London EC2 Very little on show but significant collection in store; can be viewed by arrangement

The Museum of Mankind, (The British Museum Department of Ethnography), 6 Burlington Gardens, Piccadilly, London W1

The Raffles Collection of Javanese puppets and a selection of Chinese puppets. The collection is so large that very little is displayed at any one time but other items can be inspected by arrangement.

Polka Children's Theatre, 240 The Broadway, Wimbledon, London SW19
A theatre with a varied and very well displayed collection.

The Puppet Centre, Battersea Arts Centre, Lavender Hill, London SW11.
Has acquired the Hogarth Collection (international and historical). This
is not normally on display but is available for exhibition hire.

Pollock's Toy Museum, 1 Scala Street, London W1
Toy theatres, puppets and toys

The Theatre Museum, Covent Garden, London WC1
Houses the collection of the British Puppet and Model Theatre Guild.

Victoria and Albert Museum, South Kensington, London SW7
Mainly Indian and Indonesian puppets, also toy theatres. Much of the V
and A collection is displayed at the Bethnal Green Museum and other
items in store can be viewed by arrangement.

Derby
Derby Museum and Art Gallery, The Strand, Derby
International collection of toy theatres, printed sheets, etc.

Edinburgh
The Museum of Childhood, 34 High Street, Edinburgh
A small but growing collection of exhibits

Liverpool
Merseyside County Museums, William Brown Street, Liverpool
Collection of Javanese shadow puppets

Oxford
Pitt Rivers Museum, University of Oxford, Parks Road, Oxford
Mainly shadow figures

Rottingdean
National Toy Museum, Rottingdean Grange, Rottingdean, Brighton
Small but growing collection

Sunderland
Sunderland Music Hall Museum, Gordon Place, Sunderland
Modest collection of Victorian puppets

Canada

British Columbia
Centennial Museum, 1100 Chestnut Street, Vancouver 9, B.C.
American north west coast and Javanese puppets

University of British Columbia Anthropology Museum, Library Building,
Univ. of British Columbia, Vancouver 9, B.C. V6J 3J9
Kwakiutl puppets

Montreal
McGill University, 845 Sherbrooke St West, Montreal, Que. H3A 2T5
Collection of puppets, books and toy theatres

Ontario
Royal Ontario Museum of Archaeology, 100 Queen's Park, Toronto, Ont. M5S 2C6
Northwest coast puppets and marionettes

The United States

California
Santa Barbara Museum of Art, 1130 State St., Santa Barbara, CA 93101
A modest collection

University of California, Los Angeles (UCLA), California 90024, (Ethnomusicology, ethnic and theatre collections)
Wide range of puppets from all over the world and some important American exhibits

Connecticut
University of Connecticut, Storrs, Connecticut 06268
Developing a puppetry centre

Illinois
Field Museum of Natural History, Roosevelt Road at Lake Shore Drive, Chicago, TL 60605
Includes a range of various Asian shadow and rod puppets

Michigan
Detroit Institute of Arts, 5200 Woodward Avenue, Detroit, MI 48202
Extensive collection, including many items from the Paul McPharlin Collection, extensive library, photographs and archive material

New Jersey
Gest Oriental Library, Institute for Advanced Study, Olden Lane, Princeton, New Jersey 08540
Over 2500 Chinese shadow exhibits

Newark Museum, 49 Washington Street, P.O.B. 540, Newark, NJ 07101
Selection of Asian, Sicilian and Tony Sarg puppets

New Mexico
Santa Fe Museum of Fine Arts, 107 W Palace Ave., P.O. Box 2087, Santa Fe, NM 87501
Collection of marionettes by Gustave Bauman

International Folk Art Collection, Museum of New Mexico, P.O. Box 2087, Santa Fe, NM 87503
Modest variety of puppet exhibits

Art Museum, University of New Mexico, Albuquerque, NM 87131
Selection of puppets from McPharlin Collection, also books and masks

New York
Museum of the City of New York, Fifth Avenue at 103rd St., New York 10029

Brooklyn Museum, 188 Eastern Parkway, New York 11238
Selection of Asian figures plus a few other interesting exhibits

Cooper Union Museum (now part of the Smithsonian Institute), 2 East 91 Street, New York 10028
A few particularly interesting French and Italian 18th century exhibits

American Museum of Natural History, 79th Street and Central Park W, New York 10024
Large collection of Asian and American Northwest Coast puppets

Ohio
Cleveland Museum of Art, 11150 East Blvd., Cleveland, OH 44106
Modest collection of Asian figures

Pennsylvania
Mercer Museum, Pine and Ashland Strs., Doylestown, PA 18901
Sicilian and Chinese puppets and a set of Punch glove puppets

University Museum, University of Pennsylvania, University Park, Pennsylvania 16802
Reasonable collection, particularly of Javanese shadows and rod puppets

Virginia
University of Richmond, Richmond, Virginia 23173
Caroline Lutz collection, with Japanese, Chinese and Mexican exhibits

Washington DC
National Museum of American Art, Smithsonian Institute, Eighth and G. Sts. N.W., Washington DC 20560
Includes a variety of American Indian, Hawaiian and Asian puppets

Important collections in other countries

Austria
Theatre Museum, Austrian National Library (Vienna), A-1014 Vienna, Josefsplatz 1
Richard Teschner's puppets and *Figurenspiegel* theatre

Belgium
Theatre Toone, Place de la Chapelle, Brussels
Traditional folk puppet theatre with a collection of old puppets

France
Musée Internationale de la Marionnette, Hôtel de Gadagne, Rue de Gadagne, 69001 Lyon

Musée de l'Homme, Palais de Chaillot, 75116 Paris

Germany
Theatre Museum, University of Cologne, Abertus Magnus Platz, D5000, Cologne 41, FDR
Over 1500 exhibits

Puppentheatersammlung der Stadt München, St-Jakobs-Platz 1, – 2, Munich, FDR
Largest and finest puppet museum in the world

Deutsches Ledermuseum, Frankfurter Str. 86, Offenbach-am-Maim, FDR
Contains large collection of shadow puppets

Abteilung Puppentheatersammlung, 8122 Radebeul, Barkengasse 6, Dresden, DDR
Fine collection of puppets and related material from all over the world

Sicily
The Marionette Museum, 19 Piazza Marina, Palermo
A collection of the traditional Sicilian puppets

USSR
City Museum of Theatre Arts, Kiev State Historical Museum, Vladinwskaya 2, Kiev
Theatre Arts Collection includes 18th and 19th-century puppet theatres, particularly from the Ukraine

State Central Puppet Theatre Museum, Sadovo Samotechnaya ul. 3, Moscow
The major puppet theatre in the world, with its own collection of exhibits

3 Copyright regulations

Copyright laws protect musical, literary, dramatic and artistic works, recordings and films. Protection is given to the form an idea takes, not to the idea itself; thus, if an idea that has already been used is presented again in a completely different way, there is no infringement of the law of copyright. Anything printed or even written (it need not be published) is automatically protected by copyright whether or not it is deemed of any literary value. The normal period of copyright is for the life of the author and for another fifty years after his death.

Sound recordings   Copyright of sound recordings covers their use for fifty years after publication. Unless the puppeteer uses records which are specially produced by certain firms and not covered by copyright, he must obtain a licence for any music used, whether on record or tape-recorded from records. It is illegal to tape-record from radio or television.
  Phonographic Performance Ltd (Ganton House, 14 Ganton St., London W1) issues the licences for the use of nearly all records released.
  The Performing Rights Society Ltd (29 Berners St., London W1) collects the royalties for the public performance of copyright musical works (but not dramatic works such as operas or musical plays).

The use of copyright material   The puppeteer who wishes to use copyright material must obtain permission from the owner of the copyright. It should be in writing, but in certain circumstances may be 'implied from conduct'. The owner of the copyright may require a fee in return for this licence. If consent is given without a fee being asked, the owner retains the right to withdraw his consent at any time.

4 Safety precautions and regulations

The law imposes certain requirements upon most public and some private entertainments, mainly for the purposes of safety. The regulations are quite complex and the requirements vary, depending on the licensing authority, so it is wise for the puppeteer to consult his local authorities.

There are certain precautions which are a matter of common sense, most of which are required by law.

1 The use of flameproof material wherever possible. Materials not flameproofed in the manufacture may be rendered non-flammable by using one of the following solutions:

15 oz Boric Acid, 10 oz Sodium Phosphate, 1 gallon water *or*
10 oz Borax, 8 oz Boracic Acid, 1 gallon water

Both solutions are suitable for scenery and coarser fabrics. The second is more suitable for delicate fabrics. The solutions should be tested on a small piece of the fabric to be used as they may affect the colours of some materials. After applying the solutions, the material should be dried without being rinsed.

Note: Flameproofing is not permanent: the treatment should be repeated periodically.

2 It is advisable to carry a small fire extinguisher with the equipment and keep it in a prominent place. The type now made for cars is adequate and comparatively cheap.

3 Electrical appliances should all be earthed.

4 All electrical wiring should be of the type that has a protective rubber or PVC covering. Twisted flexible, or other unsheathed, wiring should not be used.

5 For occasional performances, any wires that must run at floor level to mains sockets should be so placed that they are not likely to be damaged or to trip up anybody back-stage. Any leads that may be too long for the premises in which they are being used should be carefully coiled and tucked out of the way, not allowed to trail around the floor.

5   Where to buy materials

Most of the materials mentioned in the text are readily available from art and craft or model shops, chemists (drug stores), electrical and photographic shops, Woolworths (U.S. 5 and 10c. Stores) and large department stores – particularly in haberdashery, soft furnishings and dress materials, stationery, hardware and tools departments. Suppliers of materials not so readily obtained are listed below.

All toy theatre materials Pollock's Toy Museum, 1 Scala Street, London W1.

No. 18 carpet thread Rope, twine and string manufacturers and merchants; cord and line manufacturers and merchants; in certain areas, chandlers, sports and handicraft shops; some department stores.

Acetone (also fibre glass) Strand Glass Co., 524 High Street, Ilford, Essex.

Carpentry tools (extensive range). Parry and Sons, 329 Old Street, London EC1.

Celastic 'Celastic' is a trade name which has become, in puppetry circles, the standard term to describe all brands of this material. It is sold in a number of thicknesses. Suppliers are: *Britain* The Puppet Centre (Appendix 1) and The Luck Counter Co., Spencer Street, Oadby, Leicester

LE2 4DP. *USA* Creegan Distribution Co., 273 Belleview Boulevard, Steubenville, Ohio 43952. There is also a brand of this material known as 'Samcoforma' supplied by Samco Strong Ltd, P.O. Box 88, Clay Hill, Bristol BS99 74R.

Coloured/striped canvas (and fireproof gauze). Russell and Chapple Ltd., 23 Monmouth Street, London WC2.

Decorative papers 'Paper Chase', 167 Fulham Road, London SW6, also 213 Tottenham Court Road, London W1.

Dexion (tube and metal angle) Available in kits and separate lengths from do-it-yourself shops. A major supplier is Duval's, Armoury Way, Wandsworth, London SW18.

Felt The Felt Shop, 34 Greville Street, London EC1

Fibre Glass (or Glass Fibre) Now available from any do-it-yourself shops, and motor accessory shops have kits (intended for car body repairs) as well as sheets of matting. To buy larger quantities, contact: Alec Tiranti and Sons, 21 Goodge Place, London W1 (also for **casting plaster, resins, carving tools, vices,** etc.)

Glitter Ells and Farrier Ltd., Bead Merchants, 5 Princes Street (off Regent Street), London W1.

Glues and woodworking tools Buck and Ryan, 101 Tottenham Court Road, London W1, also: 55 Harrow Road, London W2.

Jelutong and woods for carving William Bloore, 57 South Lambeth Road, SW8.

Latex rubber *Britain* Type A443W* Latex (*stands for white; pink is also available) from D. B. Shipping Co. (Macadam & Co.) Monument House, Monument Street, London EC1. Dunlop's Liquid Rubber ('Soft Toy Mix'); for the address of nearest stockist write to Dunlop Rubber Co. Ltd., Chester Road, Birmingham 24.

USA Pliatex Casting Rubber from The Sculpture House, 38 East 30th Street, New York 16. Casting Rubber No. L200 from Cementex Co. Ltd, 336 Canal Street, New York 13.

Noise makers (bird pipes, sirens etc.) The Rhythm Box, 5 Denmark Street, London WC2.

Paints (specialist artists materials only) Michael J. Putman, 151 Lavender Hill, London SW11.

Paints (Theatre paints and materials). Brodie and Middleton Ltd., 79 Long Acre, London WC2.

Plastic wood C. Brewer & Sons, 327 Putney Bridge Road, London SW15 and most ironmongers in small quantities. Purchase by the tin, not in tubes.

Polystyrene (Styrofoam) Use self-extinguishing, expanded polystyrene. It is sold in standard block sizes by: *Britain* Vencel Products Ltd, West Street, Erith, Kent. Also Adrian Merchant Ltd, Chestnut Grove, New Malden, Surrey. *USA* Innerman and Sons, 1903 Euclid Avenue, Cleveland, Ohio. Magnus Craft Material, 108 Franklin Street, New York. Star Band Co., 800 Board Street, Portsmouth, Va.

Polythene Transatlantic Plastics, Surbiton, Surrey.

Sponge (Foam) (all grades) Pentonville Rubber Co., 50/52 Pentonville Road, London N1.

Stage Lighting Equipment Including lights, stands, dimmers and coloured acetates: *Britain* CCT Theatre Lighting, Windsor House, Willow Lane, Mitcham, Surrey. Rank Strand Electric, P.O. Box 70, Great West Road, Brentford, Middlesex. *USA* Times Square Lighting, 318 West 47th Street, New York. American Stage Lighting Co., 1331c North Avenue, New Rochelle, New York 10801. Capitol Stage Lighting Co., 509 West 56th Street, New York 10019. Also for coloured acetates: I. A. Friedman, 25 West 75th Street, New York. Arthur Brown and Bros. Inc. (see below).

Swazzles and ventriloquism L. Davenport and Co., 51 Great Russell Street, London WC1. Also Supreme Magic Co., 64 High Street, Bideford, Devon.

Theatre effects (Flash powder, etc.) 'Theatrescene Armour Ltd', 12/13 Henrietta Street, London W1.

Theatrical fabrics Borovick Fabrics Ltd., 16 Berwick Street, London W1.

Ultra-violet lighting tubes Service Trading Company, 9 Little Newport Street, Leicester Square, London WC2.

Other useful suppliers

Britain Atlas Handicrafts, High Street, Manchester 4; Dryad Handicrafts Ltd, Northgates, Leicester; George Rowney and Co. Ltd, 10 Percy Street, London W1; Nottingham Handicraft Co., Hetton Road, West Bridgeford, Nottingham; Reeves and Sons Ltd, Lincoln Road, Enfield, Middlesex.

USA American Handicrafts Co. Inc., 20 West 14th Street, New York, N.Y.; Arthur Brown and Bros. Inc., 2 West 46th Street, New York, N.Y. 10036; Bergen Arts and Crafts, Box 6895A, Salem, Massachusetts 01970; Creative Hands Ltd, 4146 Library Road, Pittsburg, Pennsylvania 15234; J. L. Hamett Co., 290 Main Street, Cambridge, Mass.; New York Central Supply Co., 62 Third Avenue, New York, N.Y.; The Puppetry Store of the Puppeteers of America, 14316 Sturtevant Road, Silver Spring, MD 20904; Triarco Arts and Crafts, Dept. 4410, Box 106, Northfield, Illinois 60093; Zims (mail order), P.O. Box 7620, Salt Lake City, UT 84107.

6 Bibliography

Many excellent books go out of print amazingly quickly, so it would be impossible to distinguish these accurately in the list below. Though there will be exceptions, the reader can be fairly certain that most texts over ten years old will be out of print. Those included are worth looking for in public libraries, the reference collections of the many puppetry organisations and in second-hand bookshops. For a quick, up-to-date check of publications, most libraries will contain the current editions of *British Books in Print* and *Books in Print (USA)*. Two useful suppliers are the Puppet Centre Trust, London, and the Puppetry Store of the Puppeteers of America; both are detailed in Appendix 1.

General: Published pre–1973

Tsurao Ando, *Bunraku: the Puppet Theatre*, Walker, New York 1970

Bil Baird, *The Art of the Puppet*, Plays Inc., Boston 1965

Cyril Beaumont, *Puppets and Puppetry*, Studio, London 1958

Olive Blackham, *Shadow Puppets*, Barrie and Rockliffe, London 1960/Harper New York 1962

J. Bocek, *Jiří Trnka (Czechoslovak Puppet Master)*, Artia, Prague/Hamlyn, London 1963

Günter Böhmer, *Puppets Through the Ages*, Trs. Gerald Morice Macdonald, London/Plays Inc., Boston 1971

—— *The Wonderful World of Puppetry*, Macdonald, London/Plays Inc., Boston 1971

Jan Bussell, *The Puppets and I*, Faber, London 1950

—— *Puppets Progress*, Faber, London 1953

—— *Through Wooden Eyes*, Faber, London 1956

Michael Byrom, *Punch and Judy: its Origin and Evolution*, Perpetua Press, London 1972

—— *Punch in the Italian Puppet Theatre*, Centaur Press 1983

J. Chesnais, *Histoire Generale des Marionnettes* Bordas, Paris 1947

J. P. Collier, *Punch and Judy*, Prowett, London 1828, Bell, London 1881 etc.

M. R. Contractor, *Puppets of India*, Marg Publications, Bombay

C. J. Dunn, *The Early Japanese Puppet Drama*, Luzac, London 1966

P. Ferrigni, *Storia dei Burattini*, Bemporade, Rome 1902

Peter Fraser, *Punch and Judy*, Batsford, London 1970

A. C. Gervais, *Marionnettes et Marionnettistes de France*, Bordas, Paris 1947

Franz Hadamowsky, *Richard Teschner und sein Figurenspeigel*, Edward Wancura, Vienna and Stuttgart 1956

Ann Hogarth, *Look at Puppets*, Hamish Hamilton, London 1960

Lothar Kampmann, *World of Puppets*, Evans, London 1972

Donald Keene, *Bunraku: the Art of the Japanese Puppet Theatre*, Phaidon, Oxford/Kodansha, Tokyo; complete edition 1965; edited version 1973

Gottfried Kraus, *The Salzburg Marionette Theatre*, Residenz Verlag, Salzburg 1966

Charles Magnin, *Histoire des Marionnettes en Europe*, Originally Paris 1862, Reprinted Editions Slatkine, Paris 1983

Ernest Maindron, *Marionnettes et Guignols*, Paris 1900

Jan Malik, *The Puppet Theatre in Czechoslovakia*, Orbis, Prague 1970

Paul McPharlin, *The Puppet Theatre in America*, Plays Inc., Boston 1969

Sergei Obraztsov, *The Chinese Puppet Theatre*, Faber, London/Plays Inc., Boston 1961

A. R. Philpott, *Let's Look At Puppets*, Muller, London 1966

—— *Dictionary of Puppetry*, Macdonald, London/Plays Inc., Boston 1969

—— *Puppet Diary*, Macmillan, London 1952

H. R. Purschke, *Puppet Theatre in Germany*, Neue Darmstädter, Darmstädt 1957

A. C. Scott, *The Puppet Theatre of Japan*, Prentice-Hall, London/Tuttle, Rutland Vermont 1964

Sejiro, *Masterpieces of Japanese Puppetry*, Trs. R. A. Miller, Prentice-Hall, London/Tuttle, Rutland Vermont 1964

E. Siyavusgil, *Karagoz*, Turkish Press and Tourist Department 1955

Sotiris Spatharis, *Behind the White Screen*, Trs. Mario Rinvolucri, London Magazine Editions, London 1967

George Speaight, *Punch and Judy: a History*, Studio Vista, London/Plays Inc., Boston 1970

—— *The History of the English Puppet Theatre*, Harrap, London 1955

—— *The History of the English Toy Theatre*, Studio Vista, London/Plays Inc., Boston 1969

—— *Juvenile Drama*, Macdonald, London 1946

Philip John Stead, *Mr Punch*, Evans, London 1950

J. Tilakasiri, *The Puppet Theatre of Asia*, Department of Cultural Affairs, Ceylon 1970

UNIMA, *The Puppet Theatre of the Modern World*, Harrap, London/Plays Inc., Boston 1967

Max Von Boehn, *Dolls*, Dover, New York 1973

—— *Puppets and Automata*, Dover, New York 1973

Walter Wilkinson, *The Peep Show*

—— *Vagabonds and Puppets*

—— *Puppets in Yorkshire*

—— *A Sussex Peepshow*

—— *Puppets into Scotland*

—— *Puppets through Lancashire*

—— *Puppets through America*

All published by Geoffrey Bles, London, between 1927 and 1938

—— *Puppets in Wales*, Geoffrey Bles, London 1948

A. E. Wilson, *Penny Plain, Twopence Coloured*, Harrap, London 1932

General: recent publications

Barbara Adachi, *The Voices and Hands of Bunraku*, Kodanscha, Tokyo and New York 1978

Richard Barnard (Ed. G. Speaight) *The Life and Travels of Richard Barnard*, Society for Theatre Research, London 1981

Zdenêk Bezdêk, *Czechoslovak Puppet Theatre 1949–1969*, Divadelni, Ústav 1973

Forman Brown, *Small Wonder: The Story of the Yale Puppeteers and the Turnabout Theatre*, Scarecrow Press, London 1981

K. and M. Fawdry, *Pollock's History of English Dolls and Toys*, Ernest Benn, London 1979

Christopher Finch, *Of Muppets and Men*, Michael Joseph, London 1982

Paul Fournel, *Les Marionnettes*, Bordas, Paris 1982

Brian Froud, *The World of the Dark Crystal*, Henson Organisation, New York/Mitchell Beazley, London 1983

Heinrich Mersmann, *Harro Siegels Marionnetten*, Propyläen Verlag, Berlin 1982

Sergei Obraztsov, *My Profession*, Foreign Languages Publishing House, Moscow 1981

—— *Puppet Theatre*, Moscow 1981

Shyam Parma, *Traditional Folk Media in India*, Geka, New Delhi 1975

Hans R. Purschke, *The German Puppet Theatre Today*, Inter Nationes, Bonn-Bad Godesberg 1979

Rene Simmen, *The World of Puppets*, Elsevier-Phaidon, London/Crowell, Inc. New York 1975

Dezső Szilágyi, *Contemporary Hungarian Puppet Theatre*, Corvina, Budapest 1978

Karin Theren, *Marionetteatern*, Liber Forlag Mälmo, Stockholm 1983

UCLA Museum of Cultural History, *Asian Puppets: Wall of the World*, University of California 1979

UNIMA, *Figur Und Spiel Im Puppentheater Der Welt*, Henschelverlag, Berlin 1977

UNIMA, *International Puppet Theatre* (50th Anniversary of UNIMA), Henschelverlag Kunst und Gesellschaft, Berlin 1980

Puppetry in education: pre–1973

Margaret Beresford, *How to Make Puppets and Teach Puppetry*, Mills and Boon, London 1966

David Currell, *Puppetry in the Primary School*, Batsford, London 1969
—— *Puppetry for Schoolchildren*, Branford, USA 1969

Educational Puppetry Association, *The Puppet Book*, Ed. A. R. Philpott, Faber, London/Plays Inc., Boston 1966

Moritz Jagendorf, *Puppets for Beginners*, Edmund Ward, London/Plays Inc., Boston 1971

Shari Lewis and Lillian Oppenheimer, *Folding Paper Puppets*, Muller, London/Stein and Day, USA 1964

(No author), *Puppet People*, Macdonald Educational, London 1972

Puppetry in education and therapy: recent publications

Caroline Astell-Burt, *Puppetry for Mentally Handicapped People*, Souvenir Press 1981

David Currell, *Learning with Puppets*, Ward Lock Educational, London/Plays Inc., Boston 1980

Tamara Hunt and Nancy Renfro, *Puppetry in Early Childhood Education*, Renfro Studios, USA 1982

A. R. Philpott (Ed.), *Puppets and Therapy*, Puppet Centre, London/Plays Inc., Boston 1977

Laura Ross, *Finger Puppets*, World's Work, London 1973

Technical (general): pre–1973

Majorie Batchelder, *The Puppet Theatre Handbook*, Harper, New York 1947

Helen Binyon, *Puppetry Today*, Studio Vista, London/Watson-Guptill, New York 1966

Jan Bussell, *The Pegasus Book of Puppets*, Dobson, London 1968

E. Copfermann, *Marionnettes, Jeux et Constructions*, Editions du Scarabee, Paris 1970

Educational Puppetry Association, *The Puppet Book*, Ed. A. R. Philpott, Faber, London/Plays Inc., Boston 1966

Peter Fraser, *Introducing Puppetry*, Batsford, London/Watson-Guptill, New York 1968

M. C. Green and B. R. H. Targett, *Space Age Puppets and Masks*, Harrap, London/Plays Inc., Boston 1969

Sheila Jackson, *Simple Puppetry*, Studio Vista, London/Watson-Guptill, New York 1969

Moritz Jagendorf, *Puppets for Beginners*, Edmund Ward, London/Plays Inc., Boston 1971

Waldo S. Lanchester, *Hand Puppets and String Puppets*, Dryad, London 1937

Desmond MacNamara, *Puppetry*, Arco, London 1965

George Merten, *The Hand Puppets*, Nelson, London and New York 1957

A. R. Philpott, *Modern Puppetry*, Michael Joseph, London/Plays Inc., Boston 1966

—— *Let's Make Puppets*, Evans, London 1972

S. and P. Robinson, *Exploring Puppetry*, Mills and Boon, London 1967

Vikki Rutter, *Your Book of Puppetry*, Faber, London 1969

—— *A B C Puppetry*, Plays Inc., Boston 1969

Alan Stockwell, *Puppetry*, Collins Nutshell Books, London 1966

H. W. Whanslaw, *A Bench Book of Puppetry*

—— *A Second Bench Book of Puppetry*

—— *Animal Puppetry*

All published by Wells, Gardner & Darton, London 1957

—— *Everybody's Theatre*, Wells, Gardner & Darton, London 1934

Technical (general): recent publications

B. Chesse and B. Armstrong, *Sponge-ees*, Early Stages, USA 1975

Audrey Vincente Dean, *Puppets that are Different*, Faber, London 1973

—— *Wooden Spoon Marionettes*, Faber, London 1976

Sydney de Hempsey, *How to do Punch and Judy*, Magic Inc, London 1976

Peter Fraser, *Puppets and Puppetry*, Batsford, London 1980

R. T. E. Harford, *The Complete Book of Puppets and Puppeteering*, Drake, New York and London 1976

Joyce Luckin, *Easy-to-Make Puppets*, Harrap, London 1975

Violet Philpott and M. J. McNeil, *The KnowHow Book of Puppets*, Usborne 1975

Judy Sims, *Puppets for Dreaming and Scheming*, Early Stages, USA 1978

Debbie Sullivan, *Pocketful of Puppets*, Renfro Studios, USA 1983

Glove puppets: pre–1973

C. Creegan, *Sir George's Book of Hand Puppets*, Follett, London 1966

Janet Evec, *Puppetry*, W. and G. Foyle, London 1950

Peter Fraser, *Punch and Judy*, Batsford, London 1970

Suzy Ives, *Making Felt Toys and Glove Puppets*, Batsford, London/Branford, USA 1971

Shari Lewis, *Making Easy Puppets*, Muller, London 1968

Brenda Morton, *Needlework Puppets*, Faber, London/Plays Inc., Boston 1964

Barbara Snook, *Puppets*, Batsford, London 1965

Philip John Stead, *Mr Punch*, Evans, London 1950

Glove puppets: recent publications

L. Engler and C. Fijan, *Making Puppets Come Alive*, David and Charles, London 1973
Esme Mclaren, *Making Glove Puppets*, Bell, London 1973
Brenda Morton, *Sleeve Puppets*, Faber, London and Boston 1978

Rod puppets

Hansjürgen Fettig, *Glove and Rod Puppets*, Trs. John Wright and Susanne Forster, Harrap, London 1973

Shadow puppets: pre–1973

Olive Blackham, *Shadow Puppets*, Barrie and Rockliffe, London 1960/Harper, New York 1962
Louise Cochrane, *Shadows in Colour*, Chatto and Windus, London 1972
E. Coleman and R. Bryan, *Making Shadow Puppets*, Search Press, London/Herder and Herder, New York 1971
Lotte Reiniger, *Shadow Theatres and Shadow Films*, Batsford, London 1970
Herta Schönewolf, *Play with Light and Shadow*, Studio Vista, London/Reinhold, New York 1968
Jane Scott-Kemball, *Javanese Shadow Puppets*, British Museum 1970
Amin Sweeney, *Malay Shadow Puppets*, British Museum 1972
H. W. Whanslaw, *Shadow Play*, Wells, Gardner and Darton, London 1950

Shadow puppets: recent publications

Metin And, *Karagöz*, Editions Post, Ankara 1977
Sven Broman, *Chinese Shadow Theatre*, Etnografiska Museet, Stockholm 1982
Louise Cochrane, *Shadows in Colour*, Chatto and Windus, 1972
Janet Lynch-Watson, *The Shadow Puppet Book*, Oak Tree Press, London/Sterling, New York 1980

Marionettes

Dorothe Abbe, *The Dwiggins Marionettes: a complete experimental theatre in miniature*, Harry N. Abrams, New York 1970
Olive Blackham, *Puppets into Actors*, Rockliffe, London 1948
Eric Bramall, *Making a Start with Marionettes*, Bell, London 1960
Eric Bramall and Christopher Sommerville, *Expert Puppet Technique*, Faber, London/Plays Inc., Boston 1964
Douglas Fisher, *Wooden Stars: the Lanchester Marionettes*, Boardman, London and New York 1947
Peter Fraser, *Puppet Circus*, Batsford, London/Plays Inc., Boston 1971
S. French, *Presenting Marionettes*, Studio Vista, London/Reinhold, New York 1964
George Merten, *The Marionette*, Thomas Nelson, London and New York 1957
H. W. Whanslaw, *Everybody's Marionette Book*, Wells, Gardner and Darton, London 1948

H. W. Whanslaw and V. Hotchkiss, *Specialised Puppetry*, Wells, Gardner and Darton, London 1948

John Wright, *Your Puppetry*, Sylvan Press, London 1951

The toy and model theatre

Arthur B. Allen, *The Model Theatre*, Wells, Gardner and Darton, London 1950

Jan Bussell, *The Model Theatre*, Dobson, London 1968

Moritz Jagendorf, *Penny Puppets, Penny Theatre and Penny Plays*, Plays Inc., Boston 1967

M. Scaping, *The Toy Theatre*, Premier Publishers, London 1967

H. W. Whanslaw, *Everybody's Theatre*, Wells, Gardner and Darton, London 1948/1959

—— *The Bankside Stage Book*, Wells, Gardner and Darton, London

Plays, stories and play production

Peter Arnott, *Plays Without People*, Indiana University Press 1964

M. Batchelder and V. L. Comer, *Puppets and Plays*, Faber, London 1959

Hans Baumann, *Caspar and his Friends*, Phoenix House, London 1967

Bill Binzen, *Punch and Jonathon*, Macmillan, London/Pantheon, New York 1971

Eric Bramall, *Puppet Plays and Playwriting*, Bell, London 1961

J. R. Brandon (Ed.), *On Thrones of Gold: Three Javanese Shadow Plays*, Harvard Univ. Press, Massachusetts 1970

Remo Bufano, *Show Book of Remo Bufano*, Macmillan, New York 1929

Nancy H. Cole, *Puppet Theatre in Performance*, Morrow, New York 1978

Educational Puppetry Association, *Eight Plays for Hand Puppets*, Ed. A. R. Philpott, Garnet Miller, London/Plays Inc., Boston 1968

Lynette Feasey (Ed.), *Old England at Play*, Harrap, London 1955

D. John, *St George and the Dragon and Punch and Judy*, a Puffin Book, Allen Lane, London 1966

Miles Lee, *Puppet Theatre Production and Manipulation*, Faber, London 1958

A. R. Philpott, *The Magic Tower and Other Plays*, Macmillan, London 1952

—— *Mumbo Jumbo and Other Plays*, Macmillan, London 1954

Violet Philpott, *Bandicoot and his Friends*, Dent, London 1970

N. Renfro, *Puppetry and the Art of Story Creation*, Renfro Studios, USA 1979

Antonia Ridge, *The Poppenkast (or How Jan Klaasen Cured the Sick King)*, Faber, London 1958

A. C. Scott, *Traditional Chinese Plays*, Univ. Wisconsin, Madison and London 1967

George Bernard Shaw, *Shakes Versus Shav*, Privately Printed (Lanchester)

Miscellaneous

C. J. Alkema, *Masks*, Oak Tree Press, London/Sterling, New York 1971

Douglas Houlden, *Ventriloquism for Boys and Girls* Kaye and Ward, London 1968

M. Hutchings, *Making and Using Finger Puppets*, Mills and Boon, London/Taplinger, New York 1973

Shari Lewis and Lillian Oppenheimer, *Folding Paper Masks*, Muller, London 1966

M. C. Skinner, *How to Make Masks*, Studio Vista, London 1973

Barbara Snook, *Making Masks*, Batsford, London 1972

Journals

The majority of puppetry organisations publish a journal; those listed are among the most notable. Back-copies are often available. Where no address is given, the organisation is listed in Appendix 1. Journals of UNIMA Centres in other countries can often be subscribed to if you are a member of your national section. Many organisations exchange journals so each should have a wide-ranging reference collection.

Publications in English

Animations   Two-monthly review of puppets and related theatre. The Puppet Centre Trust, London

À Propos   Twice-yearly journal of the American Centre of UNIMA

Billboard   Weekly entertainment trade paper. Billboard Publishing Co., 1564 Broadway, New York

British UNIMA Bulletin   Three times a year; journal of the British Centre of UNIMA

Manipulation   Three times a year. About puppetry generally, not only manipulation. 28 Macarthur Place, Carlton VIC 3053, Australia

Puppetry in Education News   Monthly during the school year. The PIE News, 164 – 27th Street, San Francisco, CA 94110, USA

The Puppet Master   Annual journal of the British Puppet and Model Theatre Guild

The Puppetry Journal   Quarterly journal of the Puppeteers of America

The Stage and Television Today   Weekly theatrical newspaper with regular puppetry features. Carson and Comerford, London

Occasional features are found in educational magazines such as *Art and Craft in Education*, *Child Education*, *Teachers' World*, etc.

Publications in French

Les Cahiers de la Marionnette   A new publication, due to appear four times a year. The first issues have each focused upon a particular country or theme. Alain Lecucq, 37 rue de Bras, 14300 Caen, France

Marionnettes   Quarterly journal of UNIMA – France

Marionnettes en Castelets   Twice-yearly review of the French-speaking section of Belgian UNIMA

Publications in German

Figuren Theater   Twice-yearly journal of the Deutsches Institut für Puppenspiel (DIP)

Meister des Puppenspiels   Occasional publication of the DIP, each edition (over 35 in all) devoted to one puppet master. Back-copies available.

Puppenspielkundliche Quellen und Forschungen   Occasional publication of academic dissertations on aspects of puppet theatre. Published for DIP by Puppen und Masken, Eppsteiner Strasse 22, D – 6000 Frankfurt/M.1, West Germany

Perlicko-Perlacko   3/4 issues per year; privately published by Dr Hans R. Purschke, Frankfurt/M.35, Postfach 550135, West Germany

Puppenspiel Information   Twice-yearly journal of the German Organisation for Professional Puppet Theatre and the Hamburg Research Group for Puppet Theatre. Fritz Leese, Zimmerplatz 13, 3582 Felsberg 1, West Germany

Puppenspiel und Puppenspieler   Twice-yearly journal of the Swiss Society for Puppet Theatre and the Swiss UNIMA Centre. Zentralstelle SVfP/UNIMA, CH – 8401 Winterthur

Other languages

Dockteater-EKO   Quarterly journal of the Swedish Puppet Theatre Organisation. Gerd Henze, Sandavagen 10, 140 32 Grodinge

Het Poppenspel   Quarterly journal in Flemish with a resume in English. Published by Louis Contryn, Kadodderstraat 14, 2800 Mechelen, Belgium

Poppenspel   Quarterly journal of the Flemish-speaking section of UNIMA-Belgium. Jan Martin, Serigiersstraat 5, 2020 Antwerp

Theatrical Animation   Three issues a year, with articles in Italian, English and French. Teatro Porcospino, 51100 Pistoia, Italy

Acknowledgements for photographs

Bracketed figures refer to chapter numbers, the following figures to the numbers of the illustrations. *PCT* indicates photographs supplied from the Puppet Centre Trust Reference Collection.

Gretl Aicher, Salzburg Marionette Theatre (2) 8, 9, 10

Art-Wood Photographs, Courtesy Rank Strand Electric (13) 5, 8, 9, 12, 13, 17, 18, 19

Ron Bailey, Courtesy Ray DaSilva, DaSilva Puppets/Norwich Puppet Theatre (15) 10

Ken Barnard (6) 32

Dora Beacham (5) 5, 6

Courtesy John Blundall, Cannon Hill Puppet Theatre, Birmingham (2) 57

Courtesy Richard Bradshaw, Australia, *PCT* (2) 69

Bura and Hardwick, Courtesy Gordon Murray (2) 61 (11) 15

Burmese Government (2) 42

CCT Theatre Lighting (13) 4, 6, 7, 10

Central State Puppet Theatre, Sophia (2) 21

Central Television, Courtesy Spitting Image, *PCT* (11) 17

David Currell (2) 37 (3) 3, 5, 6, 7 (5) 11 (10) 16, 17, 18 (12) 89/1 (13) 2, 11, 14

Courtesy Cultural Attaché, Austrian Embassy, London (2) 5

Courtesy Ray DaSilva, DaSilva Puppets/Norwich Puppet Theatre (2) 53 (15) 9, 11, 13

J. Ducker, Courtesy John Thirtle and Ian Allen, Playboard Puppets, London (8) 15 (14) 7

H. Southwell Eades, Courtesy John Blundall, Cannon Hill Puppet Theatre, Birmingham (4) 2 (6) 10 (8) 11, 20, 43

Iraj Emami, *PCT* (2) 36

Paul Fender, Courtesy Barbara Aiello, Kids on the Block, USA, *PCT* (3) 10

Stefan Fichert, Courtesy Ian Allen and John Thirtle, Playboard Puppets, London (6) 2 (7) 3, 5, 13 (9) 30, 32, 33, 75

Stefan Fichert, Courtesy John Wright, Little Angel Theatre, London (2) 62

Derek Francis (9) 35, 68

Courtesy Philippe Genty, *PCT* (2) 18

K. A. Harnisch, Courtesy Frieder Simon, Larifari Theatre, DDR (2) 19, 20 (5) 7 (6) 15, 16 (7) 6

Edward Hartwig, State Puppet Theatre Lalka, Poland (2) 27 (12) 43/3

Hausmann, Courtesy Cultural Attaché, Austrian Embassy, London (2) 6

Henson Associates, Courtesy Jim Henson (2) 67 (4) 1 (7) 19 (11) 10, 11, 12

T. E. Howard, Courtesy British Puppet and Model Theatre Guild (2) 11

Adam Idinski, Courtesy Marta Janic, State Puppet Theatre Pinokio, Łodz, Poland (2) 29 (8) 25 (12) 62/1

Incorporated Television Company Ltd and Century 21 Films (2) 59 (11) 13

Courtesy Japan Information Centre, London (2) 46

Emrys Jones, Courtesy Eric Bramall, Harlequin Puppet Theatre, Colwyn Bay (2) 63

Ptáček Josef, Courtesy Drak Theatre, Czechoslovakia (12) 36, 44/1 (14) 3, 4

Mme Keleti, MTI, Courtesy Hungarian State Puppet Theatre, Budapest (2) 25, 26 (12) 6 (14) 1

Courtesy Hana and Joseph Lamka, The Black Theatre of Prague (2) 23

Waldo S. Lanchester, the Lanchester Marionettes (now in the Polka Children's Theatre collection) (2) 49, 52 (9) 42

Courtesy Leningrad Bolshoi Puppet Theatre, USSR (2) 31, 32 (12) 62/2

Michael Little, Courtesy Richard Gill, Polka Children's Theatre, London (2) 55 (8) 21 (10) 1/1 (11) 18 (12) 85

Courtesy Daniel Llords, Llords International USA (9) 57

Marjorie Batchelder McPharlin, USA (2) 64 (3) 4

W. Meacock, Courtesy Jan Bussell and Ann Hogarth, the Hogarth Puppets (2) 54 (9) 34

Courtesy Michael Meschke, Marionetteatern, Stockholm, *PCT* (2) 1

Nat Messik, Courtesy Bil Baird, USA (2) 66

Courtesy Claude and Colette Monestier, Théâtre sur le Fil, France, *PCT* (1) 3 (2) 17

Richard Moore, from the author's collection (3) 9 (5) 12 (6) 21 (9) 12/4 (10) 1/2, 20, 22, 24/1, 24/2 (12) 62/3 (13) 3

Franciszek Myszkowski, Central State Puppet Theatre Guliwer, Poland (2) 30

Courtesy National Theatre of Puppets and Actors Marcinek, Poland (8) 26

Violet Philpott, Cap and Bells Puppet Theatre Company, London (2) 45 (6) 8 (7) 4, 14 (8) 22, 24/2

Violet Philpott, from the Lucy Claus Bequest (2) 44

Photax (London) Ltd (13) 1, 16

Oliver Postgate (11) 16

L. Postupa, Courtesy Naive Theatre, Czechoslovakia (12) 43/2

Lisa Powers, Courtesy Bruce Schwartz, USA, *PCT* (2) 68/1, 68/2

Courtesy Puppet Centre Trust, London, *PCT* (3) 1, 2 (5) 17 (8) 24/1, 37/2 (9) 1

Courtesy Alain Recoing, France, *PCT* (12) 54 (14) 2

Lotte Reiniger (11) 14

H. Rodgers, Courtesy Ray DaSilva, DaSilva Puppets/Norwich Puppet Theatre (15) 12, 15

Courtesy Albrecht Roser, Stuttgart (2) 12, 13, 14 (9) 41 (12) 12

H. Schmidt, Courtesy John Thirtle and Ian Allen, Playboard Puppets, London (2) 58

Alan Sewell, Courtesy Ray DaSilva, Norwich Puppet Theatre (15) 14

Julian Sheppard, Courtesy Jane Phillips, Caricature Theatre, Cardiff (2) 56 (12) 7, 35 (14) 6

V. Sirucek, Courtesy Milos Kirschner, the Spejbl and Hurvinek Theatre, Czechoslovakia (2) 24

Barry Smith, from the author's collection (3) 8 (5) 13 (6) 3 (7) 12 (8) 41, 42, 45 (9) 43, 55, 61, 66, 73/1 (10) 9 (11) 1, 25/1, 25/2

Barry Smith, Theatre of Puppets, London (2) 43, 48, 60 (6) 26 (8) 46 (11) 20 (12) 62/4 (15) 1, 2, 3, 4, 5, 6, 7, 8

Barry Smith, Courtesy Jan Bussell and Ann Hogarth, the Hogarth Puppets (2) 2, 15, 16, 22, 28, 38, 39, 40, 41, 47, 51 (10) 7/1

Barry Smith, Courtesy John Wright, Little Angel Theatre, London (10) 8

Edwin Smith, Courtesy George Speaight (11) 9

Courtesy Eugenios Spatharis, Greece (2) 3, 4 (10) 15

David Stanfield, Courtesy John Wright, Little Angel Theatre, London (1) 1 (4) 4 (6) 1, 12, 14, 33 (14) 9

Courtesy State Central Puppet Theatre, Moscow (2) 33, 34, 35

Courtesy John Styles, Sidcup, Kent (2) 50

Courtesy Thames Television (7) 20

Courtesy John Thirtle and Ian Allen, Playboard Puppets, London (6) 35 (12) 5

Courtesy Burr Tillstrom, USA (2) 65

Mary Turner, Courtesy Muriel and Judith Shutt, Mejandes Marionettes, London (9) 40

Tristan J. Vales, Courtesy Alain Lecucq, La Citrouille, France, PCT (1) 2 (10) 21

Votava, Courtesy Cultural Attaché, Austrian Embassy, London (2) 7

Hylton Warner, Courtesy Jane Phillips, Caricature Theatre, Cardiff (11) 19

Darryl Williams, Courtesy Richard Gill, Polka Children's Theatre, Wimbledon (12) 56/4

Ron Wood, Courtesy Gordon Straight, Yorkshire (9) 67, 74

Courtesy John Wright, Little Angel Theatre, Islington (9) 31

Index

Italicised numbers indicate page references for photographs which are particularly interesting examples of each topic listed.

Photographs are not listed under the broad categories of glove, rod or shadow puppet, nor marionette, as these would clearly include most photographs in the book.

After the title of a production, the author's/composer's name is bracketed.